KU-053-242

CONTENTS

2
WRITE

3
DELIVER

APPENDIX

FOREWORD

I shouldn't be writing this foreword. I don't believe in how-to books. Not for writing. I'm not sure writing can be taught. I believe novels need to be instinctive. I think writers need to shut their eyes and write exactly what and how they want to. Because that way their books will be organic, living, breathing, vital, full of energy, full of integrity. I think that's the only route to success. You can't do it by committee. I think that to want to do something, but to hesitate because Lee Child or someone else does it differently, is the route to certain failure. My how-to book would be all of three words long: 'Ignore all advice.'

But.

But . . . writing is also a job. It's a trade. It's a profession. Maybe it shouldn't have rules, but it does have manners. And conventions. And realities. And processes, and different stages within those processes. And tricks. Getting the words on the page isn't easy. You have to make them your words, and your words alone, but some ways will save you a little time and frustration, and some ways will cost you a lot of both.

And once the words are on the page, it's a whole new ballgame. There are blind alleys, and ways to avoid them. There are elephant traps, and ways to sidestep them. There's praise, and ways to parse it. There's criticism, and ways to respond to it. And ways not to. Once the words are on the page, you step out of the office and into the jungle. You need a guide.

You need David Hewson.

I know David pretty well. We've sat side by sardonic side through publication dinners, on conference panels, at committee meetings, and with our elbows propped on bars. We've set the world to rights many times over. There are three things you need to know about old Hewson: his bullshit meter is second only to mine. He loves the business to death, but is the least starry-eyed writer you'll ever meet. And he was a working journalist, and (perhaps therefore) the most professional and down-to-earth guy you'll ever meet.

You should listen to him. I do, all the time. You should listen long and hard. You should absolutely be prepared to ignore what he says if you're not convinced, but I think you will be convinced. By most of it, anyway.

LEE CHILD
New York, 2011

INTRODUCTION

This is a guide to practical craft not cerebral art. It is aimed at the ambitious budding author more interested in finishing a book than allowing it to linger in the purgatory of a never-ending work in progress. Success and failure in any writing project frequently depend upon matters deemed too mundane to be worthy of discussion in authorial circles. Yet the real-world challenges – how to approach a manuscript, to manage research, to fix the right point of view – represent important and recurring obstacles every writer, novice or professional, must overcome.

All too often students and teachers alike focus almost exclusively on the intellectual question of 'what to write' and ignore the more immediate yet equally pressing one – 'how?' As my title suggests, this book is designed to be a manual offering some plain-language insights into the everyday mechanics of creating a book from hazy idea to finished manuscript. Sound working habits and an understanding of the technical structure of fiction are no substitute for creative talent. But the right tools and approaches can free the imagination to work on the most difficult task of all: telling a compelling story. Years of talking to students at writing schools around the world have shown me that projects frequently fail not because of some lack of inspiration but through the more humdrum issues of poor time management, faulty working habits and plain ignorance of some of the basic tenets of the writing craft. These are the principal issues I intend to approach here.

Art is fundamental in the development of characters and themes and the creation of a compelling story sufficiently gripping to hold the attention of the reader. I have doubts about how much these elusive talents can be taught beyond the obvious. The best tutors for the subtle skills of narrative have been around us since we were children, on bookshelves, in libraries, alive in our own minds. They're the stories we've come to love ourselves and usually the reason we want to write in the first place. Every creative aspect of fiction is laid bare in the pages of the books we have absorbed as readers over the years. Better to study the work of the masters in their original form and work out for yourself what makes them great than to have someone else try to explain their achievements for you.

What can be learnt is the ability to think about writing, to understand how to control the various processes that go into the making of a book, from planning to story development, research to revision and, finally, delivery in a form which will catch the eye of an agent or publisher.

A first-time author may not be a professional in name, but there's no reason why he or she cannot be proficient in execution. Nothing guarantees failure more than tardy delivery, shoddy presentation and badly proofed manuscripts betraying the most basic of structural and textual errors. Those who come to judge your work will be looking for motives to reject it more readily than reasons to set another hopeful on the long and expensive path to publication. They will receive no better justification than the obvious whiff of amateurism. Authors, new and old, make mistakes. It is the inexcusable and the avoidable that those judging your efforts will find hard to overlook.

Budding author or professional, you should endeavour to adopt the unsung virtues of the practical side of the craft and seek to maximise your time, energies and skills in order to get a fighting chance of reaching the goal: a finished book of publishable quality. An organised writer, in control of his or her fate as much as any author can be, will negotiate the rocks ahead more competently than one who simply sets sail on the first gust of wind. He or she is also far better prepared to rescue a project from the wreckage, a prospect few busy authors will manage to avoid at least once in their career.

A significant part of the battle to become a writer lies in discovering and adopting the combination of working methods that suits your own temperament, personal circumstances and ambitions. Books make harsh taskmasters. An author has few chances for success and many for failure. It's important to maximise the former and minimise the latter.

Producing a successful novel shares much in common with architecture. While the public may see nothing more than the glorious dome of St Peter's in the Vatican, Michelangelo, who designed it, needed also to be familiar with the hidden structural issues and foundations beneath his work in order to ensure that glorious vision did not – like the bell tower of his successor Bernini – come tumbling to the ground. You must pay the same attention to these unseen yet essential aspects of your book, adopting skills and strategies that may be invisible to the reader but shore up the story, giving it the confidence, depth and resonance that are the hallmarks of the polished narrator.

This book is divided into what I regard as the three principal phases involved in producing a book: planning, writing and finally the essential task of refining a raw manuscript for delivery to an agent or publisher, or as a self-published book. I have provided examples of how the techniques I outline here might be used to develop an imaginary story called *Charlie and the Mermaid*. From time to time I cite some of the techniques I use in some of my own work, in particular for the series of novels I write around four figures in a fictional police station in contemporary Rome. You don't need to know those books in order to make use of this one, but anyone hoping to start a series should be aware that this route does require some special consideration.

Finally I should emphasise that none of the advice that follows is intended to represent that dread object, a 'rule of writing'. Fiction is too rich and flexible an art to be defined by rigid strictures invented largely for the convenience of those who concoct them. The guidance I offer here is personal and partial, based on nothing more than my own experiences from thirty years of trying to write the best fiction I can. During that time I moved from being a reporter on a small newspaper in the north of England first to national newspapers in London, then to writing fiction in my spare hours, and finally to becoming a full-time author, with more than sixteen books in print in twenty or so languages, a movie of one and now the entire Costa series in development for TV in Rome. It's been a long and interesting ride, one I could never have achieved without focusing at times on unexciting matters other authors may think are irrelevant or beneath them.

They could be right. You should question every aspect of the advice I offer here, ask yourself whether these ideas ring true for you, then cherry-pick and reject each element as you see fit. And after that . . . break your own standard practices from time to time, as I've done on many occasions. Which is another way of saying – if you read some of the million or more words I've written in my career you'll find I've contradicted some of the ideas I've outlined here time and time again.

Writing's like that: a hazy, insubstantial craft that you grasp at through a mist. Only you can define your own path to becoming a successful author, through your own creativity and a disciplined and imaginative approach to your work. I hope these suggestions help with the latter, and allow you, in turn, the freedom to devote more of your time and energy to writing a very good book.

Part 1

PLAN

BOOKS don't come into the world out of nowhere, even if it seems that way sometimes, to the author as much as the reader. Something must happen that makes an individual think: I want to become a writer.

A sudden yearning for easy riches?

I hope not. You'll probably be disappointed.

Celebrity?

Think about it. How many bestselling authors would you recognise if you saw them in the street?

Books come from somewhere else. An odd, subterranean desire to invent stories, to play with your own imagination and share the results with the world at large. There's no point in trying to analyse the creative urge. You either have it or you don't. But it is worth trying to work out where it comes from, and to set down a few basic strategies for how you intend to pursue the elusive goal of a publishable novel.

CHARLIE AND THE MERMAID

Your name is Charlie Harrison. You're a teenage boy walking in the shadows of a burnt-out pier on the seafront of a run-down English resort, watching shyly from the shore as a pretty girl stares back from the water, the still grey sea up to her waist. She's wearing a cheap, colourful cheesecloth shirt and her hair is soaking wet as if she's been swimming. The girl is crying uncontrollably and refuses to come out. She seems to want to say something but she can't quite bring herself to utter the words. A stray, bizarre thought occurs to you: she's actually a mermaid, someone stranded and in trouble, for reasons you can only guess at.

An idea, a seed is sown . . .

All books start like this whether we realise it or not. A sight, a few casually spoken words, a line on a page, an encounter with a stranger. That trigger may lay dormant for years then one day, summoned usually by something you can't quite place, it emerges. Finally, you say to yourself, 'I *am* going to write a book.'

And so a long, strange journey begins, one that ends for so many in failure and frustration. We know intuitively there's a story inside us somewhere. We have to believe we have a tale worth telling and of sufficient interest to others to make the effort worthwhile.

Why, then, is it so difficult to bring this blurry narrative to light?

In part because we often approach the problem from one direction only, that of writing, of production, of hunting for words to fill the void of a blank page. In our ignorance we think that staring at a dead white monitor will, through some magical intervention, bring forth a solution. We bang our heads against the same hard wall repeatedly wondering why we can never break through. Or if we do get to the other side we wind up asking ourselves what cruel turn of fate made the way ahead just as foggy and impenetrable, as devoid of reason and progress as the grim place we came from.

Writing is never easy, but it can be made less difficult. Some of the answers lie in understanding the process that brought you to the point at which you said, 'I have a story to tell.' Starting work on a novel is usually the culmination of years of reading, thinking and dreaming, most of it muddled and unfocused. In other words a hotchpotch of ideas suddenly fighting to come together in the form of a long and convincing narrative.

Books don't enter the world from a vacuum. Nor can they be shapeless, without some kind of form, structure and direction. Bringing a fulllength story to a satisfactory conclusion will require more than a single bright spark of inspiration. You will need to understand the nature of the obstacle course ahead, the skills required to negotiate it and the crucial decisions every writer will face along the way.

The seed is important too, of course.

Who *is* Charlie Harrison? What is his relationship with the girl in the water? What happens next? What kind of story could a starting point such as this one prompt?

Only one of those questions has an answer at the moment. That's the last one and it's dauntingly vague: any kind. This could be the opening for a tale of young love, a thriller, a crime story, even some kind of fantasy or gothic horror. The seeds for books are the same as those in your garden. You can never know what might emerge from that small brown husk when all you see is a tiny green shoot just starting to poke its way out of the top. Rose or thistle? Precious flower or not-so-welcome weed?

The temptation, always, is to seek the answer by sitting down at the keyboard and hoping some revelation will flow from your fingers. You may be desperate to get that first page out of your head and on to the screen – and if you are, then do it. Perhaps you've written it already and started to wonder . . . what next?

To finish a book, though, you need, at some stage, to walk away from the computer and try to think through some of the long and complex tasks ahead.

Don't worry. The words in your head won't disappear overnight. Why should they? If this is your first book they've been festering inside you for years, hidden away, murmuring in the dark, nagging you one day to try your hand at writing. They've been patient for a long time already. They can wait.

A WRITING FRAME OF MIND

I said in the Introduction that this book was divided into three sections representing the different phases of producing a book, its planning, its writing and finally, its delivery. The section titles you see here differ slightly, however, and say simply: 'Plan', 'Write', 'Deliver'.

Why? Because words matter. An appreciation of their subtle power is vital for anyone who seeks to use them. 'Writing', 'planning' and 'delivery' are all nouns, static, descriptive terms we use to denote things. This is fine for a description of how a book is organised. But a section title is an invitation to dive in and act. So instead I use verbs here, exhortative ones in this context that could just as easily be written as 'Let's Plan', 'Let's Write', 'Let's Deliver'.

Verbs are anything but stationary. They denote movement, vitality, effort and dynamism, all attributes that will be needed to see you through the difficult and testing task ahead. Self-doubt and negativity are not just threats to the completion of any writing project. They're an insidious poison that will seep into the text itself, instilling in it a dismal and pervasive mood visible to the reader.

Any book is a massive undertaking requiring commitment, skill, determination and an extraordinary amount of perspiration. Most people with half a feel for language and fiction can write a thousand words or so to kick off a story. Many can make it to some kind of mid-point. A few get to the end, and a small number of those few will manage to do so with sufficient dexterity to attract the attention of a publisher and see the fruits of their imagination reach, finally, the pages of a finished book. Of those only a handful will still be seeing their work published a decade or more after their debut and truly lay claim to the title 'professional author'.

Is it talent that separates the career writer from the amateur? Up to a point. But attitude, energy and resolve matter as well, which is why those section titles are active verbs not immobile, descriptive nouns. Creating a book may appear a solitary, cerebral activity from the outside. Beneath the surface it's a vibrant, exciting and immensely ambitious exercise, one that demands those traits of an author too. Successful writers don't sit down to start something. They set out intent on finishing it. You need to find the same enthusiastic doggedness in yourself.

Like the books they write, authors are a heterogeneous mix, some private, some extrovert, some deeply ingrained in academia, a few (this one, for example) with scarcely an educational qualification to their name. They do, however, tend to share some similar personal characteristics.

Here are a few. Some, you will note, are contradictory, but this is a profession of eternal paradoxes.

SELF-MOTIVATED. Most of us write our first book with little if any support or clear idea of what we're doing. Even established authors are, for the most part, lone operators, dependent on their own imagination for their ideas. You need to be able to analyse the problems you meet and find solutions without much in the way of outside help. Even when you have an agent and publisher you will find it's not their job to fix your career beyond advice and guidance. No one can write that book but you. If you're the kind of person who can't start work until you see the boss casting his beady eye in your direction something has to change.

FOCUSED. Writing requires intense concentration often to the exclusion of matters that, seen from the viewpoint of a non-writer, may appear more important. You could find yourself forced to write on planes and trains to keep up your work rate or locked in a room in your home with the sound of children in the next room and the noise of traffic outside. You will have to accustom yourself to devoting your leisure hours at the computer to work, not browsing the wastelands of Facebook and Twitter. This is a vocation for the single-minded and the obsessive.

INDUSTRIOUS. A novel may involve 150,000 words of raw text or more, research, editing, revision, liaison with editors, the occasionally fun but always time-consuming round of marketing and events. If you want to write full time in mainstream popular fiction you will usually be expected to deliver at least a book a year and risk losing your foothold on the sales slots if you're late or turn out something unexpected or not up to standard. Anyone looking for a secure and comfy job with long holidays need not apply.

PATIENT. Finished manuscript to book on sale may take two years or more from the moment a work is bought by a publisher. Add another year to that for the mass-market paperback edition if you first come out in hardback. In translation we're talking many years more. Should your book be optioned for film or television it may be a decade before you know whether there is any chance of the project being green-lighted into production. Nothing you can do will shorten any of these processes. Accept all this and use the waiting time wisely. There is no better way than writing another book.

OPEN TO CRITICISM. First-time author or old pro, your work will be judged by others and usually found wanting in some way. How do you react? Do you throw up your hands in horror and scream, 'But this is my book, not yours?' Or do you listen to the wisdom of people who have been in the business for years and have a very clear idea of what does and doesn't work? Writing involves constant learning. Even with sixteen or so books under my belt I discover something new with every fresh project. Successful authors pick up more from their mistakes than their successes. Smart ones ask a first-time editor, 'Tell me how to make this book better, please,' not, 'Tell me I'm clever and that you won't change a word.'

OBSERVANT. Books, ultimately, are about people and the universe they inhabit, about the creation of fictional characters who pass as real human beings and fictional worlds that are authentic enough to convince the reader they exist. You will never be able to achieve this small miracle unless you have the ability to listen to and try to understand the people around you, and to make notes constantly about what you hear and see and how that might affect your writing.

THICK-SKINNED. Few of us escape rejection at some stage. Those who go on to be published are often later happy to admit they should be grateful for their early rebuffs. Many books will be ignored by the critics and find little in the way of shelf space in a shop. Occasionally you will be subject to filthy reviews, particularly from the new army of so-called web critics, and rarely achieve much in the way of sales. If you crave instant public adulation or if disappointment dims your ardour, your writing career is likely to be brief and dispiriting.

REALISTIC. A sensible author understands that they are unlikely to be the next Lee Child or John Grisham, that Spielberg will not option their book, and that bestsellerdom normally takes many years and several books if it happens at all. He or she will be aware that it is an enormous achievement simply to be published, and that every book needs to be regarded as a stepping stone to a brighter future, not some desperate one-shot chance at stardom.

AMBITIOUS. You must aim high, craving a chance to sell more titles and write better books. If you don't believe in yourself why should your agent and publisher?

SELF-CRITICAL. It's no use trying to convince yourself that everything you write is wonderful. A serious author should be the first to find fault with their work and, whenever possible, correct that before passing a manuscript on to an editor. We all write rubbish sometimes. It's of absolutely no consequence provided we recognise it for the drivel it is and do our best to ensure it's never inflicted on others.

Is it reasonable to expect a novice to possess all these from the outset? No. You pick them up over the years. But you can prepare yourself for what lies ahead in some very simple ways. The first is the most obvious and pleasurable of all. Which brings us to the last universal quality to be found in all those who write for a living . . .

Well-read.

IN ORDER TO WRITE BOOKS YOU HAVE TO READ BOOKS

The publishing business likes to focus more on the positive than the negative. So here's a truth you hear rather too rarely. Agents everywhere are drowning in unsolicited manuscripts from hopeful writers that are so bad they make the poor souls who receive them want to weep.

Not bad in the sense that they're sub-standard. Bad in the sense that they are pitiable, dreadful efforts that can only have come from the minds of people who simply don't read books at all.

Are there really individuals out there who think you can be a writer without also being a reader? You bet. Anyone who has taught at a writing school has met them. Here's a somewhat disguised conversation from recent memory.

> AGENT (*to budding writer pushing an idea*): So who do you read?
> BUDDING WRITER: Read?
> AGENT: What other authors? Whom do you think you might be compared to?
> *Pinter pause.*
> BUDDING WRITER: I read a Stephen King book a while back.
> AGENT: Which one?
> BUDDING WRITER: The movie one with Jack Nicklaus.
> AGENT (*sighing*): I think you mean Jack Nicholson. *The Shining.*
> BUDDING WRITER: Yeah. *The Shining.*
> AGENT: Book or movie?

BUDDING WRITER (*hesitantly*): Both, I think.

AGENT: That was, what, thirty years ago? Anything since?

BUDDING WRITER: To be honest I don't read fiction a lot.

Long Pinter pause.

AGENT: Don't you think that would be a good idea? I mean if you want to write fiction . . .

BUDDING WRITER: They're all the same really, aren't they? So to get back to my story. There's this secret research facility, see. and some aliens. And a vampire. A really hot vampire . . .

I exaggerate. But only a little. If you're about to start a book do yourself a favour: go back to something you really like – an old classic, a title from a few years ago, one that's stuck in your memory for some reason. Read it again, from beginning to end, carefully, making notes. Try to put your finger on what it is you like and what, on a fresh reading, doesn't impress you so much. See if you can pinpoint the aspects of the story that made it memorable in the first place. The people? The concept? The location? It's more likely a combination of all three. But in what kind of order?

Think about the characters in particular. Why have they stayed with you over the years? What makes you like the ones you sympathise with and recoil from those you don't? Examine them against the sections later in this book that describe technical issues such as point of view and tense. How did the writer handle these? What difference would it have made to the story if he'd written it differently, from another point of view, say changing a first-person story to a third?

When your idea catches fire you will soon have to try to evaluate your own work. You'll find that a lot easier if you start trying to pick apart the books of others first.

Now, back to Charlie and his mermaid.

What kind of book could this be? Before we can begin to understand that we have to unravel a more pressing question.

WHAT KIND OF WRITER ARE YOU?

Robert Louis Stevenson was a talented man. Not only did he write some wonderful books but he was allowed a degree of freedom few of us can enjoy today. Stevenson produced a children's adventure classic *Treasure Island* and the dark gothic horror of *Dr Jekyll and Mr Hyde*. He penned the historical novel *Kidnapped* and *The Master of Ballantrae*, a kind of international revenge blockbuster with locations ranging from the Scotland of the Jacobite Rising to America and India. There was plenty of journalism and travel too, all in a mere forty-four years of a life blighted by sickness.

No one ever said to Stevenson, 'Stick to what you know, dear boy. You can be a kids' writer, a teller of adventure tales, a master of horror, or the forerunner of the Clavells and Archers of the century to come. But you can't be them all.'

He was lucky. Very few authors will find themselves so fortunate today. We live in the era of genre, of intense and rigid classification. In the 1960s, when I was a teenager browsing the shelves of the library in the small town where I grew up, already imagining where a book bearing my name would end up on the shelf, titles were divided into the most basic of categories. One part of the library was for fiction, one for non-fiction. The only sub-division in fiction might be an area where the sci-fi titles were kept, usually in the tell-tale yellow jackets of Gollancz. Everything else – from Mary Renault to Henry James, from Raymond Chandler to Somerset Maugham – was arranged alphabetically on the same shelves.

I grew up reading books of all kinds, not a set selection relegated to a genre, a pre-defined classification of the rich and sprawling world of literature that someone had kindly sifted and sorted beforehand. Like Stevenson, I was lucky too.

Today most popular fiction comes with a label attached. Crime, young adult, thriller, mystery, history, chick-lit, science fiction, fantasy, romance. These interbreed so we also have chick-lit mysteries and historical crime. Then there are the sub-genres such as noir, steampunk, gothic, hard-boiled, legal, police-procedural, speculative and alternative history. Some of these terms have geographical limitations. American readers are always surprised to learn that the word 'mystery' means precious little to their counterparts in the UK. The US term 'cozy' – used for a crime novel that avoids nastiness such as overt violence, sex and bad language while still managing to kill people somewhere along the way – is equally foreign to most readers outside America, though the kind of book it describes is universally popular.

Rail against the rise of the genres as much as you like, but you would be foolish to ignore it. One way or another your book will probably be defined as belonging to one of these categories, even if only tentatively. Accept that fact and start to understand how best to use it. You'll stand a much better chance selling your work as 'upmarket crime' than as 'general fiction that happens to involve a murder'.

Not that everything about genre is necessarily negative . . .

THE CHARLIE VARIATIONS

Taking on some of the aspects of a popular classification will add an important aspect to your coming book: a direction. You need that badge on your lapel not just because an agent or publisher will want to see it. Developing a clearer idea of the kind of story you want to write will also shape the progression of that seed of an idea germinating in your head. A first-time author isn't simply trying to complete a book. He or she is unconsciously struggling to understand what kind of writer might lie inside them.

An idea of the genre you're pitching for helps define the route ahead, and that's going to be important because this is a journey with many different crossroads and turnings. You need to ensure you take the right ones along the way.

Let's try to imagine some of the possibilities that could come out of the brief spark of a concept we've called *Charlie and the Mermaid* once we allow this germ of an idea to browse along a few different shelves in the bookshop.

CRIME

Crime is a broad church, one of the most popular kinds of popular fiction around at the moment. Most stories in this field tend to be about revelation, about a search for truth, one that can often be costly for those involved. A crime writer could look at our starting point this way ...

> Charlie wades into the water and discovers a drowned child at the young girl's feet. The police are called. The baby is hers. Immediately the police blame the girl and take her into custody. But she tells Charlie something before they arrive and he knows she's a victim too, not that the police will believe him, and for some reason she refuses to make this plain to them herself.
>
> The girl is released into protective custody. Charlie manages to see her again and his conviction about her innocence grows. He takes it on himself to find the real culprit, even though he knows this is dangerous and will lead him into conflict with the police himself.

Note: there's no detail here. Nothing much to tell us what happens next or even where the story is headed. It's implicit in this kind of book, as it is in most fiction, that the central dilemma – how can Charlie prove the girl's innocence? – will be resolved at the end. But we've no idea how and that doesn't matter. We're not looking for specifics. We're trying to get a general, fuzzy idea of the kind of book this might turn out to be and then use that to take the story forward.

THRILLER

Thrillers are so close in tone to crime stories the two frequently overlap. The key difference tends to lie in the thread that propels the story. In crime it is the hunt for the hidden perpetrator of some dark deed. In a thriller the narrative drive will come from something more immediate and pressing: an impending threat, a need to escape, a deadline that must be met. We'll sometimes know who the bad guy is, even if we don't know the full story about him or whether we should trust the information we have. None of this matters at the moment. Thrillers are there to thrill, to put the reader in the shoes of the protagonist as he or she tries to save their own skin, or that of someone else, and put the world to rights along the way. At this stage we simply need the starting point that propels our innocent into a new and threatening world.

> Charlie wades into the water and discovers the body of a well-dressed man in a suit lying on the sand by the young girl's feet, held down by lead weights. She stands there weeping, terrified. A group of scary-looking men are walking towards them along the beach. One of them pulls out a gun. The girl starts to howl. A fast inflatable boat emerges from behind. There's a woman on it. She's armed to the teeth and looks even more scary than the guys on the beach.
>
> She holds out her hand and makes it clear: this is their one chance to get away. They take it and as they speed off hear shots from behind. Has Charlie walked into the middle of some kind of gang war, a bloody feud over some issue his rescuer is reluctant to divulge? Is the girl he thinks of as the Mermaid a player or a victim in the endgame ahead? And how on earth is he going to get his geography homework to Mr Postlethwaite in Form 5c and avoid detention for the third week running?

There are lots of kinds of thrillers, just as there are many kinds of crime story. Some start with a big bang on the first page and hope to hook you there. Others reel you in slowly with an air of mystery and menace. This would be one of the former I think, perhaps a juvenile James Bond-style romp about a spirited kid who finds himself trapped inside some nasty drama that's deadly and threatening, but one that brings out his own character so he wins through in the end.

FANTASY

Fantasy covers a lot of fertile ground, stretching from gentle fairy tales to grim and visceral horror stories. But let's try an idea that's pretty low-key and 'ordinary' for this genre. No gates into other dimensions, no blood-sucking night creatures or howling werewolves. Just an unexpected rip in the fabric of the everyday world, one we can't even begin to understand at this stage.

> Charlie walks into the water to try to talk the girl out on to the beach. When he suggests this she becomes even more distraught. Close up he sees that she is, indeed, a mermaid. Human – all too human – above the waterline. Something else beneath. He wants to help her but she's more intent on telling him something. She knows his name somehow and tells him she has a big secret. In order to hear it he has to come back to the beach that evening, in the dark, and bring three things: a silver ring, a candle and a set of Tarot cards.
>
> Then suddenly, with the agility of a dolphin, not a human being, she turns and disappears back into the sea. He sees the flash of a silvery, scaly tail as she goes. He feels frightened but interested, almost elated too. She's done something to him. His life isn't ordinary any more and for some reason he knows exactly where he can find that ring, the candle and the set of cards.

Some fantasies take place in fantastic locations. Others, the most haunting occasionally, take place in the 'real world'. Once again there's no clue about where this idea goes next. Why does the mermaid want a silver ring, a candle and a set of Tarot cards? No idea. They're just objects to seek, to provide waypoints for the future story, places I could head towards. A note like this tells me some important basics about the story. The Mermaid knows Charlie somehow; there's a connection between the two of them. Does Charlie have an inkling what that might be? Is there a secret in his past too? Charlie has an interest in this girl, per-haps a romantic one. There's some kind of magic involved and, given her demand for some strange objects, a quest of some sort. Quests are popular devices for driving along narratives of all kind, especially fantasy.

YOUNG ADULT

The wonderful thing about ideas is that they often spawn others. It's tempting to replace one with what comes after. Resist. You're trying to build up a collection of possibilities at this stage, not narrow everything down to a single, concrete plan. That can come later. Perhaps your first option will be a mistake and it was something you rejected that will work better.

Here's a general rule you should apply to every scrap of information and inspiration you collect along the way. *Never throw these things away.*

There's another take on this story that last snapshot suggests. Charlie is a boy. He's met a pretty girl. There's attraction on his part, and a natural teenage curiosity about physical matters. Sexuality is an important human drive. Charlie sounds a nice kid but hormones happen to everyone. If this were to go to the young adult market it would be rash to ignore the possibility of some budding relationship here, innocent, tragic or simply some kind of coming-of-age story. So let's go back to the real world, and ditch silver, scaly tails . . .

Charlie walks into the water. The girl stands there sobbing. When he gets up to her he sees her clothes are ragged and torn. She doesn't speak good English but they manage to converse. She's lost something: a ring. He puts his head beneath the water and retrieves it. He thinks she may be east European – there are a lot of immigrants in the town, and the atmosphere between them and the locals is more than a little difficult – even incendiary at times. And Charlie's dad is one of the biggest immigrant-haters of all. He's a fisherman and he thinks the foreigners have been stealing his catch.

Sure enough, a boat comes along and it's full of scary-looking men who speak a strange language and take the girl on board. She holds out her hand and for some reason he comes along too. They take him back to where they live, some shacks and huts beyond the harbour. They're wary of him but he found the girl's ring and that means a lot to her. Charlie eats with them, listens to them sing, sees the girl become a little more relaxed, content again. Then he goes home and he hopes he'll see her again, though he thinks there's more to her unhappiness than a lost ring. When he gets back to his house he realises his dad saw him in the foreigners' boat and now he's in big trouble.

There's enough there for a chapter or two to see if this project catches fire. Why is the girl sad? Are the foreigners really living off illicit fishing alone? What will Charlie do when his dad says he can't see her again? You can work out for yourself where a story like this could go. In several different directions, of course, but that's usually inevitable at this stage. We're not looking for an outline here, we're simply trying to establish what kind of book this might be.

If you've started your story already you may have decided that by now. But it's always worth standing back from your work from time to time and asking yourself frankly whether it's proceeding the way you want. If you're unsure, you may save yourself a lot of wasted time by pausing the writing for a while until the idea is clearer in your head. Problems in books are usually solved by thinking them through, not pounding out words at the keyboard, hoping salvation will miraculously appear out of nowhere.

Playing with these seeds of ideas should point the way. There are other key decisions that need to be made to stamp this narrative with a particular identity. We may have narrowed down the kind of book this could be. Now we need to know how, exactly, it will be related to the reader.

POINT OF VIEW

Authors of popular fiction are primarily storytellers, building on the tradition established by early oral narrators back to Homer. This ancient Greek forebear worked before the invention of writing, and was a poet, a singer perhaps – blind according to legend. Homer memorised those fantastic tales of ancient heroism and derring-do and recounted them for anyone willing to pay his fee.

There are two conflicting theories about why human beings started to write things down. According to one, it was to enable the development of trade, so that individuals could produce lists of goods, invoices and sales receipts. Another claims we invented writing because we found the stories of poets such as Homer so entrancing we didn't want to lose them, to leave them to such a fragile and temporary thing as one man's memory. I know which theory I prefer.

One way we recognise our position as Homer's heirs is through something most readers never consciously notice: point of view – or POV, as it's commonly known.

Every scene of every book is defined and in some ways shaped by the position of the voice narrating it. Sometimes this is obvious. In a first-person book the voice of the tale comes directly from the character relating what happens. But sometimes POV is far more subtle. Popular fiction is usually divided between first-person and third-person stories, and third-person fiction sub-divided into three distinct sub-categories. Before embarking on any book you need to think about the POV you intend to use.

This decision is far from irrevocable. Sometimes it's worth rewriting an opening scene from different points of view in order to work out which is best. What matters is that you're aware of the POV as a writer, even if this technical concept goes over the reader's head entirely. Without a defined POV your narrative is likely to flounder around the place, meandering into byways where the story will become confused and lost.

The best way to envisage POV is to think of it as something Homer could never have imagined: a camera. In every chapter there's a lens through which the reader experiences the narrative. It's a very clever camera too, one that doesn't simply pass on an image of what's happening but also the words of those speaking and even at times what's going on in their minds.

This distinction between speech and thought gives you a clue to one of the trickiest aspects of POV. In order to function, that camera must understand its limitations and never range beyond them without good reason.

Let's look at some of the principal POV options open to you, how they might be used in a story like *Charlie and the Mermaid*, and some of their strong points and their failings.

FIRST PERSON

She wasn't around at first. At least I don't think so. It was as if she just appeared out of nowhere, like a ghost. Or a mermaid. One minute the beach was empty. The next she stood there, waist deep in the lazy waves of an ebbing tide, a little unsteady as if sinking into the soft sand beneath. Her long black hair was soaking wet. She wore a T-shirt that clung to her skinny body. I looked at her and shivered. For some reason I thought I recognised her, but that was impossible and soon I'd know it. Didn't matter either. Sally looked as miserable as anyone I'd ever seen.

From the outset we're inside Charlie's head, seeing what he sees, hearing his thoughts as they happen. This is a very direct and personal way to engage our audience. Readers hear the voice of the protagonist and are immediately introduced into both the plot and its key character.

Many novice writers begin their first attempt at a book writing in the first person. You only have to scan the bookshelves to see that first-person tales are very popular with readers too. For someone starting out it's an approach with many attractions. It's usually much the easiest voice when it comes to getting words on the page. You can imagine yourself into your character and describe what he or she sees through the progress of the narrative. If you're desperate to see whether you have the stamina to finish a full-length book, first person will probably help get you there more quickly than any other voice. But it's not without some serious drawbacks.

First, there's the question of character. There's another clue to the limitations of first person in that opening paragraph. We hear Charlie's thoughts as he looks at the girl in the water. We don't – and shouldn't – hear hers. Novices very often make key mistakes when it comes to point of view, errors that can get you marked down badly by any agent or publisher who reads your manuscript. One of them in the first person is the questionable use of interior thoughts. It's fine for Charlie to think he recognised her. It's perfectly reasonable for him to think she looks miserable too, since this is his observation. But what about this?

> I'd seen her before somewhere. Her name was Sally. She looked
> back and thought to herself: he's a funny-looking kid.

No. At least not within the accepted conventions of popular fiction (though there are always writers who will – and should – break these from time to time). We're in Charlie's head. He can't know what Sally is thinking, and you mustn't, in general popular fiction, pretend that he can. It's fine to say 'I watched her. She seemed to be thinking about what to do next.' That's his observation. But in 'I watched her. She was thinking about what to do next,' the omission of 'seemed' drags us out of Charlie's first-person narrative and puts us into Sally's head. And that's plain wrong. No reader will scream, 'Inconsistent point of view!' Or at least not many. But you're diluting the tightly fixed dimensions of the narrative – shifting the camera, albeit briefly, from Charlie's head to Sally's. Editors may shriek and for good reason. This is bad practice and, unless you're doing it deliberately for a reason, it will reveal you as someone who doesn't understand such a basic tenet of writing craft.

This example points to a broader problem with first-person narratives. They are, by their very nature, restricted in what they can describe. Unless you use some sly techniques the reader can only see what happens within the immediate experience of your narrator. In third-person stories you can flit from character to character, location to location. You can see inside the heads of different people, on all sides in the tale. You have a much broader field of possibilities to play with. With standard first person you're locked inside one character.

Most popular fiction is based on a conventional linear narrative, going forward from one point in time to another. In the simplest kind of first-person story your protagonist can usually only witness what is happening in scenes where he's physically present.

This is tricky. Is some bad guy sneaking up on Sally when she leaves Charlie and goes home? In the pure first person, Charlie can be scared about that possibility. But if it happens when he's not present he – and by implication the reader – can only learn about it afterwards, through some reported event. In the third person you can be there, with the bad guy, with Sally, with someone else altogether. First person denies you that flexibility and immediacy. It's a narrow, restricted, two-dimensional canvas, one that needs to be worked with special skill. In short . . . it may be the easiest way to achieve a finished story, but it can be the hardest POV through which to produce something compelling and original.

Unless you get sneaky. Here are a couple of common tricks.

The diary

First-person stories don't have to be linear narratives moving forward from a starting point to a conclusion, hour by hour, week by week, year by year depending on the timescale you've chosen. They can be more free-ranging if you play with the first-person system a little. The most common way is through a diary or letter-writing – epistolary to be precise – format.

Two of my favourite classics are *I, Claudius* and *Claudius the God* by Robert Graves. These manage to tell complex, panoramic stories of life in the Imperial Rome of two thousand years ago through the first-person voice of a single narrator, Claudius, a crippled member of the ruling family who goes on to become emperor himself. Graves achieves this through a very simple trick. The books are 'false documents' pretending to be the diaries of Claudius himself, written in old age, looking back on his life and the history of the empire, ranging from era to era, location to location.

This epistolary approach circumvents many of the problems of linear first-person narrative. Since Claudius is an amateur historian he can relate events in the furthest parts of the Roman empire with a distanced yet individual voice. It doesn't matter that he wasn't there and didn't witness what went on. Claudius knows these facts because he's now an old man telling the story of his life and times. The diary format allows him to tell stories, comment on characters, make observations of a series of historical occurrences and famous people even when he isn't personally acquainted with them.

Books written as letters or diaries bring much more flexibility and range to the first-person viewpoint. They allow the writer a considerable degree of perspective and the chance to take a panoramic view of an unfolding story. The catch can be easily seen in the nature of *I, Claudius*. Books of this nature are, of necessity, reflective, more leisurely in pace than a simple story hooked to the linear passage of time. Claudius is looking back at his life. If it's thriller-style speed you're after this is going to be a tough place to find it. That doesn't mean you shouldn't try.

Here's another take on the first-person voice:

The unreliable narrator

One of the great epistolary novels is Wilkie Collins's *The Moonstone*, often acclaimed as an early precursor to the modern detective tale. Written in 1868 and first published as a serial story in a magazine edited by Charles Dickens, this is an adventurous and highly gripping mystery about the theft of a precious Indian gem from an English country house. Collins performs an extraordinary feat in telling his tale in the first person through the recollections of several different characters, many of whom contradict each other, gradually revealing the truth behind the crime. In most first-person books we assume we can believe the voice of the person whose personality we have almost come to share as the story progresses. In works such as *The Moonstone* we've no idea whether they're telling the truth or not.

The storyteller in works such as these is known as an 'unreliable narrator', someone whose word we simply cannot trust. Children often make unreliable narrators, and may not even know it. Teenagers, such as J. D. Salinger's Holden Caulfield in *Catcher in the Rye*, know full well what they're up to, and don't mind letting on to the reader either. If you want to experience an unreliable narrator so unexpected that his revelation provoked outrage in some readers at the time, try another detective classic, Agatha Christie's *The Murder of Roger Ackroyd*. These are all works told in the first person, but with much more surprise and richness than one might expect. An unreliable narrator may be simply economical with the truth, a villain, someone who hides something for a good reason, or plain mad. Even a combination of all three. There's a lot of room to play with and, unlike in the epistolary approach, the unreliable narrator is quite happy to play a part in a conventional, linear narrative.

One caveat though: the narrator here is unreliable only in terms of what he or she shares with the reader. Internally the character needs to be working to a strict and accurate set of values which will usually only be shared with the world at the end. In order for this to work you will need to know very clearly what those values are as you go along. If in doubt read *Roger Ackroyd* and ask yourself: how did Agatha Christie handle that as a writer? At what stage do you think she managed to come up with that unexpected twist at the end? Certainly a long time before it reaches the reader.

SECOND PERSON

It's the middle of July, a hot afternoon, and you're bunking off school again, kicking pebbles on the beach near the old, fire-blasted pier, wondering when you dare go home and face the music. You look into the cool dark space below the walkway. Next to a rusting iron pylon that looks like some severed stork's leg you see her standing waist-deep in the water by a concrete stanchion green with seaweed. She's a little older than you, but she's crying uncontrollably, tears running down her shiny pale cheeks, and she's holding something in her arms, cradling it like a baby. But it isn't. You can see it's a doll, an old and battered one, with a pale face that's cracked, skull open to the sea air as if someone's smashed it. You think: she looks like a lost mermaid. You tell yourself: walk away. There's trouble down here sometimes. Gangs and louts and all the people your father says to steer clear of.

> But there's a girl too. She's pretty and she's in trouble. You can't
> walk away. You can't.

Very few full-length books are written entirely in the second person. The voice is usually employed in short stories or to add some variety to a work in another voice by introducing short passages, perhaps prefacing a chapter, told in a semi-interior second-person mode. This is, I imagine, how one would proceed with the passage here. One could move from this dreamlike image into a first-person account told by Charlie himself, indicating that this was a memory perhaps or a dream. Or segue into a third-person version that leaves the reader wondering who the 'you' referred to in the first few paragraphs actually represents.

Brief changes of voice – and as we shall discuss later, of tense – can add a slightly surreal and creepy nature to your story, beguiling the reader who knows he's being drawn into something unknown and perhaps a little unreal. Note that this opening is set in the present tense, not the customary past. That adds to the idea that this is some kind of vision or dream. Placing the second person in the past tense changes the effect substantially.

> It was the middle of July, a hot afternoon, and you'd bunked off
> school again, kicking pebbles on the beach near the old, fire-
> blasted pier, wondering when you'd dare go home and face the
> music. You looked into the cool dark space below the walkway . . .

We can imagine the first would lead to a narrator thinking inwardly, wondering about the reality of the memory. In the past tense all this *has* happened. So perhaps you'd use that to lead into something a little less loose and strange. The narrator is distanced from this event. He might even be recalling it decades later in his old age.

The possibilities are there, but the second-person past can all too easily sound a touch flat and prosaic, the report of some event, not the tantalising glimpse of the coming story that we're looking for.

Only the very brave and experimental should attempt to write a complete novel in the second person, especially if you hope it will fit into some category of popular fiction. As a voice it has all the drawbacks of the first person and none of the plus points. Best to stick to first or one of the flavours of third.

THIRD PERSON

Most books are written in the third person. In other words the reader's 'camera' lies outside the head of the principal character we're following. Third-person books are popular for a reason. They give the author far more freedom and scope than a first-person book. Readers can follow different people, go to different places at the same time, float around the author's imaginary world and examine it and its inhabitants from a variety of perspectives. This point of view is incredibly powerful if you choose to play with it. Or it can be used in a very straightforward way as a popular storytelling device that readers come to understand immediately.

There are different flavours of third-person writing. You should choose the one that best suits your own story. Rewriting chapters to see how they work in different voices is good practice and will let you see some of the possibilities such changes can open up.

Here are the principal third-person options open to you.

Third-person subjective

This is the probably the most common variation and in a way it's much like the first person transferred to a different but linked perspective. In the third-person subjective the reader's 'camera' is perched on the shoulder of the scene protagonist, so close that the reader can hear what he hears, see what he sees, even follow his thoughts. Like this . . .

Charlie asked the girl her name.

'Sally,' she said.

Perhaps she was lying. Not doing it very well either. There was something in her expression that seemed decidedly shifty.

He knew he ought to feel scared here in the chill darkness beneath the rusting pier. There were bad people around at this time of night. He wanted to go home. It was beans on toast tonight and he was hungry. Maybe the girl – Sally, if that was her name – would come too. She looked as if she hadn't eaten in days.

We're on Charlie's shoulder. We see the girl through his eyes, share his suspicion that she's not telling the truth. When Charlie feels hungry we know it without being told because we're privy to his inner thoughts. We've no idea whether 'Sally' is hungry or not because Charlie can't know that either. In the third-person subjective the camera stays on the shoulder throughout, listening, watching, monitoring the scene character's thoughts, no one else's.

How would this work through the girl's eyes?

The boy looked too old to be wearing tatty grey shorts a size too small for him.

'What's your name?' he asked.

'Sally,' she said, trying to sound as English as she could.

He thinks I'm making this up, she thought. She'd never been a good liar. Something crept into her face, she guessed, and it probably looked a little shifty.

He didn't seem scared by being alone in the chill darkness beneath the rusting pier with a stranger waist deep in the sea.

'You hungry?' he asked. 'We got beans on toast tonight. I reckon you could use some.'

'What're you called, kid?' she said, nodding at him, the way a grown-up would.

'Charlie,' he said, then rubbed his hands on his grey shorts and stuck out a hand. 'And by the way . . . I'm not a kid.'

Think about what that means for a moment. The reader and your point-of-view character are linked, tied together in a bond. It's important, then, that the two get along somehow. All popular fiction demands that readers care about the characters in the story. In a first-person story the closeness of that relationship is obvious. It's still there in the third subjective too, no less forceful but sometimes ignored. You're pushing the two together like passengers in a very small train carriage. They *have* to forge some kind of relationship pretty quickly otherwise the reader will soon get bored and think: why should I care?

Usually that's a connection based on some kind of affection. Charlie's a young kid, out of his depth perhaps. If this were his scene we'd be expected to like him and worry what he's about to get himself into – this is a story, after all, so we know *something* is going to happen.

The girl seems to be older, colder, more mysterious. Making her the point-of-view character is going to be more problematic unless she begins to reveal some inner warmth.

There is one other third-person reader-bond that can work wonderfully, of course. That's when you put the camera on the shoulder of someone utterly appalling, so bad, so nasty, so vicious you have to follow and watch, even if you're peeking through your fingers at times. Sally could easily be stringing poor Charlie along here. You choose.

Third-person objective

The camera's moved now. It's hovering somewhere around Charlie's back, following him, watching everything. This isn't the same lens at all. It can see things Charlie can't. If there was a bad guy hidden in the shadows this camera might have caught his presence. This is still Charlie's scene, but we're now attached to him very loosely. We can't see through his eyes any more or monitor any of his internal feelings. What we are aware of, more broadly than Charlie can possibly be, is the scene around him. This can have a lot of potential. One example: we can turn the reader into the audience at the pantomime screaming, 'Look behind you!' all for the benefit of an actor who simply can't hear.

> The boy called Charlie Harrison walked a little closer and asked her name.
>
> > 'S-s-sally,' she stuttered. 'Why do you want to know anyway?'
> > 'Don't sound very sure.'
> > 'You calling me a liar?'
> > 'No. Are you foreign or something?'

He shuffled on his feet, staring at the sand, and added, 'Not that I'm fussed.'

'It is Sally,' she insisted. 'Honest.'

'Shouldn't be doing this, Sally. Not standing in freezing mucky water. Like some daft person. There's bad people round here.'

Beyond the rickety iron legs of the pier something moved in the pitch-black darkness, sliding slowly, silently through the water, working its way towards them.

'Maybe I'm bad too,' the girl said. 'You thought of that?'

He wiped his fingers on his shorts and stuck out his right hand.

'Charlie,' he said. 'Charlie Harrison. We're having supper soon. Beans. Want some?'

Neither has any idea there's something sloshing slowly towards them. It's silent isn't it? We understand that. They can't. Nor can the author pass on the information that the girl has a foreign language directly. We let Charlie bring that out of her instead.

Do you have to be absolutely rigid about this? Not at all. Think of them as conventions, not strict rules that must never be disobeyed, though some editors may crack the whip if you don't stay within the accepted norm. Readers don't sit there thinking about point of view. If you wanted to write ' "Sally," she replied in a foreign accent,' most wouldn't shriek, and nor would I. In the objective viewpoint the reader is still there, inside that camera, listening. You could argue it's the reader's observation that the accent is foreign. What will break this perspective is writing ' "Sally," she replied in what sounded to him like a foreign accent.' Do that and you've put the camera in Charlie's head for a few seconds only to remove it soon after. These may seem small points but you need to remember them and not just because a publishing professional might regard them as 'errors'. Readers may not know about point of view, but it does subtly guide them through the story. If your grasp of perspective is confused and shifting, theirs will be too and most of them won't like it.

The third-person objective is a more challenging voice, and one best avoided unless you have very specific reasons for using it. One good reason would be if you want to keep your readers out of the head of the characters, to let them observe the narrative developing without being able to guess, from interior thoughts and dialogue, exactly what's going on in their minds. This can be a very useful tool if you need it. If not, this mode of writing can make for a story that is somewhat disconnected. Readers will have to work harder to get close to the key characters. This is problematic; you want to bring down the barriers between them and your audience, not erect them.

The third-person objective can very easily become a manifesto for a particular intellectual approach to writing, a literary equivalent of the Dogme 95 school of film-making, not a storytelling tool in its own right. But feel free to try it and see if you feel differently. Getting over that eternal difficulty – how do you tell the reader what your characters feel when you can't put them directly inside their heads? – is a good test of your skills and ingenuity. People are still writing many great books in this viewpoint today, though the third-person subjective remains far more popular.

Third-person omniscient

If we go back to the classics we find this variant of the third person everywhere. In the omniscient the camera has hovered up somewhere into the sky of our world and from there it will watch everything with a cold, remote and observational eye.

You can't look for better examples of this style of writing than in Charles Dickens, in particular his opening for *A Tale of Two Cities*:

> It was the best of times, it was the worst of times, it was the age of wisdom, it was the age of foolishness, it was the epoch of belief, it was the epoch of incredulity, it was the season of Light, it was the season of Darkness, it was the spring of hope, it was the winter of despair . . .

Nothing there prepares you for a panoramic work of historical fiction, flitting between London and Paris around the time of the French Revolution. Dickens establishes from the outset the kind of point of view he will use – his customary one. In the third-person omniscient the narrator possesses – as the term suggests – an all-seeing, all-knowing eye, and the reader merely has to wait for this storyteller to decide which part of the tale to reveal next. Imagine a narrative retold by God and you have it. And God, naturally, has all the time in the world.

Most of the classic novels of the nineteenth century follow the third-person omniscient model. Tolkien used it for *The Lord of the Rings* trilogy too. Modern epic writers will reach for its scope. Stephen King rarely writes using anything else. This is a voice that knows its place. When you need it, little else will do.

Unless you aspire to the epic mould it's a tough prospect. The reader of the twenty-first century is more pressed for time, more anxious for that elusive and occasionally destructive quality 'pace' than ever. The omniscient is tailored for the blockbuster tale spanning continents and centuries, with the kind of sprawling cast that a Cecil B. DeMille would find attractive. If that's the kind of magnum opus you're planning, go for it. If it's something a little more down-to-earth you could find yourself fighting a rearguard battle against both editors and readers frowning in puzzlement and asking, with good reason: but why couldn't he just write this straight? Outside the epic field the omniscient is a curiosity, occasionally seen in popular fiction but hard to pull off.

And remember . . . even epics can be written in the more standard third-person subjective. Just pick a handful of ordinary mortals and make them witnesses to history. What ensues may be more vivid seen through their eyes than through the remote viewpoint of that literally super-human camera in the sky.

How might this mode work with *Charlie and the Mermaid*? For the sake of brevity I'll have to compress things here somewhat, since it's a hallmark of the omniscient that those different sweeps over the world below rarely happen in the space of a few paragraphs. Bear this in mind and try to fill in the gaps for yourself.

It would be the hottest evening of the summer. In the narrow, winding lanes the night people lurked sweating, breathless. Gang kids in tight jeans and black T-shirts, wads of skunk and crack in their pockets. Teenage lovers desperate for some sharp stab of passion. Drunks and deadbeats, a lone cop, a solitary hooker too tired to push for trade.

The boy of fourteen, Charlie Harrison, skirted the alleys, brought his rusty old bike to a halt by the shuttered doors of the old pier. The place had been burned out by one of the dope gangs the year before, half tumbled into the sea like the fiery embers of some gigantic bonfire. Still this stranded wreck drew him, not that he remembered why any more.

No place for a girl just a year older either. She stood waist deep in the icy water beneath the moonlit pier, watching the gentle waves of the ebbing tide ripple against the crooked iron limbs of the pier ahead of her.

A memory. Back home, in the east, a place she'd fled for reasons she'd never understood, the storks flew away at this time of the year. Great white shapes rising into the sky, long, fragile-looking legs lifting beneath them. Spindly legs, too weak to support that big strong body above. Or so she thought. The rickety black supports of the pier looked much like them. She remembered how the birds left the shore so easily, rising from the ground with a single effortless flap of their wings.

It was easy for them, she thought. Easy for most people. Not her.

She looked at the water ahead, took a deep breath, and lifted her arms in front of her, out towards the sea.

'Oi!' yelled a voice from the shoreline.

She turned and their eyes locked on one another: lanky fourteen-year-old in tatty shorts too small for him, skinny girl shivering as the freezing waves lapped hungrily around her waist.

'What are you doing?' the kid screamed. 'What . . . '

She didn't get the rest of it. She was falling beneath the water, letting the cold, dead waves embrace her.

Ahead of them beneath the pier a dark shape moved. Behind the boy with his bike, there was another shape stomping down the alley head down, throwing a cigarette into the gutter, swearing, nodding, chanting to himself, getting madder all the time.

There was a time, a time, a time . . . this second one sang.

And then was silent, looking ahead, seeing the strange black silhouette rise from the flat moonlit water by the crooked stanchions, feeling the fear seep into his fury, wondering which of them might win.

The giveaway's in the first sentence. It '*would*' be the hottest day of the summer. Only a god could know that.

Since we're omniscient now we know how the weather will turn out. We understand what people are doing in the back alleys of the town. We can see inside Charlie's head and that of the girl simultaneously. We hear what this new character is chanting as he stamps angrily towards the beach and see before any of them that dark shape rising from the water.

The third-person omniscient is a wonderful voice provided you can bring the reader sufficiently close to those mere mortals your narrator is watching from on high. No one wants to spend a whole book in the company of a god.

CONFORMITY OF POINT OF VIEW

There's no rule that says you can only use one POV in a book. It's perfectly acceptable to switch voices between scenes, from first to third, if you want. This is most common in books that flit between two eras. In my own *The Cemetery of Secrets* (in the US, *Lucifer's Shadow*) I wrote a contemporary story in the third person, mirrored by a companion tale set in the Venice of 1733 written in the first.

But this kind of approach is quite complex, and anything complex mitigates the speed of the narrative. If you're after the 'read-in-one-sitting' effect, stick to something simple. Most first-person books are written in the voice of the same character throughout. Just make sure that character grips the reader sufficiently from the start in a positive and riveting fashion. That doesn't necessarily mean they have to like the person, though that will usually be the case. We're fascinated by bad people too, so a first-person tale recounted by a monster can work just as well as a story told by a saint.

But here's a confession: I wrote three books without knowing that point of view even existed. As soon as this very important aspect of fiction writing was explained to me my approach to writing scenes changed to conform with the established norm – one point of view per scene usually.

It doesn't have to be like this. There are no rules of writing, except for the most elementary one: never bore your reader. In my very first book, a Spanish thriller first published then filmed as *Semana Santa* and now back in circulation as *Death in Seville* I occasionally committed one of the cardinal sins of point of view. I switched back and forth from character to character *within the same scene*.

You're not supposed to do this. It can confuse the reader and is generally viewed as bad practice. Unless you want and expect to engage in a technical editorial argument with an editor, stick to one point of view throughout. There is one conventional exception: when your next scene is going to shift POV to a character who's actively involved in the present one. Then it can become very effective to move that camera from one shoulder to another towards the end.

Think of it like this . . . Charlie takes Sally home to his house where she eats baked beans with him and his father. We find out a little more about the greater mystery that lies at the heart of the book. Towards the end of the scene Sally hears something from Charlie or his father that rings a bell, something she doesn't want to discuss with them, a fact or possibility that will fire her into taking some action in the very next scene which we will see through her point of view. We see the present scene through Charlie's eyes, then something happens.

Charlie's dad finished his plate then popped open his second can of beer. He looked at Sally and said, 'You don't seem bad for one of them.'

'Dad,' Charlie said, suddenly embarrassed. 'Don't be so rude!'

'Rude? *Rude?*' He'd been down the pub before coming home. Did that most nights now since Mum had left. 'You tell me I'm being rude when you grow up and there's no damned jobs left. Not if you're English and want a working wage.'

'I'm sorry, Mr Harrison,' Sally said. 'I know it's not easy here. I didn't choose it. My family brought me. If I could go back . . . '

'Fat chance of that,' he mumbled.

'Dad!' Charlie whispered. 'How could you?'

He got up from the table and cast them both a filthy look.

'She's too old for you lad. Spoilt rotten probably. Like most of 'em. I know what goes on.'

'What's that, Mr Harrison?' she asked.

'Down that place you all go. You lot and the men who run this bloody town. Have fun, do you?'

'I don't know what place you're talking about,' Sally told him.

'Dad . . . ' Charlie pleaded.

'That creepy Masonic hall down Bridge Street. They won't let the likes of me in there, will they? Only you. And *them*. I wonder why.'

Sally Gulik closed her eyes and tried to quell her troubled thoughts. There was a picture in her mind: a girl two years older than her, much loved, a sister lost in their travels since leaving the old country. Gone.

'I'm sorry if I've offended you,' Sally said, getting up from the table. 'Thank you for the food. Thanks, Charlie, for your help.'

'You don't have to go!' he cried, glaring at his father. 'Ignore him. He's been on the beer. Always has by this time of night.'

She watched the two of them. This was courageous on the boy's part, she thought. Perhaps the furthest he'd ever gone.

His father just looked at the two of them and began to laugh, strong shoulders heaving, making a sound she didn't like.

'Spoiled goods,' he said again. 'They all are.'

She walked outside. Charlie followed and started to apologise.

'No need,' she insisted and briefly touched his arm.

He seemed to like that.

'Will I see you again?' he asked.

'Here.'

She wrote her mobile number on the back of his hand. He was very still as she held his fingers and worked the pen across his skin.

'Where's Bridge Street, Charlie?' she asked him.

Shifting point of view at the end of a scene this way is a bit like passing the baton in a relay race. If you're going to attempt it you need to make the exchange obvious. Here the change happens with the sentence, 'Sally Gulik closed her eyes and tried to quell her troubled thoughts.' We now know the reader is inside Sally's head. The sentence that follows contains some significant information, not that we understand *why* it's significant yet. Just to enforce the point I would make this the first stage at which we reveal Sally's surname. She withholds it from Charlie. But the reader is told and this enforces the shift in point of view, leading to the following scene which is Sally's as she goes to Bridge Street.

That is a conventional way to shift viewpoints in the same scene. But there are writers who will do more than this, changing back and forth mid-scene and getting away with it. I turned out to be one myself. When I came to revise *Semana Santa* for its republication as *Death in Seville* I rewrote the book from beginning to end. I was quite shocked to come across scenes where the point of view shifted in a way I'd no longer contemplate. It was always obvious, and usually between just two characters, often the only ones in the scene. I was entirely prepared to rewrite these scenes to conform to the 'one POV' format with a handover at the end now and again. When I asked my editor about this she thought for a moment then said, 'I think you should leave it as it is. It works.'

So you can do it, just as you can break any so-called writing rule you encounter. When? You have the answer above. 'When it works.' This is writing, not algebra. Sometimes there is no easy, pat solution. What succeeds for one writer fails for another. You can say the same for readers and for books too. What you're after is the tone, voice and approach that work for you and the book in question.

ALTERNATING VIEWPOINTS

I once got an email from a reader who said one of the things he liked about my books was the way I told the story through different pairs of eyes – multiple points of view, in other words, across scenes, not within them. It's always nice to have hit the mark but I wondered then, and I wonder even more today: what has happened to the world of writing that we find this convention so unusual it's worthy of remark?

Tales that are told through multiple points of view are simply those in which different scenes are seen through the eyes of different people. That email came just after I'd proofed my book *The Blue Demon* (in the US, *City of Fear*). Like most of my work, that book uses the third-person subjective point of view throughout, but shifts this very personal 'camera' from character to character throughout the story. The tale begins through the eyes of an assassin stalking the president of Italy in the gardens of Rome's Quirinale Palace. The second scene shifts back in time three days and is seen from the viewpoint of a kidnapped politician. After that we settle into several sections where the viewpoints move backwards and forwards between two of my cops, Nic Costa and Gianni Peroni, as they begin to unravel a terrorist plot in Rome.

I don't think that book is any more or less multiple-viewpoint than much of my work. Sometimes I will focus largely on a single third-person viewpoint – normally Costa's, as in the first book in the series, *A Season for the Dead*, and the sixth, *The Garden of Evil*. But usually we switch from character to character.

Why do I do this? Two reasons really. I feel it gives me more flexibility to tell a tale with depth and resonance than would a story seen through a single viewpoint. When I gave Costa the dominant point of view there was a reason: these were very much stories about him. Mostly, though, these books are ensemble pieces in which Nic is a key character but by no means the only one with a viewpoint that matters.

The second reason is much simpler. This method reflects the style of writing I grew up with, the approach taken by the majority of the novelists I've admired since I began to read. Most authors writing in the third person over the last two centuries have switched viewpoints as needed. Dickens wrote like this all the time, as did most Victorian and Edwardian authors. Stephen King was happily doing it from his earliest work and continues to do so today. To me it's the natural way to write.

But popular fiction has changed somewhat over the last twenty years. A new audience no longer finds its definition of story from books, but from TV and the cinema – media which, ironically, use multiple viewpoints all the time. But they do so alongside a compression of narrative and characterisation which is usually categorised as 'pace'. The casual reader often wants that kind of kick from a book too, and as a result simpler viewpoints, either first-person or third-person subjective confined to a single character, have become popular to the extent that the older technique of multiple-character perspectives is sometimes seen as almost an innovation. Odd really . . .

But none of this means you need to follow the mainstream. Multiple viewpoints are still popular, just no longer dominant as they once were. They can provide the reader with a perspective on a world that is richer and more full of mystery than one which is seen through a single pair of eyes. They also allow you more play with readers' expectations.

Theatre doesn't have points of view in the same sense as fiction. But there are similarities. Shakespeare is a master at varying the rhythm and tone of his work, switching from the main drama to a short, humorous piece of gallows humour before some bloody, climactic scene, for example. Shifting from the head of one character to another gives the author the chance to perform exactly the same trick, taking the reader to the brink of some exciting and revelatory moment, then extending the tension by taking them somewhere else briefly, for an unexpected diversion. It's a tease in other words, and like all teases needs to be brief.

In some ways this use of POV is an attempt to achieve a scene structure similar to the narrative flow of cinema. The movie camera defines absolutely the perspective from which we see a scene. It also tells us very clearly when we've gone somewhere else.

Does that make books like this a little harder to read? Possibly. Or put it another way, they will appeal to people who like to get stuck deeply into a book instead of being able to skim-read the main plot points. But literature is a broad church. No one wants to go into a library that contains nothing but the same kind of story. Reading is a two-way deal too. The more all of us put in – writers and readers alike – the more we're going to get out in the end.

The amazing thing is that for some modern readers multiple viewpoints in popular fiction are seen as something unusual. Something new even, as that reader's email confirmed, not as old as the hills.

Here's one reason why you might wish to consider this technique.

THROUGH THE EYES OF OTHERS

How do you persuade the reader to adopt an opinion about the actors in your tale? In very simple fiction it's easy. Good people wear white hats, bad people black ones. Good people are handsome, athletic, have nice smiles and pat any dog that passes. Bad guys have scars, crooked teeth, greasy hair, swarthy skin and pull the wings off butterflies.

Outside stories for infants, that doesn't work for a moment. Nor can I accept either that you disclose the personality of individuals by attaching a simple label to them. 'Renowned scientist Roger Frick' . . . 'Courageous Captain Hearty' . . . Sorry. I need more subtle tricks.

Here's one to do with characterisation that comes directly from the use of multiple characters in the third-person subjective viewpoint.

When I was starting out as a writer I thought that you established character openly through the individual concerned. You showed him being kind or cruel. You revealed him as a hypocrite or liar by showing how his inner thoughts conflicted with his outward actions and what he said out loud. You painted him directly on the page.

This is fine, and something that all writers can and will do. But if you adopt the third-person subjective fully you can approach this problem another way. Remember, if you get this right the reader is inside the head of your POV character, seeing everything through his or her eyes. When your character, and through him your reader, views other people a subtle and potentially powerful chain reaction kicks in. The response of the reader is refined and enhanced by the very fact they are discovering this person indirectly, through the eyes of another character in the book.

Think of it like this for a scene in which Nic Costa – a good guy, something already established – is the POV character.

Nic is dealing with two of his colleagues.

He clearly likes one and appreciates his opinion.

Nic does not like the other guy.

Because we know Nic, like him and trust him already, his opinion comes to colour ours. Through his eyes we understand that the one he likes should turn out to be trustworthy and decent, unless Nic's a bad judge of character (which is rare). And we suspect the other guy, even if Nic doesn't go that far, precisely because Nic is normally right about people. So we've established some personality traits without ever having to state them baldly, and they are reinforced by the relationship the reader already has with Nic.

It gets even more interesting if the POV character is less reliable. Supposing he's not a good judge of character and the reader knows this. If he then starts trusting someone, we're going to think, uh-oh, this may not be such a good idea.

In real life we judge people both directly and through the eyes of others. Books are no different. Of course you can and should use this technique with a third-person subjective story that never shifts POV. But if you apply it to a multiple-viewpoint narrative, the possibilities for building real, resonant relationships between your characters implicitly, without ever having to state something as blunt, tedious fact, become much more interesting.

Point of view is one of the most powerful implements in the writer's toolbox and worthy of a book in its own right. But it's not this one. The best way to begin to master this immensely potent technique is to play with it yourself. Try writing scenes from different viewpoints and see how they change. Ask yourself which best fits in with your ambitions for the story. Experiment at the edge of the envelope if you like, mixing first, second and third person to see how they work. I'd avoid using the variations of third person in the same book. This would confuse me. But you may have a way round that. And finally, if you are heading for a third-person story, try to evaluate the various pros and cons of approaching it through a single character or an ensemble.

These are important decisions, ones that, after a little experimentation, you need to stick to. It's no fun finding halfway through a book that you picked the wrong person for the single third-person subjective. There's nothing to do in those circumstances but to go back to the very beginning and rewrite the whole thing (and I speak from experience).

On the other hand, I should also point out that perhaps you should discount all the above. There's still a hard core of writers ignoring these rules out there, and some of them do pretty well. A century ago popular writers knew none of this and no one seemed to mind. If you want proof and the opportunity for a little creative exercise, pop over to somewhere like Feedbooks.com or Project Gutenberg (www.gutenberg.org) and pick up a free copy of *The Invisible Man* by H. G. Wells. Turn to the second chapter, 'Mr Teddy Henfrey's First Impressions'. Then try to work out whose point of view is being used throughout. Clue: it's not Mr Teddy Henfrey's for a fair bit of the time. The POV hops about like a moth trapped in a room full of light bulbs. If you want to test your understanding of modern POV conventions try to work out the changes and see how a writer today would 'correct' them. Wells clearly wasn't bothered by such things when he wrote this very successful book in 1897. So should we be now? I think so. It's a great story but for me it flounders in this chapter precisely because the modern reader, short on time and patience, can't work out the perspective.

We now need to pass just two more hurdles before we get down to writing: a decision on the simple matter of tense; and, much more fundamentally, a way to monitor the content, tone and progress of our book as it begins to grow beneath our attentions, fighting to find a life of its own and, if we're not careful, squeeze out of our control.

A QUESTION OF TENSE

Now to a very simple decision. Do you want your story to take place in the past, the present or the future? Let's deal with the last option immediately, since it really won't take long. Let me tell you the answer: probably not, if you want to be published as commercial fiction. There's always someone out there who'll disprove the obvious one day. But books are rarely set in the future. As a narrative tense it's too odd and too constricting. For a short story looking for a voice that screams 'disconnect' from the outset . . . possibly. A full-length novel? Best avoided.

Which leaves us with two basic choices . . .

IN THE PRESENT

Few books use the present tense throughout. It's not as odd as the future tense for a narrative, but it's not far off. It can also become distinctly wearisome after a while. Narrative tends to run to a rhythm, much like a piece of music. It will have slow and fast passages, loud and quiet ones. At times characters will be ruminating on the past or the future and giving the reader a chance to do the same in the context of the story so far. At other points the book will be making the story happen, moving more quickly, furiously even. It's very hard to achieve that sense of a changing tone if all you have to work with is the present tense. The voice lends a distanced, dreamlike flatness to the story. It's much like the first-person point of view in that respect, which is one reason why first-person passages often work best when set in the present tense.

There's a clue to one of the most useful functions for the present. Imagine your novel is principally written in the past tense. From time to time your protagonist has dreams or flashbacks which start to illuminate the mystery as it's revealed. The sudden jolt of the present can make these interludes more gripping.

It's way past midnight and I'm walking down the alley to the pier. Butcher's Lane, they call it. Sally's round here somewhere I think. Lost and frightened. Maybe. Or something else. Something I don't want to think about. Up ahead I hear the sound. The bad one. Screaming. Fighting. Waves and water. I run to the beach. Run to her. And then . . . and then . . . beneath the moonlight I see it. The thing. The beast. The nightmare, flapping, screeching, waving its long shiny arms, beating the waves.

There's something in its grip and I know what it is. The sea rises, the waves dash against my face. The water, the wind, the fury of the gale begins to consume me. I fight, I struggle, I beat the thing with my fists . . .

'Charlie! Charlie!'

He came to in bed, head hurting, arms off the mattress, stiff in a foetal crouch. The window was open and through it beat the steady summer rain, battered by the chop of a gusty breeze.

'Are you ever going to get up for school?' his dad barked from the doorway.

'Yes,' Charlie muttered and climbed out of his creaky single divan, soaking from the rain, and the sweat of the nightmare too. The little alarm clock on the cupboard said eight thirty. He'd slept for twelve hours solid and still he ached from the night before.

In this example the first person serves to pass on Charlie's nightmare. Note that I've put those few paragraphs in italics to emphasise that they're outside the normal past-tense narrative of the book. We'll look at italics in more detail later. They're optional when used like this, but they can be effective, provided they don't run on for more than a few paragraphs.

Another way to use the present tense is as a bookend closing a scene when something very significant is about to happen. This technique is similar to the shift of third-person perspective to a fresh character discussed earlier in the section on conformity of point of view. It acts as a relay, passing the reader into a different phase of motion within the narrative.

Charlie walked down the dark alley and called out her name. It was past midnight. He wasn't supposed to be out. Nor was she.

He heard a noise ahead. A kind of sloshing sound. Like wellington boots full of water, moving laboriously through mud. There wasn't mud around the footings of the pier. There wasn't anything that could make a sound like that.

'Sally!' he shouted.

Somewhere in the black night ahead he hears a voice. Hers.

A cry. A pained scream, muffled and distant.

Still he stumbles on, knowing this is the moment. There's a pen-knife in his hand and he realises how very small and childish it feels.

You wouldn't usually place this change of tense in italics. It's at the end of the scene, an integral part of it, designed to be a tension-twisting hook that makes sure the reader turns the page and goes straight into the next chapter. The preface earlier serves a very different purpose and, since it begins the chapter, is more easily formatted in a different way.

There are no hard and fast rules, of course. There rarely are. I'd tend to italicise internalised thoughts used in this fashion and leave descriptive prose relating to the real world alone. There are plenty of variations on these two. You could have a character suffering from some intermittent flashbacks who hears or sees them midway through a scene written in the past tense (and they'd be italicised). You could try a version of the split-screen technique from the movies and, towards the end of the scene, intercut between characters in two different locations. In the latter case the shift from past to present signals to the reader that something new and different is happening here and, hopefully, ensures they stay alert to your tricky machinations. I'd italicise those just to make sure.

These techniques repay experimentation. But don't get carried away. They're best used sparingly if at all. If they become so repetitive that the reader begins to expect them, they're liable to turn tedious soon after.

IN THE PAST

Most novels are written in what grammarians call 'the simple past tense'. Don't you love that word? Simple. Books are meant to look that way to the reader. Authors are there to deal with the complexity, then hide it underneath the carpet.

Grammarians also call it the 'preterite', which doesn't sound simple at all though it's exactly the same thing – the tense used by most authors most of the time. Stories recount things as they happen. The reader's perspective is that of a remote viewer witnessing a series of events.

Charlie went to the pier.

Sally ran away.

Later the two of them met by the railway station.

Simple past. Readers who don't even know what tense is, and probably think a preterite is something that falls from the sky, understand instinctively what's going on when you write like this. If your audience has done part of the groundwork for you, a smart author says thanks and takes this free gift with gratitude. The reason we usually write in the simple past is because it works without any explanations.

You will use other variations of the past in your book. There's the past continuous:

Charlie was swimming towards the pier when the wave hit him.

And the past perfect:

Sally had thought for a while that it was time to go back to the water. Then Charlie called and finally she knew.

If you want to write you shouldn't need me to tell you what makes those two sentences past continuous and past perfect in turn. They should come naturally as part of the narrative flow, contained within the greater context of passages written in the past simple. I'm sure there are people out there who will attempt to write entire chapters, or even books, in the continuous and perfect tenses. All I can say is: good luck. We're back in Dogme 95 territory again.

The past simple is the predominant voice of fiction, one you've been listening to all your life if you're an avid reader. My advice to the first-time writer is: don't buck the trend. Assume your book will be written in the *lingua franca*. Play with the present from time to time if you feel like it. Drop into other forms of the past tense when the demands of good plain English demand.

DECISIONS

If this were my book my mind would be fixed by now. In terms of point of view I like Charlie. I think I'd prefer to stick with him for most of this story. So while I may veer off with Sally from time to time I'll usually place my camera on his shoulder and tell his story through the simple past. But he's a dreamlike kid so from time to time I will insert the odd flashback or flashforward – not sure which yet – which could be in the first person and the present tense.

The voice and tense are fixed. I've got a seed to start the narrative and even a few characters. Can I start writing yet?

Yes. Just not, for the moment, the book itself.

KEEPING A BOOK JOURNAL

We have our story seed, some characters, a voice, a tense and an idea of the kind of narrative we want to produce. So why not fire up the word processor and start putting together some words?

If by this stage you're dying to get stuck into that first scene, by all means do so. When the writing itch hits it's best to push everything else to one side and scratch it. Enthusiasm is paramount. But here's a perpetual truth: at some stage that rush to get words on the page will run out. You'll find yourself looking at a blank screen with little idea of what comes next, even if you've tried to outline the story in advance. Stories aren't written, they're *created*. In other words, they're the result of a complex mix of actions and processes, some imaginative, some deeply practical, that need to work alongside one another from beginning to end.

Think of it this way. Full-length books are substantial pieces of writing encompassing a cast of fictional characters, an imaginary world and a story pulled out of thin air. If that idea in your head were a business project it would require a team of people, all with a variety of skills. There'd be a plan, deadlines, targets, goals. Throughout its development people would write progress reports, note problems and sticking points, and shift strategies and expectations to meet the changing reality of the idea as it matured.

A writer has to wear all those hats alone. Can you really handle them just through writing the manuscript? What happens to all those ideas you have that don't make it to the page? The sudden flashes of possibilities about where the story might be headed several scenes down the line? Your research, your ideas for character or location?

It's very tempting to think you can keep the book entirely in your head, and leave writing to the story itself. You could be right. Maybe you'll manage. But your job will still be a lot easier if you use the modern equivalent of something deemed rather antiquated these days: a filing cabinet. You could use a physical one if you liked, divided into sensible folders stuffed full of notes. But if you're writing on a computer already it's much easier to put together this practical, left-brain material there, keeping a running record of the work in progress outside the story itself.

I now begin a journal for every project I undertake. I put into it all the background material I possess, every idea, every observation I have as it progresses. The journal is the place I turn to when I want to know what colour a character's hair is, what a location really looks like, how I expected this story to develop when I first planned it. It's a resource I can work on when I don't feel like writing, a receptacle for all manner of minutiae, some useful, some eventually irrelevant, that go to make the foundations of the story ahead.

The novice writer out there may be slapping his forehead thinking, 'You mean I have to write *even more*?' Relax. The book journal may look like extra work but if you get it right it will help coax that story out of you. It could even save a project that would otherwise fail.

You could choose to write your book diary in an ordinary word processor, much like the manuscript itself. As we'll see later when we look at the process of writing, there's also software that will handle the story-writing function and let you save research, character and other reference files in the same document.

The Scrivener application has a very useful little notepad facility which opens in a separate window and is ideal for simple text notes like this.

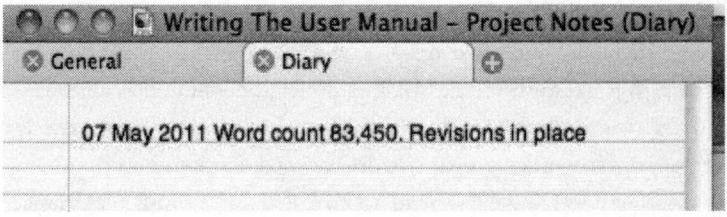

You'll find a variety of software packages to look at in the Appendix at the end of this book. I suggest you play with the ones that interest you, make a firm decision which to use . . . and then stick with them, at least for the first project, to see how they go.

I collect substantial amounts of diary and reference information and usually prefer to keep my left-brain material separate from the story. When I'm writing I want to focus on the story and nothing else. The book journal, as we'll see, is a very comprehensive package of ideas, information and research resources. I only want that visible when I need it.

A very simple solution is to buy a cheap piece of journal software. This is MacJournal, an inexpensive package for the Macintosh which has a very similar companion application for Windows.

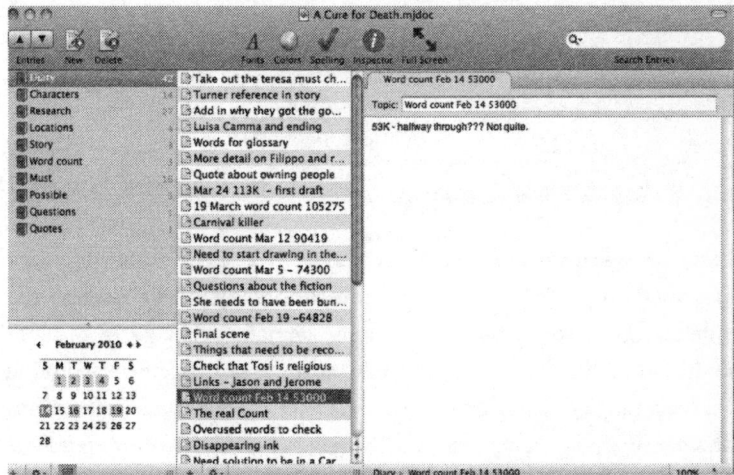

As the name suggests, MacJournal is software for keeping a dated record of different items. This is the actual journal I used when writing one of my novels set in Venice, *Carnival for the Dead*. As you can see, while it was a work in progress it went under a very different title just as a place-holder. You can see from the headings the kind of things that were noted – word counts, concerns about the story, reminders to check different items. I also have a document called 'Overused words to check'.

Another possibility is Evernote, a web-based service with client applic-ations for PCs, Macs, iPhones, iPads and Android phones and tablets. With Evernote you can view your research journal in many different ways, even from someone else's computer through the web. Here's how a book project might look using Evernote's Windows client.

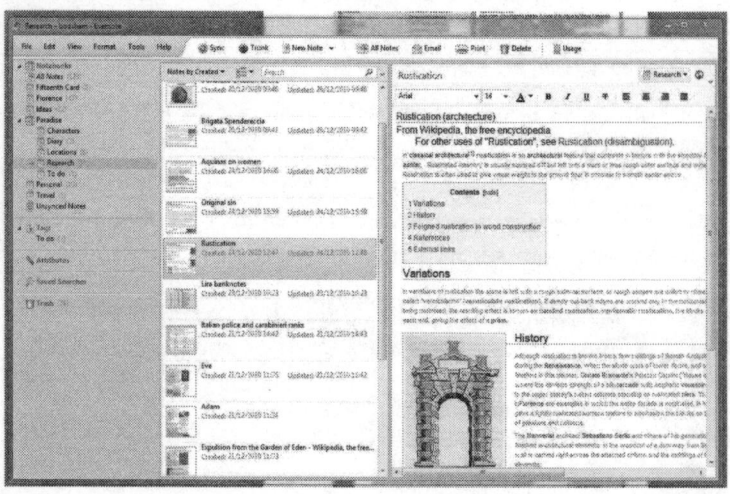

In its simplest form Evernote is free, though if you are a heavy user you may need to pay a modest annual subscription which includes all the different client applications. It has some limitations compared to more sophisticated products, but is certainly worth a look. The portability is a major boon too – you can, for example, take a photo with your smart-phone and send it straight to your Evernote research notebook.

Software like this lets you create folders or tabs for different categories. You then store your notes, photos and web clippings there. When you want to retrieve them you can find the entry you want in a variety of ways, by searching for keywords, by sifting through the different folders, or by the use of 'tags', generic labels that work across folders. We'll look at tags a little later.

Windows users who already use Microsoft Office own, alongside Word, a very usable journal application in OneNote. Let's take a look at how *Charlie and the Mermaid* might be developed using that.

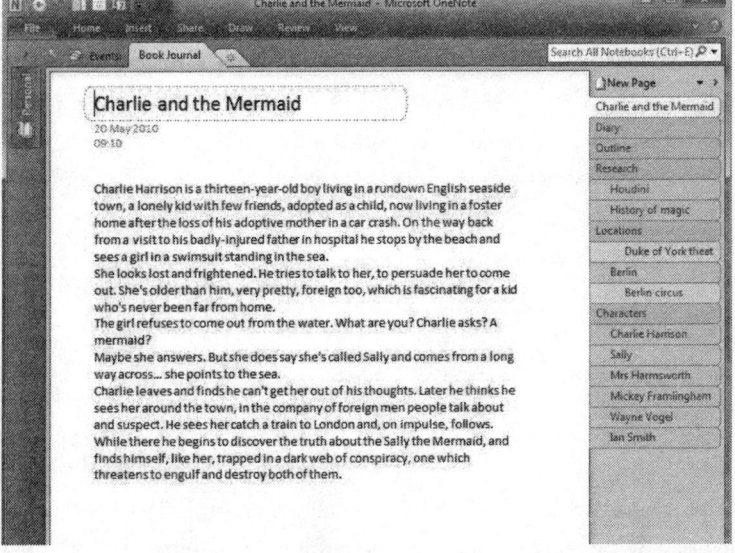

Some journal applications, such as MacJournal, work on the basis of folders and files. Some, like OneNote, more resemble an old-fashioned notebook. So here we have a tab for the book journal itself, and different pages for the various elements in the 'filing cabinet' itself. This is a fairly simple project which can be handled by a single page for each element, with sub-pages – those indented beneath a master page – as you can see above. If your project involves substantial organisation you might want to break the journal down into a number of different tab sections to make them easier to control.

The first page of the diary is devoted to a description of the 'seed' that kicks off the tale. This will change, of course, as the work progresses. But one of the joys of keeping a journal is that nothing needs to be 'corrected' to reflect the way a manuscript is developing. You can keep your new ideas alongside the old and compare both quickly and easily. Very soon they should turn into the foundations that will underpin your finished novel.

You can divide your journal into as many different sections as you like. Here are the ones I tend to use.

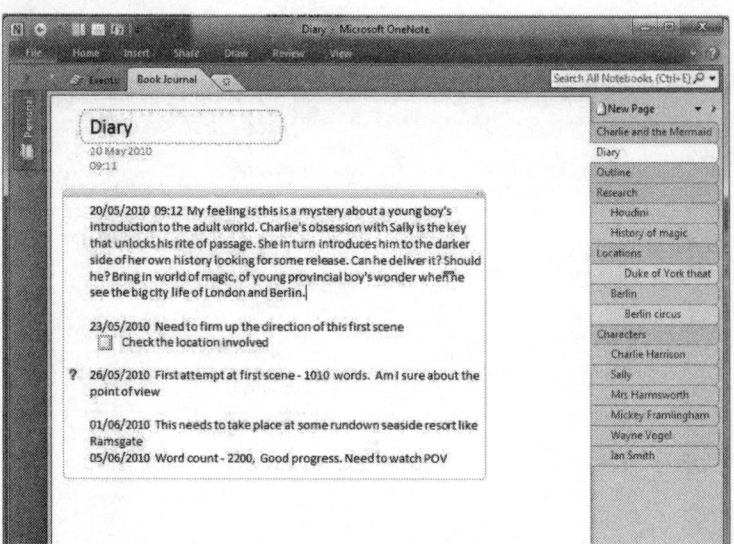

The diary is what it says – and incredibly useful too. Throughout the writing of the book I will refer back to this growing record and see how the story shapes up against my earlier expectations of it. You don't need to keep a daily diary. I just write down thoughts about the project as I have them, putting a date stamp on them to make sure I know when they cropped up. Time has little meaning when you're writing a book. You can never remember when you had an idea, or what the context was, unless you write everything down. This is the place to do it. A good chunk of the possibilities you raise for yourself here will never make it to the finished page, but that doesn't matter. And you will be writing another book after this one, won't you? Perhaps the seed of it will lie in something that occurs to you during the writing of this one.

You can write anything you like in the diary, but I tend to focus on specific areas. Ideas obviously go here. I also make a note of the current word count for the book, usually every Friday at the end of the working week. Word counts aren't necessarily a sign of progress but they're always good for morale.

Tags – labels to remind me of things to do – are an important part of any journal application. In OneNote they look like this out of the box though you can invent and use your own.

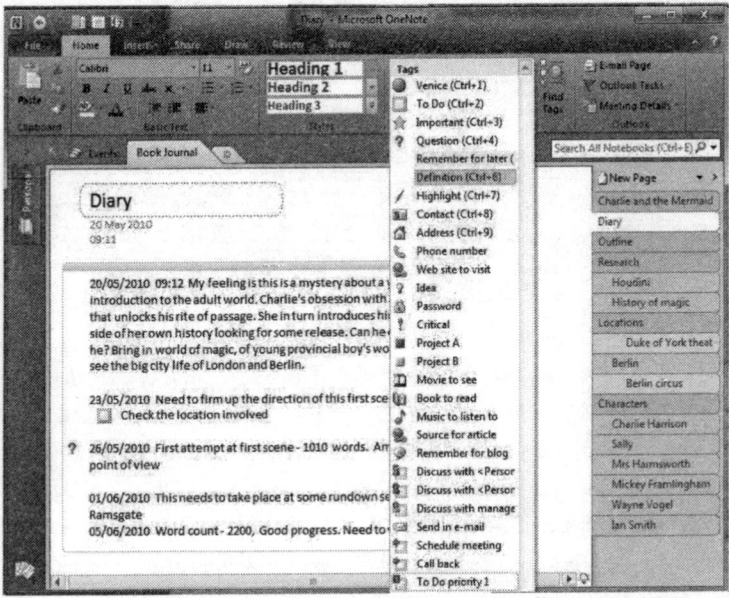

You place a tag against any item you want to mark for later retrieval. The check box just means it's something I have to do at some stage. The question mark is for a doubt or a question.

You can see the tags I used for the journal for *Carnival for the Dead* at the bottom of the left-hand column in MacJournal. 'Word count' lists every entry that relates to a word count so I can see instantly how the book progressed over the months. 'Must' is attached to anything I feel is so important it has to go into the book – such as that reminder about overused words. 'Possible' relates to entries I'm not sure about but I'm not ready to reject just yet. 'Questions' are those things that I think need answering at some stage. And 'Quotes' are chunks of dialogue that have occurred to me as useful in terms of defining a particular character, but have yet to find the right place in the book (and may never do).

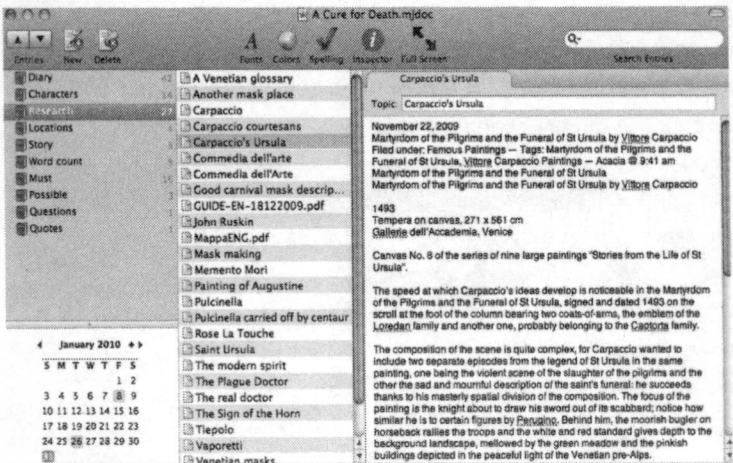

In MacJournal I go to the smart folders with those names at the bottom and immediately see every entry in the main folders that carries that tag. OneNote is slightly different. You use the 'Find Tags' command. All your tags are listed in the sidebar. If you hit the 'Create Summary Page' button you get a very useful new page that displays every piece of tagged content in your notebook.

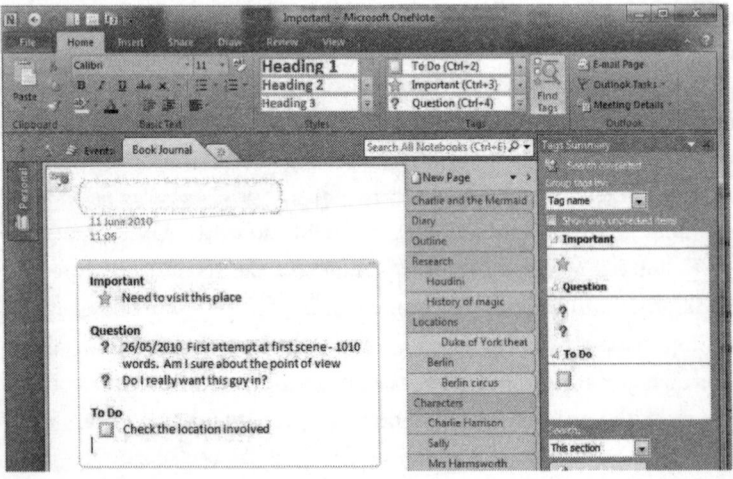

Tags are important because the notes they refer to can be retrieved whether you know where the information you're seeking is stored or not. They'll even pop up and remind you if you've forgotten about the item altogether. As your book and your journal grow alongside one another you will begin to lose sight of some of the basic ideas and facts that fired the story in the first place. This is only natural; you're inventing a new world and a cast of characters to inhabit it. Prosaic matters will be left to one side. You'll probably forget half the things you thought were important when you set out. Tags will make sure they're not lost for ever.

I always keep a to-do list of items, ranging from weeding out unnecessary phrases to visiting locations I may want to put in the story. As I complete the task I remove the tag. When the book is done the only tags left should be the ones I've decided really don't fit the story. It's a simple, logical process, and you can't say that about a lot of writing.

OUTLINING

Now to the compound question all authors get asked more than any other: do you know the end of the story before you begin? Do you outline every step of the way before sitting down to write your tale? Depending on how you intend to work, your answer to that question may need to go into your book diary, or be handled directly in the manuscript itself. The choice is yours and depends very much on scale. If your outlines are going to be simple, then the word processor should do. In Word they're very adequate. In a specialist program like Scrivener you have even more outlining tools, such as a corkboard and synopsis options.

If you plan to outline in great detail, then you could consider something more substantial. There are lots of ways to plan books if you want to go the complex route. I know people who use Excel spreadsheets, 'brainstorming' software, flow charts, posters on the wall, whiteboards. None of that works in my case. I'm a simple soul. I like practical solutions. If I wanted a detailed outline I'd write it directly into the book journal. OneNote is perfect for this kind of work. An outline looks like this:

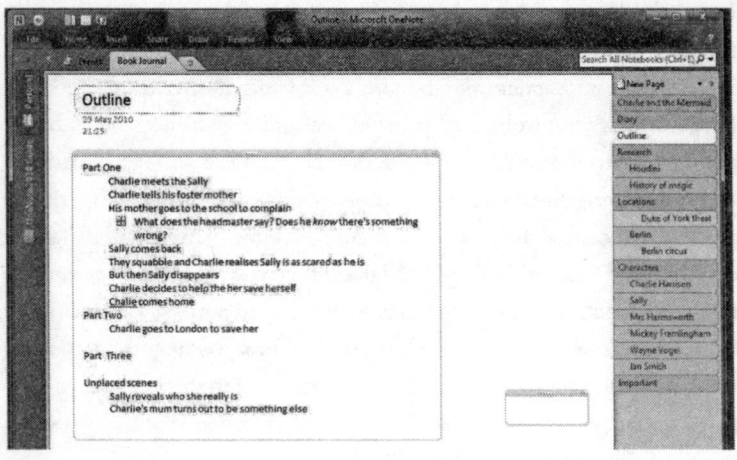

You type your main headings normally – here Part One, Part Two, Part Three and Unplaced Scenes (more of the last one later). Then hit tab to create individual chapters. If you wanted to break this down further you simply tab again and create the hierarchy you want, typing in detail as you need it. It may look like plain text but it's not. Hover over any of the lines and you get the little icon you see here. That means you can drag the contents anywhere outside the sequence and move it to a new position, bringing along any of the text or 'children' heading attached to it. In MacJournal you'd set up a folder called outline and place different posts in that, creating subsidiary folders for any hierarchies you want. Both applications offer a variety of approaches involving pages and folders depending on the complexity you need.

That, in essence, is outlining. You type a series of scenes, name them and give them some kind of description. Then you reorder these elements of your story and reprioritise them as you see fit.

How much advance planning should you do? There's scarcely an event I attend where people don't ask that. The honest truth is . . . every writer's different. Most of us work in different ways with different books and rarely, if ever, ask ourselves these questions at all.

If you look on Youtube you'll see a video from a few years ago about the group audio novel *The Chopin Manuscript* in which Jeffery Deaver,

Lee Child and some of the other authors involved (this one included) talk about the project. *Chopin* was a strange kind of distanced relay race in which story chapters were handed over from one writer to another. Part of this video involved a three-way interview with Jeff, Lee and me and concerned our own working methods.

Jeffery Deaver is the most organised writer I know. As Jeff will tell anyone, outlining is central to his working method. He will spend up to eight months on a step-by-step structure of his story, detailed to a very fine degree, before he sits down and writes it (which made it all the more brave he took on something like the disorganised chaotic madness of *Chopin*). If you get the chance to hear Jeff talk take it. You will not, I guarantee, be disappointed. Whether you can produce a book the way he can is a different matter (I've tried and I know I can't).

These are his working methods. Lee, in the same interview, made it clear that his are the absolute opposite. When he begins a new Jack Reacher book he's no idea at all where it's going. He sets up a beginning then lets Reacher walk off into the wilderness to see what happens. With a character like Jack Reacher, Lee knows – as does every one one of his millions of fans – it's going to be something gripping.

As I said in the same interview I'm somewhere between the two, in the semi-structured land which is, I suspect, the native territory of most writers. I have some rough idea of the story – a beginning, some way-points, a resolution. I really don't know how it will get from one staging point to the next. I'm also acutely aware that the end I have in mind will undoubtedly be changed when I get there because the characters them-selves will have demanded that.

I can't work the way Jeff does because I have to discover the story through writing, not planning. I'm driven to carry on with the narrative because I want to know what's going to happen, what surprises lie in store as the narrative emerges from the rough sketches and notes I have so far. So I use a fuzzy modus operandi to get from one waypoint to the next, always keeping my eye on the near and far horizon.

Here's a very common scenario. You're part way through the book and you come up with an idea for a scene. A great idea. One you don't want to lose. But it's not the next scene in the book. In fact you really don't know where such a scene is going to fit at all. The only thing you do know is it sounds perfect for the story and could, at some stage, move the narrative along. Perhaps it's even occurred to you that the scene *has* to happen in order to get to your planned conclusion.

Example . . . 'Sally kisses Charlie.'

When? Don't know.

All I understand is that at some point it simply must occur.

So what do you do? All too often you bury it in the project notes in the diary and, if you're not careful, pick it up later, when that bright spark of inspiration appears too late to affect the book.

We need a better, easier solution. You can see it in the outline here: the Unplaced Scenes folder. This is a temporary home in your outline for those events you think are necessary but currently have no logical place in the narrative. Yes, you can – and perhaps should – make a note of them in your book diary. But a simple heading in your outline can be so much more effective than a note buried deep in a sea of other material. It's there, visible every time you come back to the structure of your narrative, nagging you to pay attention to it.

Direction is essential. I need to have an idea where I'm headed even if I've no clear idea of how I get there. Somewhere along the way you'll look at those unplaced scenes and think – OK, now I know where to go. Or . . . that's just not needed. Either way you have a signpost. It's always helpful to know what you want to write. But it's equally useful sometimes understanding what you *don't* want to.

Something quite subtle and important is happening here once you get the hang of outlining, even very loosely, outside the linear, sequential order which your book will one day take. Narratives consist of bridges between the 'islands' that make up the string of events in your story. If you keep those potential islands stored in that Unplaced Scenes folder, they will, when they bounce back into your head, prompt the construction of the bridge that makes them work. You've got something to write when you might otherwise be banging your head against the wall.

At least that's the way this simple little trick works for me.

LOCATIONS

We'll look at creating the world for a book later in the section on writing. But it's worthwhile dispelling a common myth here, and placing a location tab in your book journal from the outset. I write books that are usually set in real places – Rome or Venice. They're tales concerned with history and culture, often wrapped up in actual buildings or paintings. Of course I need to keep track of the locations I use.

But what about the many writers who set their stories in an imaginary landscape? A city or town that doesn't exist? A universe all of their own in the case of some science fiction writers?

Answer: you still need to stay on top of the world of your book. If it's going to work for the reader it has to appear real. That means it needs a consistent appearance, geographically and visually, one that becomes apparent to the reader as you share it with them.

I have an inkling *Charlie and the Mermaid* might begin in some kind of slightly rundown English seaside resort and then move to London, taking in some odd events at a theatre. It's easy to track down some potential theatres for location on the web then paste the details into my diary like this:

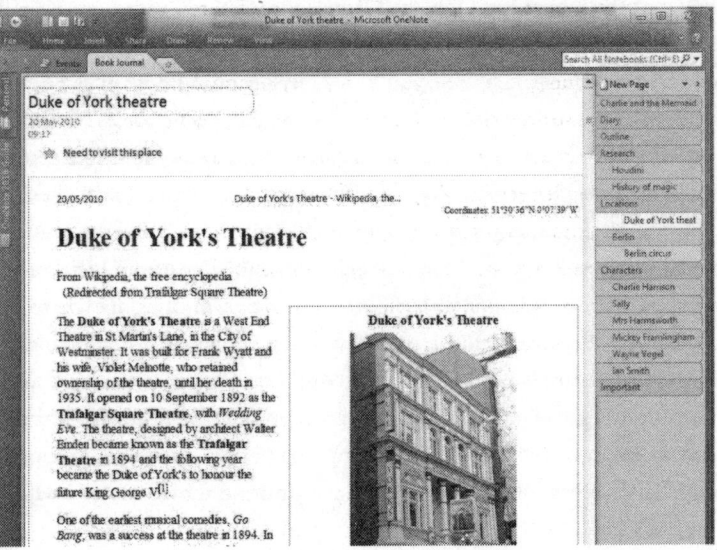

There's a picture and some history, enough to give me an idea of what this place looks like. I've tagged the entry 'Need to visit' to remind me that, if I really want to use it, I ought to go there and walk around the area too. I'm obsessive like that. You needn't be.

Photos of people don't appeal to me as character avatars, but pictures of locations are particularly useful. I have a camera with me when scouting locations as a matter of course and take hundreds of photos. Be deeply mistrustful of your own memory. *Carnival for the Dead* is set in Venice during carnival in February. I spent a couple of weeks there to see what the real thing was like, firing off snaps all the time. It was a bitterly cold winter with occasional snow in the Adriatic. Most of the story is set in dark Venetian alleys around the Rialto. The atmosphere was vivid and unique, and easily felt when I was there.

But that book was finished later, in England during early summer. I very much doubt I'd be able to re-create that frozen city from the previous February without being able to return to those original research photos. They let me track down a particular corner of the city and a certain view and remember: that's what it was like. As always in writing, you never know what's going to be useful in the end. So keep everything and sort the wheat from the chaff later.

These days you can even do away with the camera. Serendipity is a large part of writing. When you're wandering round with that book in your head you never know when you're going to come across something that might be useful. Any half-decent modern phone will take a picture, let you make a note, or even record a video. You can email them to yourself or store them in a web clipping service such as Evernote. As the work progresses, you build up a steady stream of ideas from pictures and memos you can write to yourself on trains, buses, in cafés, anywhere.

Some will prove useful. A good few will be rejected. It doesn't matter. The thirty seconds it takes to snatch a photo or type a couple of words costs nothing, and could add texture and depth to the story you produce. Just as importantly, you'll be bringing your book with you, keeping it alive in your head even when you're away from the manuscript itself.

CHARACTERS

All authors need a mechanism through which they record the traits and appearance of their characters. Leaving it to chance or memory is a sure way of risking that dangerous inconsistencies may slip through to the final manuscript, and label you as 'unprofessional' in the eyes of an agent or editor. How do you do it?

One way is to keep a character record. Some writing software will even offer to do this for you. You write – or even fill in a form – detailing physical appearance, age, job, temperament and any other information you feel is relevant. You then use this as a reference template for the character throughout the book.

This doesn't work for me for one very practical reason. I don't envisage characters fully formed before they appear in a work. I don't want to sit down and think them through beforehand. It seems an artificial way of working, unintuitive and, most importantly, out of sync with the way a reader will meet these same characters. They won't see your cribsheet here. All they will have to help them are the words in your book.

So my approach is to use those words to populate my character records. I have a rough idea of what someone looks like, their age, what kind of human being they are. Then, when they appear in the book, I just write them as I see them at that stage of the story. Note the word 'see'. I think visually as I write. This is very important to me. I need to visualise what's going on. Having some index card of a character pre-written would hinder this, not help it.

When I've finished writing the character, I cut and paste the exact words I've written into a character entry in my book diary, in the Characters folder. On the next page is the entry for Alberto Tosi, a retired Venetian pathologist who is a key figure in *Carnival for the Dead*. With Tosi my life is made easy by the fact I've met him before. He appeared as a minor figure in an earlier instalment in the series, *The Lizard's Bite*. So the first thing I do is go back to that earlier book and paste in the descriptions of him here, in this case in MacJournal:

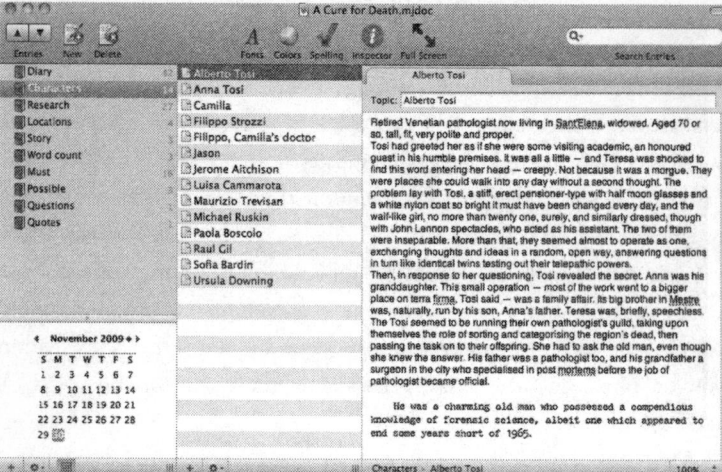

If a character is entirely new I'll give him a name and a brief description in terms of age and appearance. Then I simply write the person as they seem to fit in the story. After that I copy and paste those words into the entry in the character record, at the top. I always remind myself: this is all the reader will see. Readers don't have access to your book journal. If it contains essential information which isn't in the book you've still got work to do.

I find this makes much more sense than a pre-planned index card. I can go back and view the character in isolation, outside the book, make notes about things I need to address, then return to the manuscript and try to fix them.

Some people love index cards and thinking through a book before they start writing. Some are very fond of another technique to visualise their characters. In addition to a written description they will find a photo from somewhere, in a personal collection or on the web, and paste that into a character record for inspiration. Well-known actors often seem to work in this respect. It's not a habit I've ever followed but it's certainly worth a try. Here's a possible Charlie on the opposite page.

A quick OneNote tip. I often think of new characters while writing about a current one. OneNote has a very clever way of saving time as

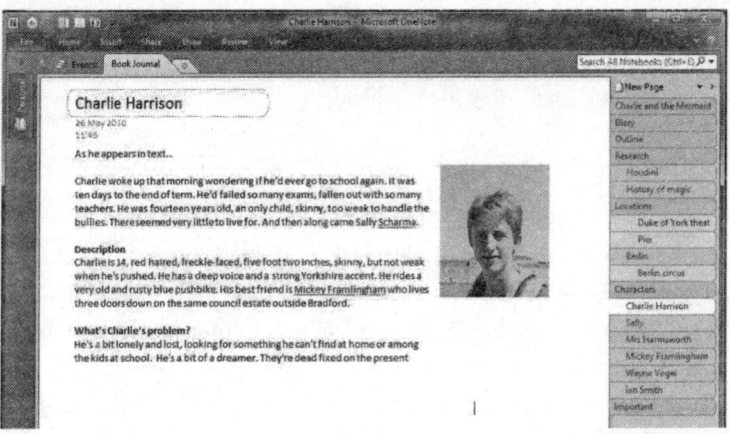

you deal with entries in your journal. Let's imagine I'm writing about Charlie and decide to give him an enemy called Jonathan Black. OneNote uses what's known as 'wiki' conventions for linking items. I will type this: 'Charlie is hated by the school thug [[Jonathan Black]]'.

The software recognises anything surrounded by two square brackets. First it looks for an entry with that name. If it finds it, a web-style link will be created to take you straight to it. If, as in this case, the name doesn't exist, OneNote will create a page of that name automatically at the end of the page list. You then drag it to the location you want.

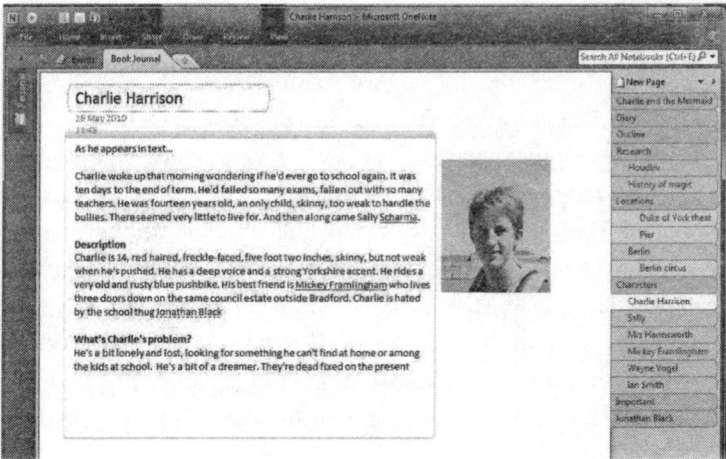

This is a very quick and easy way to build up a reference file you can navigate swiftly. If your project is going to involve a lot of research those automatic links will come in very handy.

RESEARCH

Some books require mounds of research. Others barely any. There must be a few that require no research at all, though I can't quite imagine them. The world of a book needs to feel real. In order to achieve that it must be populated by characters who appear to be alive, in places the reader can imagine in their own head, and with some kind of idea of the society in which the story is taking place. Characters and location we've dealt with. Research represents the texture of your fictional world. It provides colour and depth that can't be found in people and places alone.

Let's imagine two factual strands that might run through *Charlie and the Mermaid*. We know the story begins at the seaside. I also have a vague idea that the tale will at some stage move to London and the theatre. The opening scene seems to take place around some derelict pier destroyed by a fire. I'm also intrigued by the idea that when Charlie gets to London he discovers that Sally is the daughter of a very mysterious theatrical magician.

Whatever journal system you use for your book, you will find that you can store your notes in a variety of different ways, all of which have their own pros and cons. It's essential you understand these so that you can retrieve the information easily and in a useful form later.

British seaside piers are just the kind of subject that will generate a stack of results on Google. There are some very interesting ones too on the English Heritage site. It's not so much the location that interests me here. It's how long a pier might be, what it's made of, when it might have been built. The English Heritage site describes many different kinds. One in Mumbles in South Wales looks just like the kind I imagine for this story. Let's bring it into OneNote so that I can turn to it when I want to remind myself what this fictional pier might offer in the way of texture.

I'm already interested by a few things I can see here – that deck built on cast-iron piles and the wooden buildings that have been built around it like the lifeboat house ...

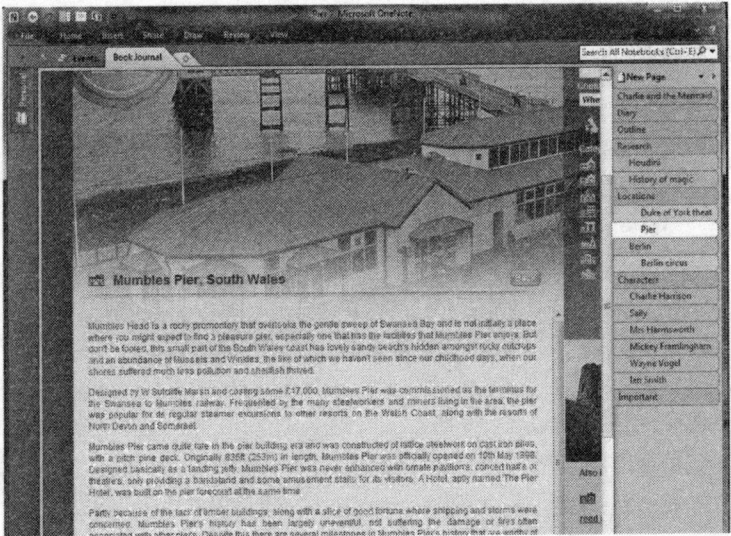

Charlie and the Mermaid is fiction, not a guide to some imaginary seaside town. I'm not going to dwell on the age of the pier or the fact that, as it says here, this one does not have the ornate pavilions found elsewhere. Charlie and Sally wouldn't know about that last fact, so it's irrelevant. But the atmosphere of abandoned amusement arcades, perhaps a wrecked fairground ride, its skeletal frame still jutting into nowhere, and the physical dimensions – half a mile long, quite a size – provide possible images that can be passed on to the reader.

Research can be addictive and get in the way of writing a book. Confine yourself to getting just as much as you need and no more. If you find something's missing it's simple enough to pick up some facts later on.

Capturing information for your journal is easy, but you should take a moment to understand some of the technical limitations involved. For this entry I just hit the Windows key-S combination in OneNote. This takes a screenshot of anything I want to capture on the page – text and photos. It's exact and precise, essentially a photograph of what is in front of you. While this may be a picture of the page, OneNote can still 'read' it. So if I type in Mumbles in the search field it will take me straight back to this page. But MacJournal won't do this – to it this is just a picture. If you use screenshots in that – and most other journal apps – you will have to label each entry manually.

Another way of keeping research is as digital printouts or PDFs. I may want something about magic in this book. Perhaps Charlie comes to see himself as a kind of junior Houdini at some stage. Here's the Wikipedia page on the magician and escapologist printed straight to the research notebook from within a web browser.

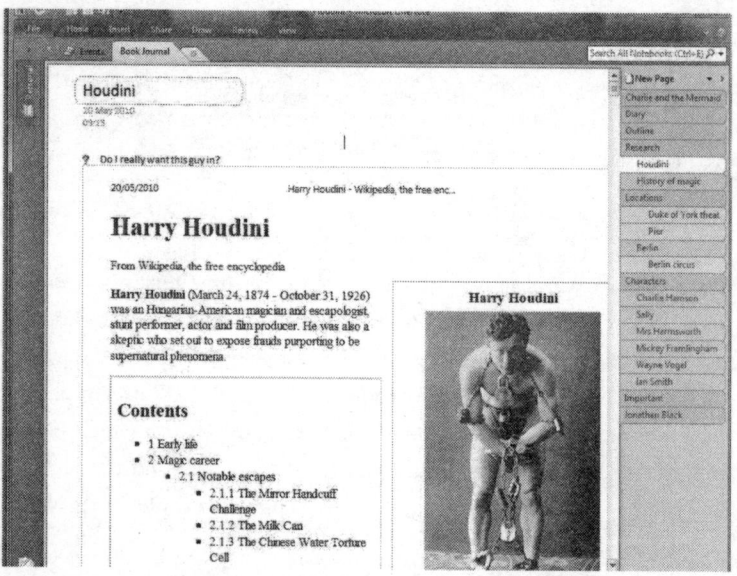

This will be 'read' by most journal applications out there, so you can find text within it very easily. But web links in the original may disappear and usually you can't change the text at all though you can annotate it separately. Here you can see I've added a question tag at the top: 'Do I really want this guy in?'

Finally you can simply copy and paste material straight into your research entry. Text is preserved and also any images the original post contained. Any web links should still be there but you may well lose the layout of the original page and occasionally some key elements.

You can mix and match the kind of data you grab off the web. But your painstaking research will be useless if it turns up mangled or in a form which doesn't allow you to retrieve it. Anyone planning to put together considerable amounts of research should spend a little time ensuring it is in the right format. Otherwise there may be some frustrating moments later. The basic choices are . . .

➢ Screenshot. Fast and easy but only searchable in something like OneNote.

➢ Print to file or PDF then imported. Keeps the original format and is searchable. But you can't change the text and web links will be lost.

➢ Paste direct from web page. You get proper text, images and web links, but the original layout may disappear along with some page elements depending on the source.

None of this applies if your research entries are original work, of course.

QUOTATIONS

It's always a good sign when a book won't leave your head. If you're fully absorbed in your story, ideas and possibilities will occur at the oddest of times. Commit them to paper in a notebook or type them into your phone. Then add them into the relevant part of your journal. Ideas sometimes come in the form of dialogue. Imagine the relationship that's going to develop between Charlie and Sally. That will be played out in part in the way they talk to each other.

We'll look at dialogue in more detail later. But you should reserve a place in your journal for imaginary conversations or simple, one-sided statements that could fit somewhere in your book. It doesn't matter that you don't know where. Perhaps they won't be used at all. But it takes very little time to set down possible exchanges or a few sentences that illustrate character. This kind of thing . . .

Sally: 'I want you to leave, Charlie Harrison. You're fourteen years old. A kid. You shouldn't be here.'

'I *am* here.'

'Why? I didn't ask for it. I didn't ask for you. *Go away!*'

He picks up his things.

'What are you doing?' she asks.

'Going! Like you said.'

Sally sits down and looks at him.

'I didn't *mean* it. God, Charlie. You can be so childish sometimes.'

There could be something to work with there. Charlie older than he seems, and getting no credit for it. Sally thinking she's more mature than he is, and fooling herself, though perhaps only a little. I'd put something like that in my Quotations section because it might prove a starting point from which I could begin to explore the relationship between these two. No story in there, no plot point, no narrative. Just two people speaking, trying to understand one another. Sometimes writers crave a thread, some small piece of string we can tug on hoping it might lead to something more substantial. Notes like these can provide that kind of help, just when you need it. Scribble them down in your spare moments and see what happens.

AND NOW IT'S TIME TO START

Good news. The planning phase is coming to a close. How do you reach that conclusion? What do you need to know in order to commit to a project and feel comfortable that it's worth pursuing? Here are some pointers.

➤ You have a beginning. An event that kicks off the story and a clue where it will go shortly afterwards. These are the shots that will hopefully pull the thing into focus at the start and make the reader think, 'OK, I'm with this one.'

➤ You've worked out some characters. The key ones are sufficiently clear in your head that you feel you're getting to know them. Others are just cards with names and brief descriptions. But that doesn't matter. The narrative will flesh them out.

➤ You have an idea of the principal locations, the canvas for the book, the world which will enclose it.

➤ You've fleshed out that world with some kind of material that goes beyond people and places. A context – the seaside and magic in the case of *Charlie and the Mermaid* perhaps – that will give the book some resonance and depth.

➤ You know what kind of story you want to write. Not just 'a good one' but a book that will fit inside a specific area that readers, agents and publishers will recognise and say, 'Ah yes. It fits there.'

Fine. Now let's list some of the things you don't have.

➤ A detailed outline, unless you demand it. If you're the kind of writer who wants to work that way, fine. But don't feel it's essential.

➤ A precise idea how the story will end. Is Sally all she seems? Is she 'good'? Is Charlie for that matter? My feeling at the moment is that Sally isn't all she seems and may have wicked intentions. But she's virtuous at heart and something in Charlie will bring that out of her, in a way that will involve some sacrifice on someone's part. That's as far as it goes. The details are something they will need to reveal as we go along.

➤ Any idea how long this is going to take. Deadlines are for established authors – and even they frequently miss them. Beginners should push all ideas of finishing dates out of their mind and just work on the manuscript at a speed that suits them. The truth – which you probably don't want to face – is that this is going to take a lot longer than you think. Best put that out of your mind for now. No one climbs Everest staring upwards at the peak all the way. It's easier and more comforting to focus on the obstacles you'll meet as you struggle to get there.

➤ A name for the finished book. *Charlie and the Mermaid* is fine as a working title for something in the young adult field. It may even fit as the final one if the book didn't get too dark. Too early to say. Titles tend to be either easy to find or desperately difficult. Either way they can wait. It's pointless to obsess about them now and deflects the mind away from the real business – which is writing the narrative. Better to have a finished book lacking a title than the reverse. Always avoid the trap of obsessing about small details to such a degree they get in the way of doing some real work.

There's one more ingredient required and that's, perhaps, the most important of all. What ambitions do you have for a project? What, in broad, general terms, are you trying to achieve? I imagine most new writers starting out will have some very simple ones.

➢ To finish the blasted thing.

➢ To sell it.

➢ To see it published successfully.

These are admirable sentiments, but scarcely count as aspirations. They're fundamental objectives in most writing projects any author is going to undertake. Why else would anyone spend all this time slaving away over words? As Samuel Johnson once blustered, 'No man but a blockhead ever wrote, except for money.'

Fine man, excellent words.

Individual books need specific aspirations, ones that are narrow and reasonably well-defined. You should set them out at the beginning so that you have some idea of the goals you want to achieve.

Here are some that might apply to *Charlie and the Mermaid*.

➢ Paint a picture of the world of a solitary fourteen-year-old boy on the cusp of adulthood, excited and a little scared by what he's beginning to encounter.

➢ Try to peer inside the mind of Sally, a strange and eccentric teenager who has very little in the way of self-knowledge and is a victim in a fashion she fails to understand.

➤ Take the reader to the grimy, creepy atmosphere of a rundown seaside town.

➤ Explore what draws people to the world of magic.

➤ Look at the tough and occasionally unforgiving world of impoverished immigrants struggling to make a living at any cost, a world that somehow touches Sally, though I'm unclear how.

Aspirations, like the other techniques outlined here, help provide two essential elements in the writing of any project: focus and control. They let you home in on what matters and keep your concentration on those essential elements once you establish them. And they will, of course, change along the way, the peripheral ones cast to one side as your story grows and comes into focus.

Now ... let's start to produce some fiction.

Part 2

WRITE

ARTHUR CONAN DOYLE brought Sherlock Holmes to life in long-hand. Ernest Hemingway liked to write standing up at his Royal typewriter set on a tall bookshelf at his home Finca Vigia in Havana – the Royal is still there today. One way or another most modern authors are blessed – for the most part – with the technology of the personal computer. Even if you insist on writing out your book with a pen and paper, as a handful still do, someone, somewhere will type it into a word processor at some stage. Changing the names of characters, making sweeping revisions and monitoring changes and word counts were once painful and tedious chores demanding hours of unrewarding work. We can now cut through these boring but necessary tasks with a few clicks of the mouse.

You'll do yourself a big favour if you can find the right combination of tools, processes and routines from the outset for one very good reason: time. None of us has enough of it. Careers can't be built – usually – by completing one manuscript a decade, however good it may be. In the field of popular fiction frequency – preferably once a year – is essential.

One element in this equation is the apparently simple question: how do you write a manuscript? The practical detail is often overlooked. Would-be authors fire up the word processor, set the line spacing to double and begin to tap out some words, hoping the rest of the process will fall into place at will. Not long after they find themselves staring at a blank page, with doubt and bewilderment creeping into an idea that seemed so alive and promising when it began.

We've already seen how planning a book project can help give it some firm foundations before a single word is written. You're going to spend a lot of time with your chosen implements over the months, possibly years, to come. It makes sense to take a little time choosing the right ones before you begin. Changing in mid-course is likely to be time-consuming and wearisome. There is also one great fallacy that needs to be dispelled from the very outset. Yes, those first few pages are important. But not as important as you may think.

WRITING TOOLS

No one needs much to write a book: a computer, some software, a printer at some stage and a few good ideas. You probably have most of what you need at home already. But producing a full-length fictional manuscript is not the same as tapping out a one-page letter to the bank manager. When your project starts to take off you will find yourself with a writhing tangle of ideas, possibilities and potential potholes. A book journal will help provide firm foundations. You will still need to maintain focus and control directly through the manuscript too, in the pages readers will see. In short, you have to choose the right writing tools. Here are your options.

HARDWARE

Windows or Mac? Desktop or laptop? Big screen, little screen?

The honest answer is: it's a matter of personal taste and how much you can afford to spend. For many years I was a great fan of the Apple Macintosh. More of my books have been written on the Mac than on any other computer, often with applications specifically designed for the creative writer. The Macintosh is a great computer system with a reputation for being cool, creative and something of a cultural icon to its followers. Readers can't tell the difference between a book written on a Mac and one produced using something else. Pick the solution that meets your personal taste and budget.

When projects struggle it's tempting to blame the objects that seem to stand between you and the page. Perhaps some new word processing software, a different screen, the latest wireless mouse will make a difference ...

Don't fool yourself. There are no silver bullets. A well-organised working routine is important since it will help you achieve more in the time available. But it's no substitute for creativity, imagination and sound craft.

I travel a lot. If you do too then sharing your work between a desktop and a laptop for writing on the road should help you keep the manuscript alive. It took me a while to get into the habit of writing in hotels, on planes and airports. Now it's ingrained and I never give it a second thought. Working away from your normal writing environment can give you something all writers seek – a sideways look at your work. That looming black hole in the manuscript back home may seem less of a problem when you view it on a laptop screen in a new and unfamiliar environment.

I once set off for Italy wondering how exactly a book I'd just started might pan out in the end. My flight was delayed for ninety minutes on the apron. In that time I took out a pen and notepad and sketched out the entire story in rough. It was finished before we took off, and pretty much represents the finished book. I would never have achieved that if I'd stayed at home. Perspective is good, and that laptop in the hotel room or on the train takes away any excuses you may have for not spending a few spare hours working on your book. From time to time I've tried writing on nothing but a small laptop too. It's wonderful when I need no distractions – and that includes research. If you make sure you see nothing else on the screen – no email, no Twitter or Facebook – you can find yourself on a small island of concentration where nothing else in the world matters.

There's no need to buy anything expensive. Word processing doesn't require any great horsepower. A good screen and a keyboard you can type on comfortably are more important than badges on the side. Pick your writing tools for their practicality, not their fashion value.

SOFTWARE

The computer you use may be of minor relevance but software is different. The choice can be much wider than you think. Over the last decade conventional word processing packages have been joined by a growing number of dedicated writing programs aimed specifically at the creative writer. You'll find a list in the Appendix. Most will have free trials for download and give you up to thirty days in which to work with them before you have to make up your mind. So the first choice you face is . . . do you write in one of the big company word processors, usually Microsoft's, or choose something that's trying to give you some extra options designed to make writing a book a lot easier?

Word processing

One thing can be said with certainty: the *lingua franca* of publishing is Microsoft Word. Publishers and agents will expect a manuscript to be delivered as a Word file which will form the basis of the typesetting for the finished book. This does not mean you need to write in Word if you prefer something else. Rival word processors will export to Word format, as will specialist writing packages, when you want to send off the book. It would be wise to read through that file in Word itself first. Mistakes and format errors can creep in. It would be rash to allow them through for the want of a quick check. This does mean that few of us can really hope to take a book all the way through to publication without, at some stage, viewing it in our own copy of Word.

Where's the problem? Word is a long-established, rather over-complex word processing package that has, for years, attempted to be all things to all users. If you want to run off a quick letter it will offer a template. It will also handle long manuscripts, deal with footnotes and endnotes, and perform design tricks that were once restricted to desktop publishing.

None of these things is of much interest to someone wanting to write a novel, though that doesn't stop thousands of writers using Word as their first weapon of choice, usually because they've tried little else.

Taking a little time to fine-tune your word processing skills to the arcane business of fiction writing is worthwhile. You're going to spend a lot of time inside your writing application as the book develops. It's important you feel it is on your side, not one more obstacle to overcome.

Word and most other off-the-shelf word processing apps have traditionally stumbled at several key tasks that authors should crave to keep their project in check. Three fundamental tools essential for managing a long and complex manuscript come to mind . . .

➢ An easy and visual way of managing and reordering scenes and sections of a book in an Outline view. Usually this has been left to a complicated and unintuitive system of hierarchical headings which was confusing and occasionally unreliable in use.

➢ A simple way of calculating the word count of individual scenes. Authors need to know the length of the component parts of their story.

➢ A tool to find words in context. The standard 'find' function in mainstream word processors hasn't changed in decades. If you want to hunt for an instance of the word the program will find the first, then the second, then the third . . . and so on. In a brief document that may not be a problem. In a book running to more than 100,000 words it can make tracking down elements a dreary and time-consuming chore. Specialist writing apps have known this for years. Most offer instead a context-sensitive find. Instead of seeing just the next instance of the word you're looking for you are offered all of them, and a sample of the text surrounding them.

These navigational and structural tools make the storyteller's job a lot more agreeable but they have usually been absent from office word processing packages. Software does get better though. Office 2010 for Windows has them if you know where to look. Unfortunately its sibling on the Mac, Office 2011, doesn't, not with the same fluency anyway.

Setting up a project in Word 2010 for Windows is very simple and visual. Let's suppose this is a book that will be outlined entirely within the word processor, with no detailed scene-by-scene synopsis held separately in a journal. We go to the Outline view and type in some headings.

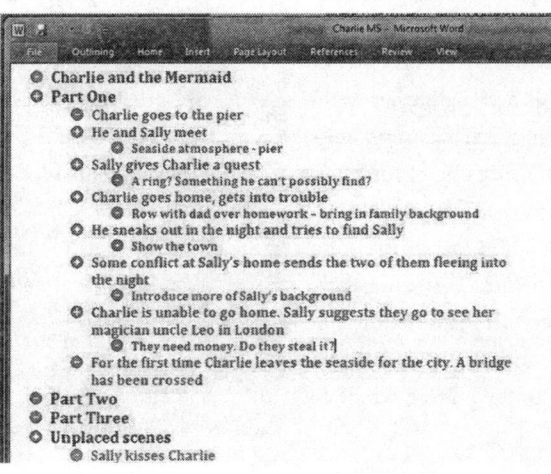

This is very similar to the standard outline view seen in earlier versions of Word and other mainstream word processing packages. The outline is based upon the paragraph style. The principal entries are top level headings. Hit carriage return, then tab, and you will, in Outline view, find yourself in the subsidiary Heading 2 style automatically. Do that again and you're in Heading 3. For most projects three levels of heading will suffice. If you're having a rush of inspiration just sit there and type, hit return, tab and then type again as you map out a line of scenes and events that will begin the book.

The titles here are for the writer's convenience, not publication. So pick headings that mean something and give you a sense of the direction of the story. Move any of those titles to a different location and any body text – the scene itself – you have written beneath it will follow. Shifting events around is a good way of exploring possibilities. How might the story change if a key event happens earlier or later than planned? Outlining makes it easy to play with 'what if' ideas, and it's a cinch to undo them or try something else by simply dragging elements to a new location.

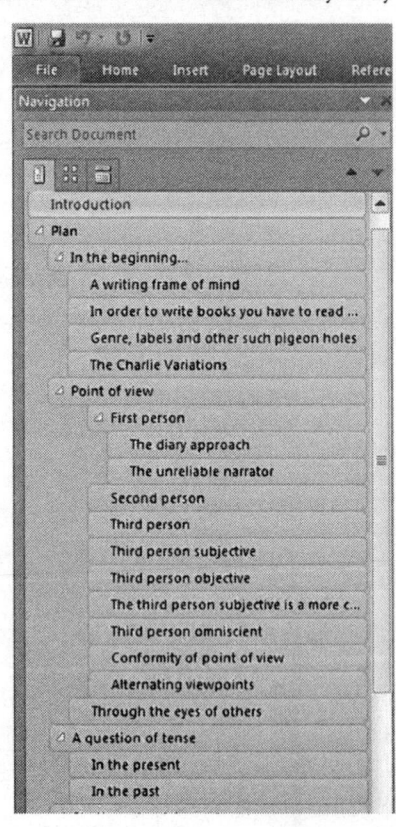

Seen as a straight page outline headings can become somewhat confusing once your book expands to multiple scenes with text attached. One of the new features in Word 2010 is a navigation pane that reads the outline structure and displays it as a live bar next to the editing window.

The timeline of your book is visible on the left when you need it. You see this as a formal book layout – parts, chapters and scenes. In an instant you can visualise the direction of the story, the events you're aiming at.

The hierarchy is now very flexible. You can collapse parts into the heading above if the list is so long something is hidden at the foot. Once again dragging a heading to a new location will take the text with it. If you want your chapters numbered you can even set up Word so that you get an automatic renumber when things float around too.

Scene headings are for your benefit, not the reader's. You're outlining narrative possibilities in a way that will let you navigate and manage them easily. Once the scene is written you can remove any of these headings altogether or, if appropriate, replace them with chapter numbers or headings intended for publication.

We also need a way to get notes into our scene from the very beginning – ideas and observations that are attached to the text but not a part of it and too long to be a subsidiary heading. Most conventional word processors will let you insert comments. They're ideal for this purpose.

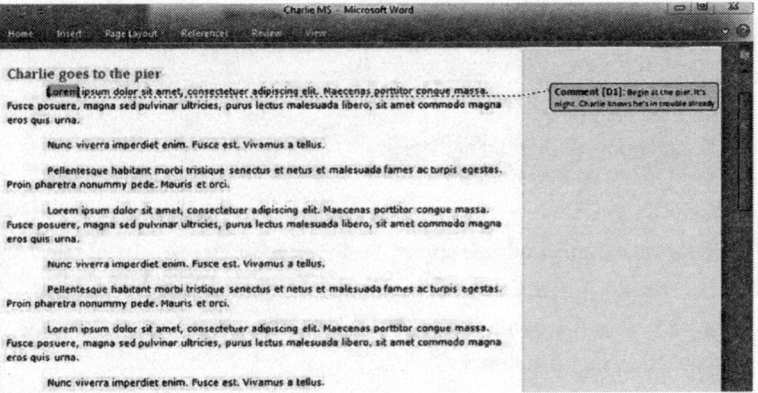

Put your cursor where you want to make a comment, insert it and you get this box at the side. If we're starting the scene this can be used for a brief synopsis or note of an idea. Comments can be hidden from view or seen in their entirety as a list. Use them for thoughts, notes, scene synopses and planned word counts.

With Word 2010 there's now a very simple way to get accurate statistics for any story element based on an outline heading.

Select the scene you want in the navigation bar and right click on the heading. You will see this. Pick 'Select Heading and Content'. At the foot of the page you will get a split word count. The first number gives you the count for all the text beneath that heading. The second (which is always there) is the word count for the

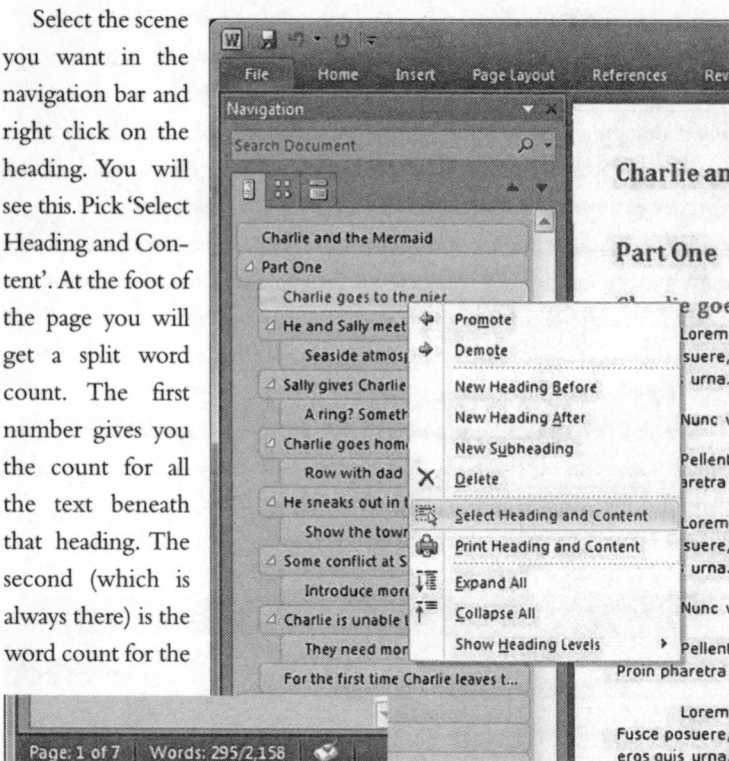

whole document. Note that you can perform this trick with section headings containing multiple scenes. So we can quickly get a word count for the whole of Part One simply through a right click and a glance at the screen. This is a great advance on the old days of manually selecting text and hunting for statistics.

Many works of popular fiction try to standardise on scene word counts so that the reader sees chunks of text that are of similar lengths and demand similar amounts of time. Use this technique and it's very simple to check the length of one section against another.

Lastly we need a way to navigate the book swiftly and accurately. Here is what conventional 'Find' looks like.

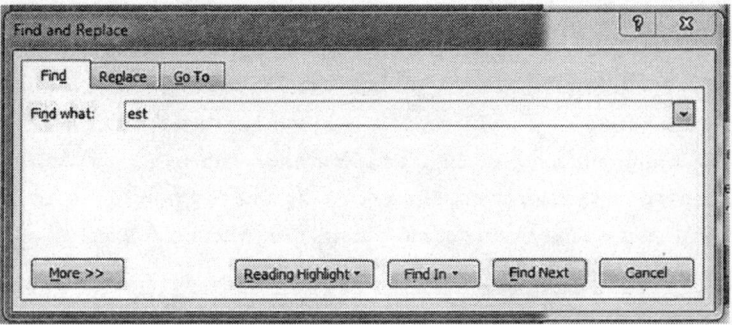

In Word 2010 if we go back to the new navigation panel to type in a search term we see this.

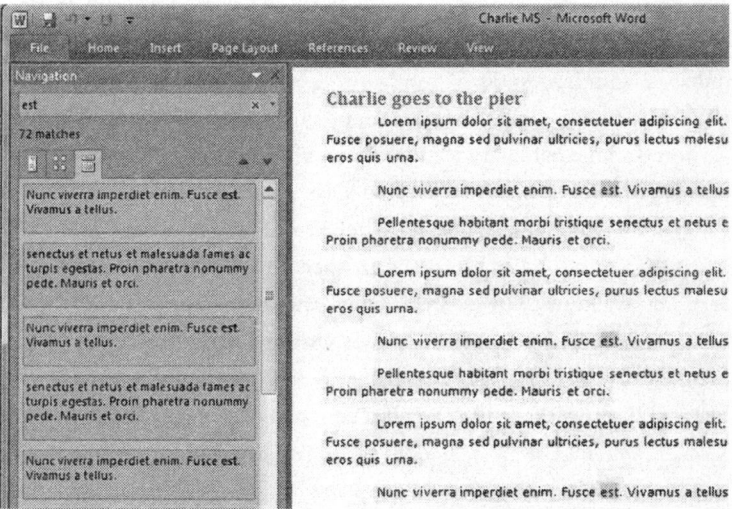

The right-hand tab will give you a preview of each occurrence of the word in the context of the sentence surrounding it. The middle tab shows you pages containing the term. The left-hand tab displays all headings where it appears and will, like the other options, highlight any instances in the text. Use this for quickly tracking down any item you need to look at in the manuscript. If you're worried you're overusing a particular word or turn of phrase, a search here will show you how often it appears.

This is a giant leap from earlier versions of Word and probably sufficient for many established writers out there. But beginners may need more control and structure. Apple users should also bear in mind that the current version of Word for the Mac lacks some of these features, notably the flexible outlining in the sidebar. You may wish to explore Apple's Pages word processor as an alternative. At the time of writing it still has its foibles, but is rather better at most things than Microsoft's word processing offering on the Mac.

But what about software written specially for writing fiction?

Specialist writing packages

Scrivener is one of the best-known specialist writing apps, used by many professional writers around the world. It's the work of an English schoolteacher – now software developer – who wanted to write a novel but was unhappy with conventional word processors. The first version appeared on the Mac but you'll find it on Windows now too, though the Windows version is a little behind in features. Scrivener is far from alone in the field of software for writers – see the Appendix. But it is a great and powerful example of what these applications hope to add to the game.

In Word a book can all too often appear to be a single, long slab of text. This is illusory. Novels are more mosaics than monolithic structures. Conan Doyle knew that when he was writing Sherlock Holmes. So did Hemingway standing up, tapping away on his Royal typewriter in Havana. Both worked with the physical medium of paper. They wrote in a standard fashion, so many lines to the page. They could gauge the length of a chapter very easily by picking up and counting the pages. Then they could set that section to one side and work on another, monitoring the progress of the next chapter through the pile of sheets on the desk.

Word processing has hidden the mosaic of writing to some extent. We have no physical concept of length, no weight of paper to show the extent of a scene. Just those blunt word counts which, until Word 2010, were restricted to the document as a whole without a lot of fiddly extra work.

Packages like Scrivener attempt, among other things, to bring back the piecemeal nature of writing. Books are no longer single, very long chunks of text. They appear as individual linked scenes, each with their own statistics, notes and place within the novel structure.

Here is *Charlie and the Mermaid* as it would appear in Scrivener.

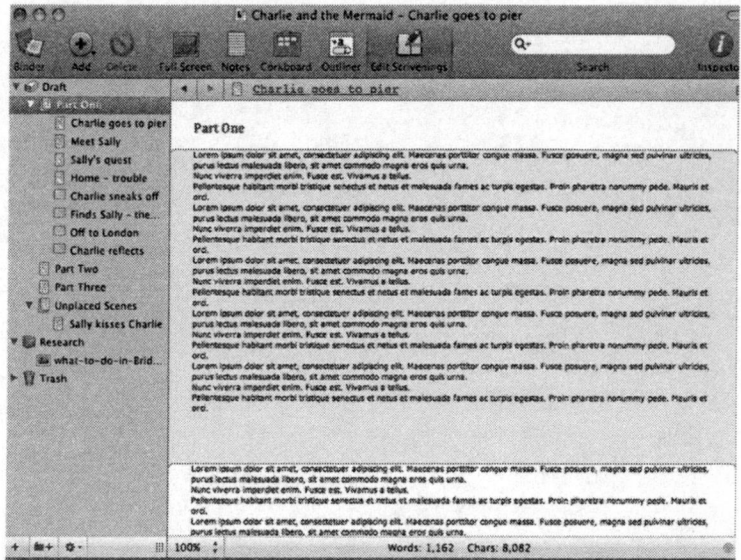

The outline idea is pretty much the same: hierarchies of main headings and subsidiary ones. There's a word count for the whole of Part One at the foot of the screen because that is the section selected. To get the entire word count you'd choose 'Manuscript'. You can divide the work into as many chapters, scenes and parts as you want, and drag elements between them. And you get a template for a proper title page, too.

If you hit the Inspector button at the top right and go to an individual scene you start to see some of the key differences, as in the screeenshot at the top of the next page. The word count now applies to this individual scene. It is, if you like, a separate writing document contained in a binder for the project as a whole. On the right we have a synopsis box and some other tools. We can label this element of our book – chapter, scene, concept, or anything else we choose. Or we could tag it with a keyword as a particular character's point of view. Beneath the label is a status option. Here we can mark the phase of this scene – to do, first draft, second draft,

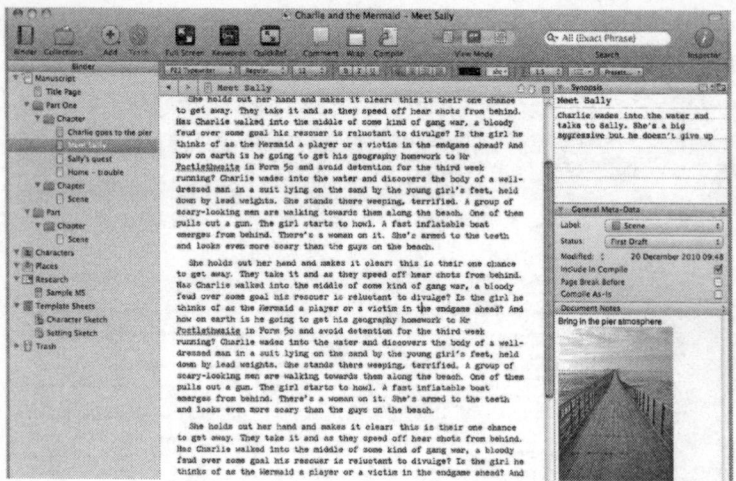

revise or finished. We know when we last worked on this scene because the 'Modified' option tells us. We can also write scene notes in the panel below and store photos there to remind us of a location or a character.

We also have far more flexibility over our outline. Choose the Corkboard option in group mode and you see this.

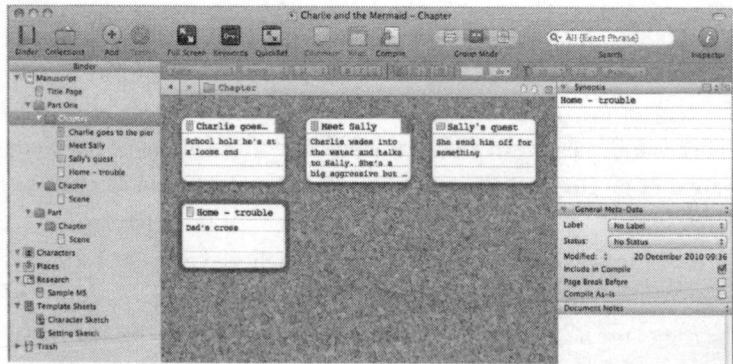

Imagine a set of index cards. Whatever you type into that synopsis field populates the cards. You can write and rewrite the contents here and drag them around your story structure at will. Just as with the headings in Word, any scene text contained in these documents will follow to the new location.

Alternatively you can look at the same book structure as a conventional outline by choosing the third group icon.

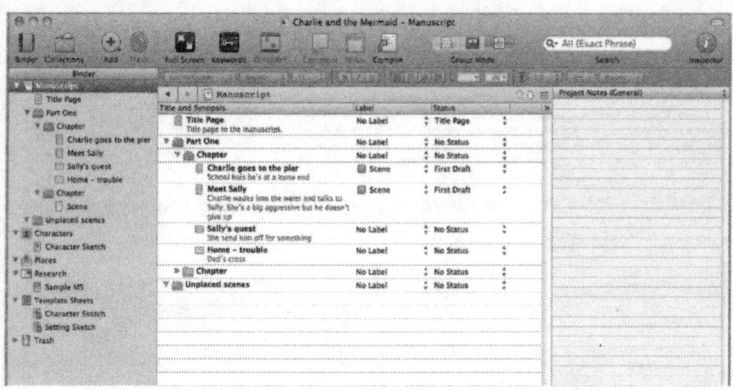

Scrivener is full of well thought-out features aimed at fiction writing. If you add a keyword to scenes recording specific information, such as character point of view or, in the case of a book written across different eras, the year concerned, the software will gather all these items together so you can see them in one place as a 'collection'. This doesn't change the order of the scenes in your narrative. It simply gives you a quick way to look at specific aspects of the book, based on POV, time or location, very quickly to check for continuity for example.

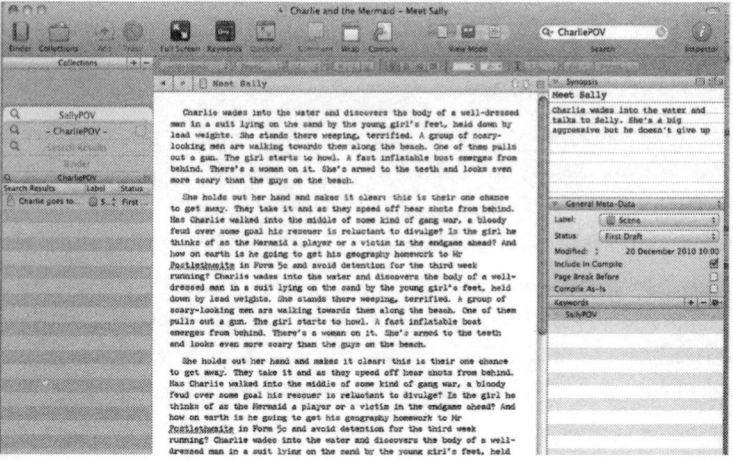

So we could now see every scene in which Charlie is the point of view character and make sure they follow logically.

You can also comment very easily in the sidebar.

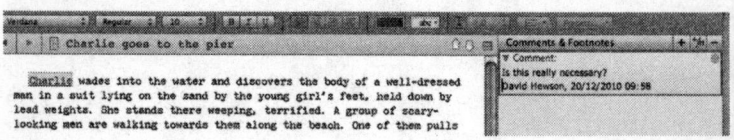

Save different versions of the same document as snapshots, seeing the old version as you work on a revise.

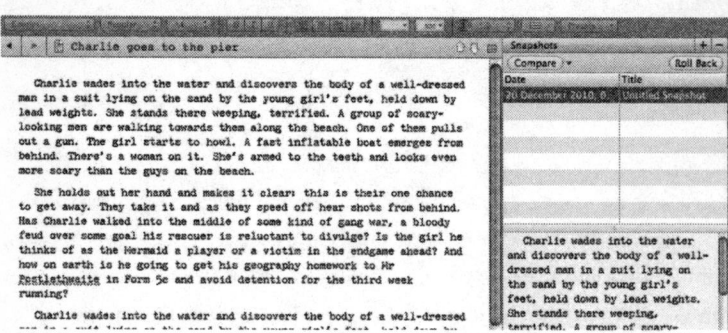

One other handy tool is a sophisticated word count target. Set the number of words you want to write – both for the book as a whole and your current session – and the software will let you know how you're doing. It's a small

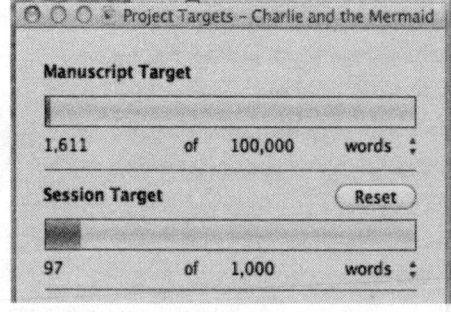

thing, and one should avoid obsessing about word counts. But useful for those who need it.

Templates come with pre-formatted folders for character sketches, research and locations. You can store text, photos, PDFs, even videos.

There are also templates for keeping character and location details. Fill in the form such as this . . .

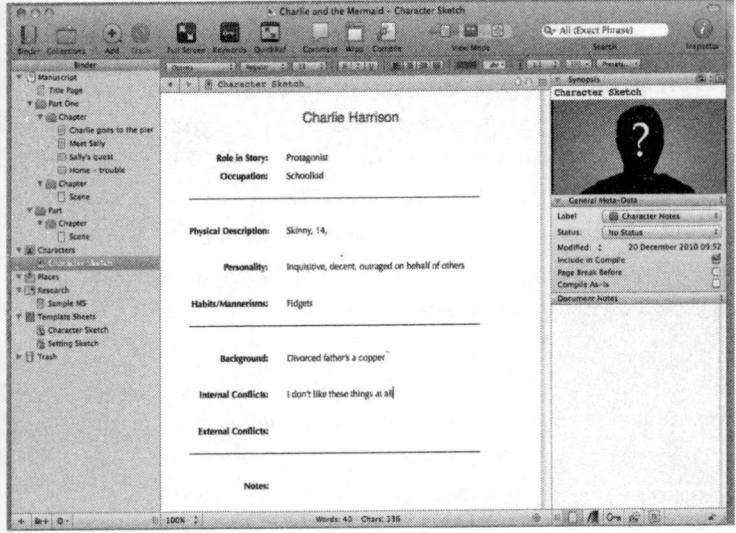

. . . and you can record what your characters look like and what drives them, and drag in a suitable photo. You can edit these templates to get rid of stuff such as internal and external conflicts, by the way.

So all the material that can go into MacJournal or OneNote could equally be accommodated here. Is that a good idea? For me, no. I like to keep the left brain and the right separate. One is for planning, one is for writing. For the first I like to put the manuscript to one side altogether. It's another instance of perspective. But you may feel differently, and you could simply set up a separate Scrivener document as your left brain information store, keeping practical material there and writing the book in a different file.

Scrivener also boasts a Trash folder. If you delete something it won't disappear. Instead the file goes into the trash and stays there in case you need to retrieve it at some stage. Delete something in an ordinary word processor and (unless you have a change-tracking option turned on) it will disappear for good. Another useful feature (only in the Mac version of Scrivener as I write, though coming soon to Windows) is the ability to export an entire book, with cover and bibliographic information, to an electronic publishing format such as Kindle or epub. In other words Scrivener, along with many other specialist writing apps, is now a dedicated end-to-end epublishing system that will take you from bare manuscript to finished ebook ready for upload should you need that.

If this were simply a battle of features, specialist writing apps would win hands down against word processors. But it's not really as simple as that. Most of us know our way around Word already. Software like Scrivener can take more than a little learning before the light bulb finally goes on. That export process into a Word file for delivery adds work and complexity. While it's a good idea to think of your book as a mosaic of scenes and chapters you also need to be able to see your work in full too. You can manage that at the revise stage by running that final read-through in Word, not a book-writing app. But you still need to refer back to the end of one scene at the beginning of another, for example.

Scrivener handles this full-book view very well, but not all scene-based apps are quite this slick. Sometimes all you see on the screen at any one time is the scene or chapter in question. You have to click from one to the next to follow or go back in the story, with no combined view for both. If you're testing something else, best check. I've found that writing apps that offer only the scene/chapter view, not the whole manuscript, become progressively more annoying as the narrative grows larger, so much so I've always abandoned them halfway through and moved to something else.

Like most software, writing apps are full of powerful tools, some essential, some frankly esoteric. Find the ones you want and ignore the rest.

It's best to settle on your writing application well before embarking on your book. The pros and cons are relatively straightforward. Conventional word processors may be limited in power in some areas but they are ubiquitous and, in the case of Word, you will probably have to run your book through it at some stage anyway.

Word 2010 for Windows is light years ahead of any previous version and certainly worth the upgrade. It doesn't have to run in a vile shade of bilious blue like its previous version either. Word 2011 for the Mac is a pale imitation, however, and best avoided if possible. Try Apple's own

Pages, which reads and writes Word files, as a speedier, though still somewhat limited, alternative.

Specialised writing apps tend to come from small companies and have more than a few quirks. All will give you a Word-compatible file export option at the end. But exporting may be a little tricky and you may well want to revise in a conventional word processor in any case, for reasons we will look at later in the section on delivery. They will offer tools you won't find easily anywhere else. But these can come with the cost of complexity. Scrivener 2 is a fantastically powerful application and can look a bit intimidating at first. Frankly my brief description here scarcely does it justice. The program is positively brimming with tricks and tools, so many that I doubt the average writer will discover some of them. Complexity is fine if you need it and can master it. But as I said earlier . . . readers have no idea what you use to write your book. They just see the words.

Is the pain of learning a new and sometimes slightly baffling bespoke program worth the gain? Hit the downloadable demos and spend a little time deciding for yourself.

FORMATTING

Picked your writing app? Good. Now let's decide what your screen is going to look like while you're writing. The vast majority of wannabe writers out there labour under very odd illusions about this. They set their font to Helvetica and opt for double spacing and think they're being professional.

Er, no.

Back in the days of typewriters we all wrote double-spaced in the same kind of font, pretty much turning out the same numbers of words per page. Editors demanded manuscripts with all that white space because they needed the extra blank lines to write in edit notes and changes. Do they work like that today? Sometimes. We'll deal with the detail of delivering a manuscript later. But even if your editor is adamant that only double-spaced Helvetica will suffice, that does not mean you have to write that way. This is a computer you're using, isn't it? Changing fonts and line spacing are simply a matter of tweaking the style details in your word processor, or selecting the whole manuscript and choosing something else.

Don't try to second guess what your future editor wants to see on the page. You've no idea, and, with the arrival of ereaders there's no longer such a thing as a 'standard'. Find a screen layout instead that suits you and gives you power over the page.

If you write in double spacing half your screen is blank. You don't need that white space – your comments will go in the margin of your software. All that emptiness is doing is preventing you seeing more of the page you're writing. That can be highly detrimental. Writers always repeat themselves. The less you see of your work as it progresses, the easier it is to let those annoying echoes escape your attention.

Here are two paragraphs with 1.15 line spacing, the way they were written.

Don't try to second guess what your future editor wants to see on the page. You've no idea, and, with the arrival of e-readers there's no longer such a thing as a 'standard'. Find a screen layout instead that suits you and gives you power over the page.

If you write in double spacing half your screen is blank. You don't need that white space – your comments will go in the margin of your software. All that emptiness is doing is preventing you seeing more of the page you're writing. That can be highly detrimental. Writers always repeat themselves. The less you see of your work as it progresses, the easier it is to let those annoying echoes escape your attention.

Here's the text with the same amount of screen in double spacing:

Don't try to second guess what your future editor wants to see on the page. You've no idea, and, with the arrival of e-readers there's no longer such a thing as a 'standard'. Find a screen layout instead that suits you and gives you power over the page.

If you write in double spacing half your screen is blank. You don't need that white space – your comments will go in the margin of your software. All that emptiness is doing is preventing you seeing more of the page you're writing. That can be highly detrimental. Writers always repeat themselves. The less you see of your work as it progresses, the easier it is to let those annoying echoes escape your attention.

You lose two lines of text out of seven by moving from 1.15 to double spacing. That's 30 per cent of your page gone. Think of that white space. Do those two paragraphs feel as connected as they should?

You wouldn't read a book in double spacing. You've no practical need to write the way authors had to twenty years ago. Choose a font and a size you find easy on the eye. Most people feel that sans typefaces work best on screen and serif ones on paper. So write in something like Arial, Helvetica or, as in the extracts above, Calibri.

If you want to be adventurous try writing in a monospaced typewriter font such as Courier or P22 Typewriter. Sometimes an old and rather battered font can work wonders on the mindset. It reminds you that you're trying to produce a work of fiction, not a letter to the bank manager.

When you're happy with the font, tweak the line and the paragraph spacing until it's as tight as you can get for comfort. Single spacing will look odd but I find that 1.15 is fine provided you put a little extra space – 10 pt in this instance – between the paragraphs. If you like looser line spacing then cut down or delete the gaps between paragraphs. Then write away to your heart's content. When you have a finished book we'll decide how best to deliver it.

Now we have the words looking right, let's deal with the rest of the screen. Get rid of any rulers and minimise any toolbars. While we're writing we want to focus on the words, nothing else. Certainly not formatting, which you should set up very simply as a body text you like with the necessary headings.

Here is what Word 2010 looks like out of the box (once you've turned off the vile Avatar blue standard colour theme).

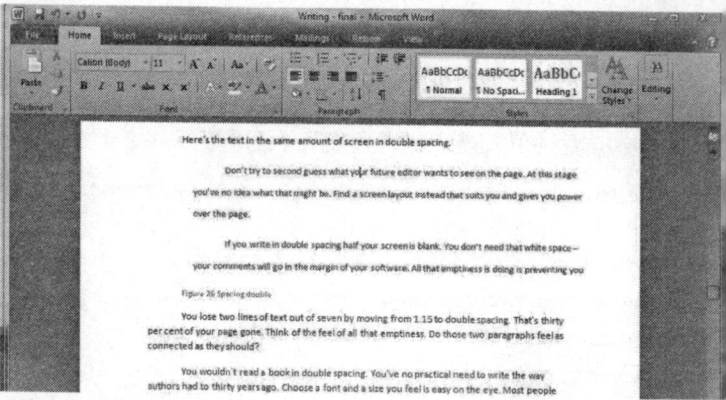

For the sake of your sanity do not spend all day long staring at that ribbon. Also I have absolutely no need of 'Mailings'. I started writing books in order to stop wearing a tie. I'm not starting again now. All of this is easily changed in Word's options panels and by flicking up the ribbon. This gives us . . .

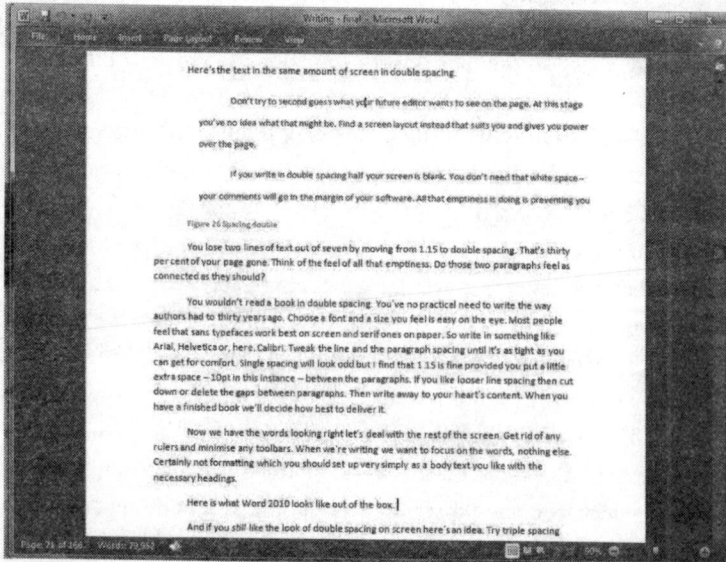

I feel a little calmer already. I write in what Word calls Print Layout view with the headers and page numbers turned off too. There's absolutely no need for them at this stage of the game.

Finally, hunt around and see if your chosen software has something akin to full page view. This is a special way of presenting text designed to let you focus on nothing but your draft. Scrivener, below, does it beautifully, fading the background to black and showing you nothing but a screen of words, with your notes and other reference material if you want them (you use the control bar at the bottom to decide what else you want to see).

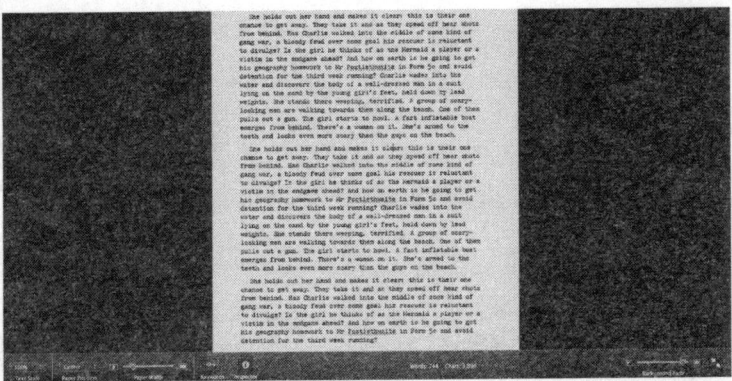

In Word things are a little more obscure. We have instead something called 'Full Screen Reading View' which fills the entire screen with your text, either single page or two pages next to one another like this:

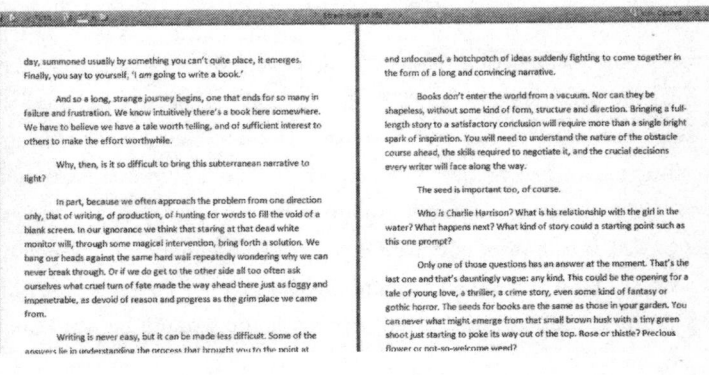

If you find yourself tired of looking at your words through the
same up-and-down screen it's
worth taking a peep at your book
like this, with the pages side-by-
side. It's perspective again.

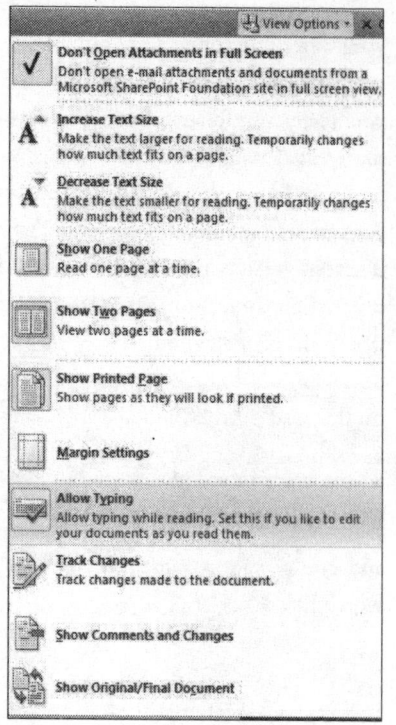

For some strange reason Word
won't let you edit text in this
view by default. No problem. Just
go to the Reading View Options
in the right-hand top corner and
tweak a few things there. You can
allow typing, turn changes and
comments off or on, and fiddle
with the screen layout to your
heart's content. On a laptop this
is lovely for reading and offers a
different view of the work in progress too, one almost like a paperback book.

Short of using a Kindle or iPad for revision, full screen view is the
closest any of us can have to that Royal typewriter Hemingway used. Just
words and the electronic equivalent of paper. Highly recommended.

BACKUP AND SECURITY

There's one final practical matter so prosaic and obvious you might feel
it's scarcely worth mentioning. Losing ideas and possible storylines is bad.
Losing your entire manuscript is unforgivable. The importance of keeping things can never be over-emphasised. That applies to basic common
sense over your computer files too. Houses burn down, laptops get stolen,
files go bad. If your story goes with it you could lose months or even years
of work. I know of one budding author who gave up altogether after his
half-finished book vanished along with his laptop. I doubt he was alone.

There really is no excuse not to keep some kind of daily backup of your work. Get into the habit of placing a copy of your key files in progress somewhere safe whenever you get to the end of the writing day. If you want the job automated, investigate one of the many online backup services offering automated storage for around $5 a month upwards.

Investing in a local USB home storage drive with backup software is a good idea too. Not only will that keep your work safe but many will store different versions so that, if things go badly wrong, you can go back in time and retrieve something that would otherwise be lost. That way even if you delete a chapter from Word you can get it back later. Businesses don't rely on a single form of backup and nor should you. And if you're on the road with no internet access a USB memory stick is excellent for keeping a working copy of your files in case your laptop goes walkabout.

Something in the way the universe works tends to dictate that those who take care to keep backups rarely ever have to use them. Ignore them and one day soon something will surely go walkabout for ever. It's not worth the risk.

STRUCTURE

Here's an old saw: all stories have a beginning, a middle and an end. A true saying too. Authors may play around with the way those elements are delivered from time to time instead of serving them up straight as a linear narrative dish. But a story that doesn't establish a starting point, a middle section which elaborates upon the beginning, and some kind of resolution at its close will not be regarded as a story at all by most readers. There are branches of literature that step outside these ideas and attempt to write their own rules. But in the field of popular fiction, of books read by people who often don't think of themselves as 'readers', these cardinal points are usually essential.

This division of the narrative into distinct component parts is often known as the 'three-act structure' – one that can be found in books, plays and films. The movie industry in particular obsesses over the finer points of those acts. You can read any number of learned tomes and attend quite a few university courses where the minutiae of the 'three-act' idea will be picked apart in scrupulous detail. I don't have space – or the inclination – for that here. I'm temperamentally opposed to obfuscating matters that are uncomplicated at heart, and truthfully this is not a convoluted subject.

But the challenges of writing a book do vary from act to act. Some of the problems that will arise, such as characterisation, are universal and will apply throughout the narrative. A few are specific to an individual stage of the story.

It should be very easy to establish where these different acts begin and end, like this . . .

First act

Begins at the beginning and goes on to introduce the problem, the main characters and the story world. The act comes to a close when our protagonist understands that this dilemma belongs to him and decides, for whatever reason, he has to solve it.

Think *Hamlet*. Forlorn son still mourning his much-loved father discovers from his father's ghost that his dad was murdered by his uncle Claudius. Then, to rub salt in the wound, the uncle has gone on to marry Hamlet's mother Gertrude. His father's ghost demands vengeance. Hamlet resolves to act mad until he can work out what to do about this.

Second act

Starts at the point the protagonist has decided he has to fix whatever bundle of trouble he's lumbered with. In order to do that he needs to understand it better and pursue a variety of options to bring about its resolution. The act ends when he sees what he believes to be the means to deliver what he seeks, and embarks upon the endgame to bring the story to a close.

Hamlet again. Our troubled prince ponders suicide, emphasises his madness, toys cruelly with Ophelia, and agonises over what to do. A group of travelling players arrive at Elsinore to give a performance. Hamlet sees them and a light bulb goes on in his head. In structural terms the second act ends when he utters the words, 'The play's the thing wherein I'll catch the conscience of the king.' His course is set. Somehow he will hunt Claudius down, reveal him as a murderer through the players, and avenge his father.

That line happens to occur in the second dramatic act of the play. Bear in mind that dramatic acts in the theatre are not the same as structural acts in narrative. Theatrical acts are in part to do with practical matters of the performance such as scenery changes. Structural story acts are staging posts along the journey of the overall narrative.

Third act

This starts at the moment the protagonist thinks he sees the way forward – catching the bad guy, finding the object of his quest, curing that broken relationship. It ends when the problem is, in some way, resolved. In simple stories and fiction for children we might say 'solved' instead. Cue that line: 'And they all lived happily ever after.' That won't work for many adult narratives. We expect our world to be restored to some kind of order, but we're realistic enough to know that rarely happens without a price.

Back to *Hamlet* . . . our troubled prince sets the endgame in motion by staging a play that re-creates the murder of his father by Claudius, who understands that his secret is revealed. He plots to send Hamlet to England and assassination. Hamlet's madness is no longer feigned. He kills Ophelia's father Polonius. She commits suicide. Claudius enlists her furious brother Laertes in a plot to murder Hamlet in a fencing match with a poisoned blade. Cue Tarantino-style ending in which Hamlet, Gertrude, Laertes and Claudius all die violently.

Those three structural acts are rarely of equal length. The first and third are frequently quite short, the second long and by far the most difficult from the writer's point of view – and the reader's at times. But there are no rules.

Hamlet is a variation on the usual theme. The prince's determination to unmask and wreak vengeance upon Claudius is made plain when he sees the players in the dramatic second act. But we have three more theatrical acts to run before the story approaches its conclusion. During that time Hamlet's determination slips, and in the fourth dramatic act it needs to be revived as he leaves Elsinore (to would-be assassination if only he knew it). On the way he meets a group of soldiers going to fight over nothing more than the territorial claims of the Norwegian king. Their willingness to die for something without personal meaning shames him for abandoning his pledge to avenge his father. He declares, 'O, from this time forth, / My thoughts be bloody, or be nothing worth!'

In a sense this is the end of the second act revisited. Shakespeare often plays with narrative conventions in order to heighten the sense of drama. The idea of the reluctant hero, one who walks away from his duty only to see something that reminds him he must return to it, is just as valid today.

Now to construct a first act for *Charlie and the Mermaid* and see what issues that prompts, and how we can overcome them in order to kick this story into life.

THE FIRST ACT: IN THE BEGINNING . . .

A protagonist, a problem, and a world. Those are the essential ingredients for a first act. Not much really. Hit the right idea and you may well find this is the easiest part of the book to write.

If this is a love story the problem might be, 'I love you, you don't love me. How can I change this?' In a crime story it's pretty obviously some kind of crime. In an adventure tale we'd expect a quest, a hunt for something lost and precious. There are many variations on the original theme but the problem, the grit in the oyster we hope will turn into a narrative pearl, always remains. If your characters lack something they want to fix on and change they don't have a magnet to draw them together – not in mainstream fiction anyway (things can be different in other parts of the bookshop).

So in order to start we need to establish that problem and make it one that someone, somewhere has to tackle. Then we have to work out who that someone is and why they want to take on this responsibility, so obsessively readers will be desperate to know how they progress. We need to fix the world in which this story will take place. Note that word: *world*. Not location. A location is simply a collection of buildings or geographical features. A two-dimensional picture postcard. We're going to need more than that. Finally we must set the tone of the story, the subtle inner character the book (rather than its individual players) passes to its readers.

When we close the first act the momentum of this tale will have changed. The reader should no longer be asking himself: 'What's this all about?' He should have a rough idea and be held to the page wanting to know how a character he has come to know and empathise with will approach the difficult path ahead. Enter the second act . . . eventually.

THE GREAT OPENING SCENE MYTH

First, some good news. There's a hoary old chestnut you hear in writing schools sometimes. It says if you haven't grabbed your reader by the third (or so) paragraph of your opening scene your book's doomed. No one will read it, least of all any busy agent or editor.

This is balderdash, and dangerous balderdash at that. I've seen wanna-be writers swallow it whole then agonise for weeks on end trying to formulate the perfect few opening paragraphs for a story that rarely ends up getting written. Why? Because all they've done is sweat over producing a beginning that's supposed to be smart and clever and attention-grabbing, never giving much thought at all to what comes after: the book.

Any agent or editor will tell you that they have a pretty clear idea from that first page whether or not the person who wrote it has any chance of becoming a published author or not. But I doubt that's because they've been blown away by three perfect opening paragraphs. Publishing professionals have a nose for potential. It's part of their job. They spot bad writing a mile off. They can read a short extract and understand very quickly whether the author reads books too, has thought about how narrative works and what he or she would like to bring to the party.

Writing that has potential possesses a confidence, a sense of direction, and an unhurried feel that's hard to nail down but obvious by its absence.

If you've been in the business for a little while you learn to spot those tell-tale signs, and the marks too of an over-anxious, hurried approach or a sense that someone is trying to be rather too clever or imitative for their own good. Those are the pointers people hunt for in a first page mostly, not some ornate piece of look-at-me writing principally designed to display how brilliant you are.

Focusing on producing a few stunning opening paragraphs, even if they're very good indeed, doesn't really tell anyone much about the book as a whole. They're just the slogan on the tin. The contents are what matters. And this kind of showy writing can become so desperate and needy in itself that it's a bit of a turn-off. What most publishing professionals want to know from a first page is that they're in the company of someone who's literate, interesting and trying to produce something original, not a wisecracking smartass trying to outdo everyone else. The average reader feels the same too.

So relax. You're setting out on a long and hopefully enjoyable journey. There's no need to shout as your audience climbs on board the bus. You've got other things to worry about.

THE PROBLEM

Charlie's seen this distraught girl in the water. Something's wrong and he doesn't know what it is, only that he wants to help, to save her somehow. We have the opening moment. The rest of the first act will draw him nearer to Sally, make him want to ease her pain, perhaps even get close to her in a way he's never achieved with a girl before. At the end of the act he will have gained a clearer idea of what's wrong and undertaken to put it right – no ifs, no buts, no going back. Charlie's the protagonist here. He's determined to fix things. He just hasn't a clue how to do it.

Problems should appear relatively simple even if they don't always turn out to be quite what a protagonist expected in the first place. A stolen figurine called the Maltese Falcon. A missing person. A crime. A fractured relationship someone would like to mend. The nature of the problem will engage with the character of the protagonist. Charlie's personality is revealed from the outset as someone who's shocked and worried that a young girl like Sally should be acting strangely, upset, perhaps even considering suicide. Sometimes the character of the protagonist will influence the nature of the problem. If you're a cop you're going to be looking for a crime. It's part of your job. Equally, if you're a pathologist or a doctor you're going to encounter medical problems – the sick, the dead – as a matter of course.

Not everyone will react to a problem in the same way. A cop chasing a criminal has access to professional resources – intelligence, computers, forensic services, firearms. A civilian who takes on the same task has little but his or her own ingenuity. The problem and the protagonist need to fit in both directions, one against the other. That's about the only restriction there is. Feel free to improvise around it, but there is a reason why so many books are classified as crime, thriller or mystery. Murder, theft, violence and general pandemonium provide problems we can all recognise.

CHARACTERISATION

All three of these story elements – people, problem, world – are important, but characterisation is the most vital of all. Quests can be a little ridiculous, worlds either flat or far-fetched, but if the voice of the protagonist is original and compelling the reader may well forgive those things, particularly if this is a series book. A strong, engrossing personality will help any narrative fly, sometimes against the odds.

Where do characters come from? Some writers filch from people they know or characters on the screen. I find that confusing. I'd constantly be asking myself: what would the real person do in this situation?

Serendipity and an idea of what I'm looking for usually work better for me. Here's an example. Back in 2002 I was stuck with a problem. I was writing the second book in the Costa series, *The Villa of Mysteries*, and struggling like mad with a character. He was Gianni Peroni, an older cop who was to be Costa's sidekick in the books to come. The man just wasn't working. He was predictable, two-dimensional, unreal somehow. I didn't know what made him tick.

This didn't worry me much at the time. The book was in its early stages and I was due to go back to Rome for more research. Then the day of the flight came . . . and the airline cancelled. Worse, they said they wouldn't fly me out to Italy for another four days at the very least.

Great. I set off by car, through France, through Switzerland, down into Tuscany, eventually settling in the hillside town of Sinalunga, trying to work out what the hell I was going to write.

The problem with Peroni at that time was simple. I didn't know where he came from. I don't mean geographically – I'd already decided he was Tuscan, which was one reason I diverted to Sinalunga trying to pin him down. I didn't understand his background – what made him, why he became a cop. I wanted him to be a sympathetic character with a bit of mystery. He's big, he's ugly, he's got scars. He looks as if he can handle himself and if the occasion arises he surely can. But there's more to him than muscle. He's actually very gentle, kind and thoughtful. In some ways the most 'emotionally intelligent' of the lot. Why?

Sinalunga is a modest little place, a small hilltop Tuscan town a long way from the tourist traps of Chiantishire. That appealed to me as a place from which my character could come. I poked around for a while and still didn't have a clue what else I could add to the man. Then there was a local holiday. The streets at the bottom of the hill filled with stalls selling food and trinkets. The little place was suddenly full of visitors all, except me, Italian. I wandered round chatting to people, most of whom were utterly baffled why a solitary Brit should have strayed so far off the beaten track.

The event had a whole line of *porchetta* stands, where locals were selling slices of roast whole stuffed pig. Must have been a dozen or more, mostly stout husbands and wives holding out bits for you to try for free and nodding at their neighbours, laughing, saying, 'Don't try his, try *ours*!'

I've never seen anything like it or tasted so much wonderful roast pork in my life. These people were mainly farmers who'd raised the beasts they were selling and had spent all night roasting them for the fair. All utterly contented with their lives, without ambition, fired by nothing more than a love of the moment and this beautiful, unspoilt part of Italy. Some of those I spoke to hadn't even visited Rome, or seen much need to.

In a flash I had Gianni Peroni. I still remember excitedly scribbling down what drove him on a little notepad in a café, fingers greasy from all that free meat. Gianni came from here and was destined to be a farmer too, happily roasting *porchetta* for the locals, handing it out for free, chanting, 'Don't try his, try mine!'

But circumstances – difficult, tragic circumstances – dictated otherwise. He was, in other words, defined by what he was not. By failure if you like. The memory of what might have been – selling *porchetta* in rural Tuscany instead of chasing bad guys in Rome – informs his personality to this day every time he walks into my head.

That backstory is explained in full in *The Villa of Mysteries*. It gets mentioned with diminishing brevity in the books that immediately follow, and not much any more. Peroni is who he is, and while I wouldn't rule out his Tuscan origins re-entering a book in the future I don't need to keep mentioning them. If readers are sufficiently interested, all they have to do is go back to the early books and find out for themselves.

What did I learn when I was looking for the 'real' Gianni Peroni?

> ➤ The things that make books work aren't gifts; you have to go out and track them down. You don't have to go all the way to Tuscany, of course. Look around you. Take a walk. Catch a bus. See the real world and imagine how some aspect of it might add something to the imaginary one you're trying to create.

> ➤ Characters, like real people, can be formed as much by what doesn't happen as by what does.

> ➤ The subterranean qualities of characterisation remain important even when they never make their way into the book. They colour and create the individual in the writer's head. They help you *see*.

> ➤ If you want some great *porchetta*, go to Sinalunga at festa time.

I've never been back. I've never needed to. But I'm glad that flight got cancelled. If it hadn't Peroni would never have turned out the way he did.

Characterisation is a subtle, tricky business. It's never so simple that you can think from the outset, 'In this scene I will establish that Fred Nark is a coward and a bully.' It's often best to let characters reveal themselves gradually. The writer has to be observant in order to recognise these personality traits as they surface, then watch for the right moment to make them plain. Unless you're one of those rare beasts, an author who knows every step of the way before starting the journey, a book is not a movie performed from some pre-planned script. When you write what you're actually embarking upon is a set of structured improvisations based around fixed ideas and narrative points loosely thought out in advance. It's up to the characters to produce the detail of how we get from point to point, and if they're to do that you need to listen to them carefully because you're the one who's got to chauffeur them to the place they want to go.

Let me spell that out once more because it's a critical point. If books are to feel alive characters must drive events, not the other way round. That's not to say characters aren't affected by plot occurrences. They have to be. But if you fit your people to match what you want to happen in your story, the tale is likely to have a mechanical, artificial flavour to it. Authors are deities of the little world they invent. To be a real god you have to accept that your creations should, sooner rather than later, discover the power of free will. 'Real' characters in a book aren't puppets to be pushed around according to some story template or plotline. They should have distinct and occasionally unpredictable personalities. If they don't shout at you at some stage, 'But I just wouldn't do that,' you should be worried. I love that moment, even though it always demands some rewriting. You should whoop with joy when you hear those words in your head. Finally your creations have taken their first steps on their own. They're *alive*.

Another of the big character fallacies is consistent personality. Consistency is a good thing to expect of your doctor or car mechanic. But not of someone playing a key role in a piece of drama. You want them to surprise you, to have odd, quirky moments. Yes, perhaps 95 per cent of the time they conform to the picture you've come to expect. But it's the 5 per cent of nonconformity that makes them memorable.

A touch of the asymmetric and the imperfect can lend them a more familiar, recognisable appearance. Perfection's best admired from afar. Few of us aspire to it, or meet it, in our daily lives. In my Rome books, Nic Costa can get things horribly wrong sometimes, his inspector, Falcone, is often arrogant, and Teresa Lupo incredibly stubborn. All the same we know their hearts are unfailingly in the right place. They're good people trapped in a fractured world, trying to do the right thing and constantly asking themselves: but what is that really?

That sense of bravery and frailty mixed together in the same frame makes them sympathetic (and yes those 'how to write' books are right on one thing: you do need sympathetic people). The trick is to bring out the sympathy subtly because human beings are a lot more complex than they sometimes seem. 'Sympathetic' is not the same as 'nice'.

Part of the narrative journey is the discovery of those concealed personalities, the revelation of the true identities of those involved. The job of an author is to chip away at the formless shape in front of you in order to uncover the story in hiding, not concoct some mechanical fabrication you hope will fit some flimsy and artificial outline for a book.

PICK A NAME, ANY NAME

How do you decide what your characters are called? With difficulty usually. Mostly my stories take place in foreign countries, too, which complicates things even further. My first published book, *Semana Santa*, now rereleased as *Death in Seville*, was set in southern Spain. It's a part of Europe I know well. But when I started the story I didn't have the time or money to go there to research the thing, or any inkling it would be finished, let alone published. So I worked from my memory of writing travels books in Andalucia several years earlier.

The book opens with a curious old aristocrat called Caterina, which sounded a pretty decent Mediterranean name. In Italy it is. But I now know that in Spain the equivalent of Caterina is Catalina. That's a flying boat to most people in the UK, not a woman's name at all. I got it wrong, and if I'd got it 'right', using Catalina instead of Caterina, it would have sounded weird. So in the rereleased version she's called something else altogether.

Character names need to sound true, and that can be tricky. It's easy enough to pick a common first name – Jack or Harry, Jill or Jane. No one is going to find that strange. But if you then combine that with a very popular surname people will scratch their heads. Jack Smith? Jill Jones? They sound too plain. I'm happy with Charlie Harrison. That's plain but just a touch distinctive.

Sally is a bit more unusual. So, for reasons that will become apparent, I'm going to abandon the idea that she's foreign and give her the surname Whitby. That's a place name, a seaside town as it happens. I've never heard it used as a surname but that doesn't matter.

Charlie Harrison and Sally Whitby. They sound memorable, easily recognised. I hope they'll stick well enough for the reader not to think, 'What's his second name again?' I'm not sure about Jonathan Black for the antagonist. I want something more mysterious. Let's make him Matt Giordano for now.

Nic Costa got his name by the easy route. I wanted something short and simple, and a little unusual too, to mark out the fact that he's a little different to his peers. When I started writing these books I'd no idea they would be published anywhere outside the UK. It never occurred to me they'd be sitting in Italian bookstores in translation one day. So I wanted a name that was easy to pronounce in English and sounded a touch international. Nic's father appeared in the first book. He was very much a man of the world, not a parochial Roman. I could imagine he would have been happy with that.

People sometimes say to me, 'But isn't Costa Spanish?' Yes, there are plenty of people called Costa in Spain. But there are lots in Italy too, and I even know roughly where they live. You can check out the geographical distribution of any surname in Italy on the internet. You'll find lists of popular first and last names on Wikipedia, broken down country by country. There are scores of genealogical sites out there which you can plunder for inspiration. Some software – Scrivener for example – comes with a name generator. Use these resources. None of them existed when

I was writing *Semana Santa*, otherwise I would never have made that mistake about Caterina.

When I start a book I have a rough list of the main characters in my book diary. Obviously the regulars never change. But the names of the 'guest stars' do as I work on the story. I'll often just try using a different name to see if it suits the character better as he or she develops. Names can also reflect the background of the person involved. The ninth Costa book, *The Fallen Angel*, features an aristocratic English family who come from a very posh Anglo-Scottish background but have fallen on hard times. After much casting around I came up with the last name Gabriel for them. The father, a very patriarchal figure, got the first name 'Malise'. This is an old Scottish Christian name, used mainly by the gentry. I found it by looking up some of the family histories of Scottish aristos on the web. It seemed to fit perfectly.

Peroni, of course, came from the beer, which was largely unknown in England when I invented him and is now actually brewed here. Nor did I ever see the link that people would make between Costa coffee and my young Roman cop – that coffee chain was a lot smaller ten years ago.

There's no way you can pick a series character name and hope to avoid such coincidences years down the line. If I were starting a new series now, though, I'd try to stick to some basic rules:

➢ Choose simple names.

➢ Make them memorable and easy to pronounce.

➢ Under no circumstances make a name indicative of some character trait, or vaguely ridiculous, not in a straightforward piece of story-telling anyway. If you're dealing with pastiche or comedy then have all the fun you want. But if you want people to take your story seriously you usually need to use names that readers think they might meet in real life.

Oh – and one final thing. Whatever you call someone you will, before long, get an email from a real person with the same name asking, 'Why did you steal me for your book?' And here let me tell you a curious true story of synchronicity, something that happens from time to time in this strange trade.

In 1957 the actor Lex Barker starred as a character called David Hewson in a very noir movie called *The Girl in Black Stockings*.

I was four years old at the time. How on earth did someone come up with that name for a character? Actually I know. The movie was based on a story by a South African writer called Peter Godfrey. In the early 1980s when I was a reporter on *The Times* a very interesting and knowledgeable old sub-editor introduced himself to me there. None other than the same Peter Godfrey, now doing a bit of subbing on the side.

'I used your name in a movie once,' Peter told me one day when we were talking about books (I was already itching to become a writer at the time and he had lots of useful advice on the subject).

'Where did it come from?' I asked.

Peter thought for a moment and said, 'Made it up, of course.'

WE DON'T NEED ANOTHER HERO

Can you sense something heroic in young Charlie, looking at that distraught girl in the sea, wondering how he can help her? I can. Heroic, that is. Not a 'hero' necessarily. You need to be wary of them, modern ones anyway. Classical heroes are fine. They're flawed, miserable, doomed creatures, nothing like the too-perfect marionettes you meet on occasion today. If you're thinking about writing about one of the latter – you know the kind, great teeth, perfect hair, indefatigable, always willing to pat small dogs on the head between saving people – please stop for a moment and consider what you're doing.

Here are some of the characteristics stereotypical heroes tend to have. They're . . .

➢ Handsome

➢ Decent

➢ Brave

➢ Invincible (and often seemingly incapable of noticing pain)

Are you yawning yet? I am. Children and people who move their lips when they read apart, who the hell wants to hang around goody-goodies like that?

The ancients understood this problem intrinsically. From the outset they gave their heroes flaws. So Achilles came with his heel (and we all knew from the moment that came on the scene where his fate would one day lie). They also made them difficult human beings. Achilles was a blood-thirsty, bad-tempered maniac. The first two lines of the Iliad run . . .

> Sing, Goddess, of the rage, of Peleus' son Achilles
> The accursed rage, which brought pain to thousands of the Achaeans.

And that's just the beginning. In a little while he starts to get really mad.

Modern heroes try to pick up on the Achilles trick but it's often an afterthought. Superman was born in 1932. Kryptonite, his Achilles heel, first appeared in a radio play in 1942. It wasn't until 1949 that the one thing that could kill Superman finally made its way into the comics. So for seventeen long years the guy was utterly invincible, bound to win every encounter in the end because no one could do him any serious harm. Fine for a comic, obviously. Boring if you only have words.

The most intriguing characteristic of a real hero is something very simple. It lies not with a hero's strength but with his weakness, his falli-bility, the revelation he's human after all. Not every reader likes this idea, of course. I once got one of those whiny so-called Amazon 'reviews' from a punter railing against a Costa book simply on the grounds that Nic was a 'bad detective who makes mistakes'. That reader wanted a comic book hero: the perfect good guy bringing evil to book. Costa certainly wants to do the latter, but he often struggles to define precisely what evil is, and he fumbles things along the way. He's a mere mortal after all because that's the kind of fiction I write. I stoutly defend my Amazon correspon-dent's right to hunt for Superman in fiction but why he was looking for him in one of my books is beyond me.

Heroism in heroes is predictable and liable to induce yawns without something to add a little texture and interest to the mix. They would act like that, wouldn't they? Wouldn't you too if you knew you were invincible and couldn't feel pain?

What can be much more illuminating is heroism in ordinary people, people who don't think of themselves as heroic in the least, yet discover an inner, unknown core of strength when some extraordinary situation demands it. There's a news story you read from time to time that sums this up. It's the one where someone jumps into a river to save a drowning child, or a dog even, and dies in the attempt. Only later do we discover that they couldn't actually swim.

That says more to me about real human heroism – the sense of self-sacrifice, the hatred of seeing a life going to waste, the blind determination to do something whatever the cost – than some bloke flying around in a cape and red underpants.

There's something of that blunt, simple bravery in Charlie Harrison and I'm determined to bring it out. Not that Charlie feels he's heroic. He's simply about to witness something that's going to make him mad, aware of a tear in a universe that's supposed to be in harmony. Charlie will want to mend that tear because he's a decent human being. That's all the hero – and character – I need for now.

DIALOGUE

Most people speak to their fellow human beings with little difficulty day in and day out. Sit them down at a computer and ask them to try to write believable dialogue for a made-up story and nine times out of ten they will flounder. Awkward conversations are never comfortable to experience, in real life or fiction. Finding a fluent easy tone of speech for your characters can be a struggle, often for the simple reason that writers try too hard. Remember what you're trying to do here: reproduce spoken interchanges between 'real' people (who aren't real at all, of course).

I had a minor argument at a writing school once. A student had submitted the first few chapters of his finished novel for my consideration. He was immensely proud of what he'd achieved. It was promising too, apart from the dialogue. It was full of verbal tics, each carefully allotted to individual characters to indicate who they were.

So one chap would say 'Umm . . . ' a lot, another was in the habit of coughing, and a third stuttering. After ten minutes it felt like being trapped in a theatre with an audience composed entirely of people who were either sick or suffering from extreme nervous exhaustion.

When I suggested that perhaps these recurrent twitches and splutters added nothing to the story the affronted author replied, 'But that's how people really speak!'

Let me repeat myself because this is vitally important. We are not dealing with the real world. Fiction is a tissue of lies from beginning to end – ones told, we hope, with sufficient skill and conviction that they fool the reader into suspending his natural disbelief. A crime story that mirrored real life would be unreadable. The first half of the book would consist of little more than serious men and women seated at desks poring over computers and CCTV footage. Authors make things up for a living, and one of the most important things they make up is the way people speak to each other.

Good dialogue serves three specific purposes.

➤ It tells you something about the person who's speaking.

➤ It moves the story along.

➤ It brings the reader closer to the characters, the narrative and the world, making them feel at home in the book, part of it, not some stranger peering in from the outside.

Real speech is often fragmented and, yes, broken up with illiterate utterances and meaningless umms and ahhs. We can take a bit of that in a book if, say, we want to paint the indecision or weakness of a character. When it becomes a habit or character trait, it soon turns annoying.

Read your dialogue out loud and ask yourself: could you imagine someone actually using those words? Do they sound natural, or odd and stilted? The best dialogue is, like much of the best writing, invisible, unremarkable in that we read it and barely notice how fluently it's taking us further into the story. It may not resemble the way we'd talk in real life, but it's very often the way we would speak if we were able to think through a sentence a bit more carefully before uttering it.

Take a potential exchange between Charlie and Sally's grandfather.

'What was it like?' Charlie asked. 'The pier? Before it burned down?'

Mr Whitby went to the theatrical chest next to the fireplace, sorted through some papers there and came back with a programme.

'It was a magical world, Master Charles,' he said, placing the programme on the table. 'Quite unlike the present.'

Charlie laughed and looked at the pictures there: singers and dancers, magicians and ventriloquists.

'Why do you call me that? Why do you speak so *funny*?'

Mr Whitby beamed, arching his eyebrows like a ham actor in one of the kids' shows on TV.

'The stage! The stage! One never leaves it, dear boy.' His smile fell a little. 'Though the audience isn't quite what it was.'

Charlie waited. The old man was watching him intently. He had an audience then and they both knew it.

'Say the word,' Mr Whitby told him. '*If* you can remember it . . . '

'Abracadabra,' Charlie murmured, a little embarrassed. He felt like a little kid again, at someone's birthday party.

'Shazam!' the old man declared with glee.

A bunch of bright paper flowers burst out of Mr Whitby's flying fingers.

'For the lady. ' He reached over and offered the bouquet to Sally, who sat silent, smiling, in the corner, taking them with a shrug that said she'd done this a million times before.

'I'd like to do tricks like that one day,' Charlie said.

'So you shall, Master Charles. I warrant it and I am the Grand Master. The wizard. Never forget.'

This is a pretty innocuous event: an old man performs a magic trick. What do we learn through the dialogue?

➢ Charlie's an intelligent, observant, forthright kid who's already made a note of Mr Whitby's oddities and must have played this game before since he knows 'the word'.

➢ Mr Whitby has an archaic, forced theatrical mode of speech, one he seems to use wryly, knowing himself it's part of the act. There's something sad about him too.

None of this is stated as plain fact, of course. The reader should work these things out by following the exchange and wondering what it means.

How 'real' is this exchange? Not very. Most kids like Charlie would probably feel intimidated by a strange old showman like Mr Whitby. The words would be different too. The opening line – 'What was it like?' Charlie asked. 'The pier? Before it burned down?' – sounds authentic. In truth though it would normally run something like this: 'Mr Whitby?' Charlie asked. 'What was the pier like before it burned down?'

We tend to pose questions in a single sentence, not broken up as you see in the original text. But the fragmented version – and the fact we don't know what Charlie's 'it' is until we go on – make the construction just a touch more interesting.

CONTRACTIONS

It's important that dialogue sounds natural. Normally that will involve the use of contracted speech. Charlie would never say, 'You are late again, Sally. It is time for breakfast.' It would be: 'You're late again, Sally. It's time for breakfast.'

In the exchange above Mr Whitby doesn't always contract his words. Take the sentence, 'So you shall, Master Charles. I warrant it and I am the Grand Master.' Why not? Because of character. Mr Whitby is an old ham who likes to appear grand and a touch pompous, even if it's all a joke. The signs are there in his speech and the use of a word like 'warrant'. There's the matter of emphasis too. Imagine him saying, 'I am the Grand Master.' What he's really telling Charlie is, 'I *am* the Grand Master.'

Most speech will be contracted. It's a matter of personal choice and style whether you contract the rest of the narrative, reported speech and action for example. But don't ignore the possibilities for bucking these conventions from time to time. Mr Whitby's mode of speech here gives us an insight into his character without any overt statement of fact. This is good because we need to avoid . . .

EXPOSITION IN DIALOGUE

Most books have recap moments. They're the point in the story where you need to remind the reader where we are in the tale so far, what's known and what's unknown. They can often be handled very slyly, in the form of a meeting or some inner thought process.

Here's what you don't do.

Charlie's father looked at him over the breakfast table and said, 'Let me make sure I understand what you're saying. This girl Sally's being pestered by Matt Giordano. She's got this dodgy grandfather who used to be Giordano's partner once upon a time when they performed in that theatre on the pier, back before it got burnt out in that mysterious blaze. Sally's mother went missing around then and you think this Giordano bloke's got something to do with it. Now you've had a look in the pier yourself, even though you're not supposed to, and you think you've found something that might bring him to justice. Am I right?'

Mother, fetch my gun.

This is unacceptable for so many different reasons. It's clumsy. It's unbelievable. It turns characters into puppets who exist for no other reason than to spout plot devices when required. Passages of this nature will get your manuscript thrown into the bin by any discerning agent or publisher, and with good reason.

They are also very easy to avoid:

Charlie rode his bike down to the promenade, fuming at the conversation he'd just had with his dad. He was a policeman. He ought to know things. Was it so ridiculous a crook like Matt Giordano was pestering Sally all the time? Charlie had shown him the photocopies of the news stories from the papers in the library. It was all there. The blaze at the pier. Sally's missing mother. The fact that Giordano had worked alongside her on the stage. And anyway . . . his dad was a boy himself back then, living in the town. Surely he would have remembered?

Keep your recap moments to a minimum. If more are demanded by an editor they're easily inserted later. And *never* try to handle them solely through dialogue.

THE INTERIOR CONVERSATION

I was wandering back from the Indian takeaway one night, head stuck in the book I was writing, when a conversation popped into my head. It was an argument between two characters discussing, roughly, why their world had gone wrong. One of them, commenting on something the other had just done, said, 'You should set a better example.'

The target of this remark is the sort of character who questions everything. She responds (roughly) . . .

'Better example? *Better example?* You've got Jesus, Buddha, Gandhi, Mother Teresa of Calcutta and a million others out there already. Who needs one more? And from me?'

Reasonable point. To that character, anyway. It never made it into the book but the exchange was valuable nevertheless. It was one more interior conversation that helped me shape the story.

Do all authors talk to themselves? I think so, even if they don't admit it. Part of this strange job is to create (hopefully convincing) characters who take on a life of their own, run around your head, then pop on to the page reasonably fully formed ready to kid the reader they're real too.

Most books aren't silent movies. Real characters communicate. So writers need some way to re-create the dialogue between the people in their story inside and outside the book itself. You need your characters to talk to one another constantly, making everyday small talk that never finds its way on to the page. They have to live inside you before you can reproduce them fully for the world at large. There are few better ways to do this than to cultivate the habit of the interior conversation. Talking to yourself, in other words, out loud or in silence, in the character of the people you're inventing.

Here's one of my routines. When I'm in Rome I love spending time in local cafés. I listen to the people there, I talk to them. I almost always learn something. Roman cafés are places for conversation and, on occasion, argument. Football, Silvio Berlusconi and the general state of the world are subjects that are guaranteed to generate a squabble, usually, though not always, a genial one.

The game I play is simple. I imagine that my four main characters – Nic Costa, Gianni Peroni, Leo Falcone and Teresa Lupo – are in the café with me, and then try to work out what their contribution to this particular argument would be. Let's say, for example, that Lazio have just beaten Roma at football and someone at the bar has voiced the opinion that this means Lazio are the better side who will sweep all before them for the rest of the season. Being good citizens of the *centro storico* – the historical heart of Rome – all four find this blasphemous (Lazio is the posh team from the suburbs). But they're different characters, and would have their own responses. Roughly this . . .

Nic Costa is a very decent, reasonable and intelligent young chap who likes to put his point of view across but in a way that doesn't involve confrontation. Also he's not terribly interested in any sport except rugby. He'd shrug and say something like: 'It's only football. Now if you want to talk Italy versus Ireland next week . . .'

Gianni Peroni is older, emotionally intelligent, likes to hold his own but can sidestep an argument if he wants. 'Ah, but it's only October. If you remember two seasons ago they whipped us in autumn and then we whipped them in the spring *and* won Serie A. So who knows?'

Leo Falcone would want to slap down the speaker but, being more than a touch arrogant, would feel it beneath him to enter in argument directly. He'd tap Peroni or Costa on the shoulder and say: 'Go tell that idiot to shut up.'

Teresa Lupo doesn't suffer fools gladly either but would never dream of asking someone else to do her dirty work. She'd simply march over, prod the guy in the chest and say: 'People like you make me wonder if Darwin got it wrong all along and the human race really is getting stupider by the day.'

Four different people, four different responses.

None of this would make it into a book. But by inventing these conversations in your own head you refine and differentiate your characters. If all of them had the same response then alarm bells should be ringing.

When we come to locations we'll learn there's a question we need to ask ourselves. A test: can we move our story elsewhere and it wouldn't matter at all? If the answer's yes then something's wrong.

Dialogue follows the same convention. Your characters should stamp their personality on the way they speak, so much that most of the time the reader will quietly recognise that individual voice. Look at the direct speech in any scene and ask yourself: is it interchangeable? Could the same sentences be said by other characters without changing any of the words? If most of your dialogue can be switched that way, you're missing a trick. You haven't built individual voices into your people. They're the same. In truth they all probably sound like you.

These silent, slightly batty interior dialogues can help you pin down the detail of the characters you're trying to bring to life and give them identities of their own.

HE SAID, SHE SAID

There's an old saw you'll hear at writing schools from time to time. It says you shouldn't have to attach a name to dialogue except at the outset, to identify who's speaking. So . . .

> Charlie looked at her and said, 'What's wrong now, Sally?'
>
> 'Who said something was wrong?'
>
> 'I did. I can tell.'
>
> 'Charlie Harrison. Mr Know-It-All.'

We identify Charlie as the first speaker, and he identifies Sally as the other person in the scene so we know she's the one replying to his question. Just to remind us, she uses his name later in a sarcastic way.

It works fine here, but this is only two people and the exchange is quite short. What happens when the conversation involves a fuller set of characters and carries on for a couple of pages? We all want to avoid a 'He said . . . She said . . . ' sequence of sentences. Can you really rely on dialogue content and characterisation to carry the job of identifying who's speaking?

The supporters of this idea say: yes, you can, if you're sufficiently skilled as a writer. I say: balderdash. You can check this yourself, and with anyone out there who reads fiction. How many times have you found yourself in the middle of extended, unattributed dialogue only to lose the thread over who's speaking and have to backtrack, checking alternative paragraphs along the way, until you finally find a name attached to some speech that lets you work out the pattern?

Quite.

Do not run long passages of speech, particularly between more than two people, without reminding the reader from time to time who's doing the talking. Be inventive. For example, find an excuse to drop briefly out of constant table-tennis-style dialogue and reinforce the speech sequence through some physical act.

> 'No, no, no. It can't be true. I don't believe it.'
>
> Charlie pushed the show programme across the table, tapped his finger on the photograph of Matt Giordano and Sally's grandfather and said, 'It is true. You can see it in his face, can't you?'

There's no 'He said . . . She said . . .' or any direct names attached to the speech here but we know exactly who's talking and can gauge the preceding dialogue order if necessary. Constant back-and-forth speech can become tedious in any case, especially if the reader loses the thread and is no longer sure who's talking. Short breaks like this make for a more interesting rhythm and give you a chance to reinforce the identity of the speaker.

TO SAY OR NOT TO SAY

You may come across two companion 'rules' to the 'you should never need to identify the speaker' idea. Let's deal with the first, which says that one verb only can be applied to speech: to say. In other words your characters may never bellow, moan, mutter, murmur, shout, declare, scream, hiss or even whisper. It's always 'say' or 'said'. It's up to you whether you follow this mandate or not. To me it's twaddle.

Most of the time I will use the verb 'to say' because it's short and straight to the point. But if someone is whining, moaning or yelling there's really no good reason why you shouldn't use one of those verbs instead. Just remember to sprinkle them sparingly through the text. An exchange where everyone is bellowing will soon become as wearing on the page as it is in real life. The same goes for a conversation where everyone is whispering, murmuring or muttering. Moderation is all.

Note, too, one convention about the use of the verb 'hiss'. Many editors will reach for the red pen if you use this in conjunction with a sentence that does not follow a sibilant consonant – the 's' sound. So it's OK to say ' "Be quiet, Sally," Charlie hissed,' because the sibilant sound of 'Sally' justifies 'hissed'. But you can't say ' "Be quiet, Charlie," Sally hissed.' Where's the sibilant consonant? It's a small point, and one I suspect that goes over the head of most readers. But editors are there to pick up small points . . . and they will.

None of this should stop you sticking to the 'never use anything but say' rule if you feel like it. But do be aware that most people (and every editor I know) don't give this rather daft dictum any credence. So long as you stick to everyday verbs that are clearly associated with the act of speaking you're fine. If, on the other hand, your characters suddenly find themselves orating, asseverating or otherwise declaiming, I will be the first to walk swiftly to the other side of this argument and cry, 'You have *got* to be joking.'

Use the right words, deploy them sparingly, and never put anything in the way of the reader that makes him think, 'What the . . . ?'

I LIKE ADVERBS — THERE, I SAID IT, BOLDLY

Now to the second 'rule'. A while back I was on a panel at a writing event with a bunch of American colleagues. Someone on the floor came up with what seemed to me a bizarre question. How did we feel about adverbs? Those words that usually, though not always, end in -ly and modify verbs and adjectives? The ones that make people walk *slowly* or be *really* bright when it comes to mathematics?

Funny one that, I thought. It opened the floodgates. The poor old adverb got kicked from pillar to post. In some quarters, it seems, adverb use is akin to wife-beating or bull-baiting, a nasty old-fashioned habit that should have been laid to rest years ago.

Remember. We're trying to produce works of the imagination here, not business plans. The only rule is: keep the reader entertained. I'd never heard of this decree before I started going to talk at writing schools in the States. Nor has any reader or editor of my acquaintance ever voiced the opinion that adverbs are so, like, nineteenth-century, dude.

One particular habit that seems to infuriate the Anti-Adverb Party is its use in qualifying speech. For example: '"I don't suppose there's somewhere we could stop for some lunch?" Charlie asked hopefully.' The haters say this should never happen. Sometimes they're right. I don't need the word 'hopefully' here. Charlie's a normal, growing lad. I suspect that by this stage of the book I would have established that he doesn't like going without his food. Anyone hearing that spoken sentence should understand the tone of his voice, hopefully (there I go again). But the word requires excision here not because it's an adverb. It's unnecessary, plain and simple, and redundant words should go whatever label they carry on their backs.

Adverbs are fine when they add something. When they don't they should come out.

One instance I cited at that panel was when people were speaking in a particular way – quickly or slowly, for example, which could be indicative of a mood or a need to act swiftly. Ah, said an adverb-hater. You can handle that through punctuation. So for slow speech, you got people to s-p-e-a-k v-e-r-y sllllloooowwwllly. Or something.

Mother, I need that gun again.

Also, how do you deal with the opposite? Speaking very quickly? Never did get an answer to that one. And what about 'nervously' and 'forcefully' and 'tentatively', all of which can, in the right circumstances, add more meaning to the text?

Adverbs exist because, used properly, they bring something to writing and have done since we learned to communicate beyond grunts. This is why we find them in Romance languages, in Japanese, Scandinavian, Greek and, of course, Latin (the term was actually invented by a fourth-century grammarian, Charisius, from 'ad-verbium', literally adding something to a verb). Are we really such clever-clogs today that we can dismiss centuries of literary usage through some blunt rule that means little or nothing to the average reader?

This is my opinion, of course. You're entitled to differ. The great Elmore Leonard certainly does, as he said in an article in the *New York Times* a few years ago. He feels the only allowable verb to be used to carry dialogue is 'say', and it must never ever be qualified by an adverb under any circumstances. I'm with him on most of the other points he made in that piece. But in truth it was principally a great article for anyone wanting to learn how to write and sound like Elmore Leonard. If you're trying to define your own voice, ignore so-called rules and find it for yourself.

SPEAKING IN TONGUES

Charles Dickens's first novel, *The Pickwick Papers*, met with little interest from the public when it first appeared as a magazine serial. It was only when Dickens introduced the character of Sam Weller in Chapter Ten that people started to take notice of his story. Very soon Weller, a loquacious Cockney who enters the tale while cleaning boots at a London inn, was a star. Here's an early appearance he makes ...

> 'Vy didn't you say so before,' said Sam, with great indignation, singling out the boots in question from the heap before him. 'For all I know'd he was one o' the regular threepennies. Private room! and a lady too! If he's anything of a gen'l'm'n, he's vurth a shillin' a day, let alone the arrands.'

Dickens has Weller speaking a language of his own, one which replaces 'w' with 'v' on a seemingly random basis, a usage which was archaic even in the author's day. Weller invents new words and mangles real ones, sometimes to the point where they're barely recognisable. It's a comic act, and one that worked spectacularly well. When our Cockney cheery chap came on the scene Dickens's career took off, and Weller mementoes and souvenirs soon began to fill the shops of Victorian England.

Try a trick like this today and you'll be lucky to be published at all. Weller is, to the modern ear, very hard going indeed. In mainstream twenty-first-century fiction readers are unlikely to possess the patience to struggle with dialogue which tests their comprehension to the limits. Accepting vampires and complex systems of magic and mythology is one thing. Trying to come to terms with what's tantamount to a different language is another.

This is an entirely modern phenomenon. Go back fifty years and you will still find English writers trying to differentiate between classes and races through the way they speak. Working-class Londoners called you 'guvnor'. Posh ladies declared, 'My good man!' Some of the phrases that were inserted into the mouths of foreigners frankly beggar belief.

So how should a modern writer reflect accents and foreign languages in a book? Indeed, should you at all?

Ernest Hemingway made a brave and instructive attempt at anglicising Spanish in his civil war classic *For Whom the Bell Tolls*. Spanish is one of the many languages which distinguishes between the singular and plural second person. In English we simply say 'you'. In Spanish singular and plural are different, and just to complicate matters there are different words for formal and informal usage too.

To deal with this in the book Hemingway, writing in English, resurrects the old English second person singular 'thou' and puts it directly into the mouth of a Spanish character. He also uses Spanish curses literally, or tried to until the sensitive editors of the day marched in with a red pen. A curse used in the book is '*me cago en la leche*'. This translates literally as, 'I shit in the milk', an odd profanity, but there you go. Readers of the 1940s couldn't handle the word 'shit'. So what appeared in the original was, 'I obscenity in the milk.' Which sounds rather worse to me.

It's a wonderful book. You should read it. But these linguistic contortions get in the way. They're only there because the writer is trying to make a point about anglicising a language which, at times, clearly refuses to play ball.

People still try, though. Another common ploy is to throw in well-known foreign words as some kind of flag. So a French character will frequently ask for a cup of coffee and add, '*S'il vous plaît.*' Shouldn't we know he's French already? Does the fact he can say 'please' tell us anything? Given that we don't routinely put 'please' and 'thank you' into straightforward English conversations without reason, not if we want to sell our book, why would we need to do it for foreign ones?

Then there are the concocted foreign accents, such as Manuel's in *Fawlty Towers,* 'Pleeze Meester Fawlty. I no had done nerthink!'

We're back with Sam Weller declaring, 'If he's anything of a gen'l'm'n, he's vurth a shillin' a day, let alone the arrands.' Manuel, like Weller, is a comic character, which goes some way towards defending such practices, though I do wonder in these sensitive times whether such stereotypes will find favour the way they once did.

In most cases it's a mistake to try to manhandle language into some convenient regional, national or racial pigeonhole. This is fiction. None of it represents the world as it is. When they were making the movie of my first book, *Semana Santa*, I flew to the set in Seville, solely as an observer, and talked to some of the crew. One of the key actors, an American, asked me, 'What kind of accent should I play this character in?'

I was baffled. What sort of accent do you fancy? I asked. Spanish, the actor said, because that was the nationality of the character.

I thought for a moment then said, 'But the Spanish don't speak Spanish with a Spanish accent.' Which didn't go down too well. What I meant, I think, was this. We live in a very international world. It's not unusual to bump into someone from the other side of the planet while waiting at the supermarket checkout. Being foreign is no longer special. It's just part of everyday life. There's a very good argument for letting your characters speak as people first and icons of some region or other country second, if at all.

No one should need to buy a dictionary of slang or a primer of foreign grammar to read a novel. If you feel accents or some other form of non-standard English are essential to your manuscript, fine. But make sure your dialogue is comprehensible to the everyday reader and your usage is there to further the story, not for unnecessary decoration or to make a linguistic point that few, if any, will grasp.

CREATING A WORLD

I talked about the synchronicity that hits when you start writing books. People with the same name, doing the same job sometimes. Real-world events that parallel fictional ones. Here's a true story from the publication of my second book, *Epiphany*. At the beginning there's a scene where a character is walking down University Avenue in Palo Alto, northern California, and notices the strong smell of cinnamon waving out from a bakery.

Not long after the book came out in the UK I got a letter from someone in San Francisco who'd bought it while in London and loved it.

'I particularly liked the scenes in Palo Alto,' he said. 'This is quite a coincidence but you know something? My grandfather owned and ran that bakery you wrote about there.'

I sent a polite and grateful reply and never told him the truth: I made it up. I never knew there was such a bakery, not consciously anyway. I knew

University Avenue vaguely. I knew what kind of area it was. It made sense to put the place there, with a couple of other stores that fitted the story.

Here's another anecdote about location that tells you something too. I was at a book signing in the mid-west of America once when a fan came up and said to me, 'I love your books. They make me feel as if I'm right there, in Rome, alongside the characters.'

'Do you visit Italy a lot?' I asked.

The lady shook her head and said, 'No. I've never set foot in Europe.'

When fictional locations work they spark something in the reader. There's a sense of recognition. An act of relocation. Point of view puts the audience inside your character's head. A successful location places them in their world too. If you can make your fictional place come alive, if your reader can't just see it but smell it and feel it too, then half your battle in this first act is done.

Places rise from the page in two different ways, through the connections readers feel for them, and the way they're painted.

CONNECTIONS

'I've never set foot in Europe,' said the woman from the mid-west. Yet the books made her feel she was in Rome. I'd like to think some of this was down to my own skill as a writer. But let's be honest. Rome has done quite a lot of the work for me already. It's a city everyone's heard of, a place we can all picture to some extent in our heads. Rome gave us much of the language we use, many of our concepts about law, justice, society, good and evil. Simply by setting my stories there I immediately forge a bond with the reader. It wouldn't be the same if they were located in Bologna, say. A beautiful city, full of history and interesting tales. Nothing there sparks that same frisson of familiarity. That doesn't stop anyone setting a story in Bologna, but it does mean your world doesn't come partly built before you've even written a word.

Fictional locations come in four basic flavours: big, well-known places; big, little-known ones; small, unknown ones; and worlds that are created out of nowhere, fictional to the last detail. All pose different challenges but in each case you face the same fundamental problem: how do you convince the reader to step into the page and believe in the world you've invented? How do you make them connect?

Big, well-known places, especially those in the English-speaking world – New York, London, LA, San Francisco – look easy. There's a reason why so many stories are set in familiar locations. They're cinema lots, with a familiar visual appearance, waiting to be populated by the writer's imagination. Their celebrity works against you too. Set your book in Oxford and people will soon be asking whether your version is as convincing as the one Colin Dexter created for Inspector Morse. Place a private detective in New York or LA and a whole host of established rivals will walk out of the shadows and ask, 'You looking at me?'

Going back in time can help. Imagine a detective story set in late Victorian London. Everyone will compare it with Conan Doyle's Sherlock Holmes but in a way that scarcely matters. Conan Doyle has long since departed to the writing room in the sky. Holmes is out of copyright and in the public domain. You could, if you wanted, have him walk in to your story and no one will sue (though you'd best do it well or the purists will reach for their daggers). The past is a foreign country, as L. P. Hartley wrote, familiar but also malleable.

Most stories are set in the present. Pick one of those familiar, well-trodden cities and you will have to work to make it yours. There are plenty of possibilities. Set your story in a little-known neighbourhood, for example. Look at the world from the perspective of a character type who isn't associated with the place. Invention and originality can get writers out of all manner of holes.

Big, little-known locations are problematic in a very different way. They may be provincial cities in the English-speaking world, Manchester, or Melbourne or Memphis. Or foreign places, Oslo, Beijing, Jeddah, Buenos Aires. We've all heard of them but, unless we have some direct experience or they're particularly famous, as is Rome, we've no idea what they're like. An author's personal connection with a place does not translate into a connection for the reader. In fact it can be decidedly dangerous to write about somewhere you know intimately. It's easy to take the location for granted and skip the details readers need to make it real. If you are going to set your story in a real-life place that is unfamiliar to most readers you will have to establish its look and feel and atmosphere thoroughly, and tell them why the tale is set there, not somewhere else.

Here's the good news, though. When obscure places work they can work wonderfully, in ways that set conventional book-world wisdom on its head. Fifteen years ago anyone predicting that the next hot location for crime and thriller stories was going to be Scandinavia would have been regarded as a lunatic. Today novels set in these cold, unfamiliar and – let's face it – unlikely climes fill the charts. There's always hope in this business, and sometimes it lurks in the last place you'd expect to find it.

Small, unknown locations and those that are invented entirely are, to the reader, very much the same thing. They've no idea where they are, no clue what they look like. There's a lot to be said for pitching your tale somewhere like this. You have free rein to do what you like without bumping up against the dead, cold hand of 'reality'. It's a lot easier to mess with the truth in Llandudno than in London – fewer people will know the original. Nor will there be such an expectation of 'accuracy', except for those who live in Llandudno, some of whom will doubtless point out the 'errors' in your portrayal.

There is a simple, instant answer to this kind of complaint, a whine authors get all the time. We write fiction. *It's not true.* Your Llandudno isn't their Llandudno. If that idea worries you, find a fictional name and simply think to yourself, 'This is Llandudno really.' While I wouldn't worry about getting the real place 'right' in terms of geographical detail, I would take some care to make sure the cultural feel remains true. There's no point in setting a story in north Wales if people speak and behave as if they're in south Wales. That is a different kind of inaccuracy, and one to be avoided. The connections you make to unknown places need to possess the same kind of conviction that comes for free with large, familiar international locations. You're not going to be tied by the geographical and cultural restrictions of the real world. You are going to have to work to make this invented one three-dimensional, sufficiently alive to fill the reader's head with images of what it's like.

The invented seaside town where Charlie Harrison has met a strange girl standing in the water beneath a wrecked pier fits into this last category. It's been a while now since I first wrote down that story 'seed' and began exploring the possibilities of where it might lead. I've recalled the seaside town where I grew up myself. I've looked at photographs of a few shabby resorts. The more I mull this over, the more I think it could be a great location for the book.

It's an old cliché in this business that locations are characters too. A true cliché for once. If you're inventing a place it's no bad idea to give it a quick profile just as you would for one of the players in your story. Let me do that now.

Charlie's town (which has yet to acquire a name and may not need one) is a small, rundown seaside resort in England. It was once genteel, but the economy has been devastated as holidaymakers have moved to foreign parts. There's little employment beyond a depleted fishing fleet working from the harbour. The pier was burned down years ago and the seafront, once a bustling tourist destination, has been reduced to a couple of squalid arcades and a few fairground rides.

In summer there are a few sad donkeys on the beach and a steady stream of impoverished visitors who turn up and don't spend much. The grand Edwardian houses on the promenade which were once hotels and posh residences are now flats for people living on benefits, many of them asylum seekers who form a separate, mistrusted sub-group. There's a park that's got a dodgy reputation for drug dealing and prostitution. But when the sun shines and the sea's fresh Charlie's happy enough there, and loves swimming in the freezing grey sea.

Most English readers will have some experience of a place like that. So will many in other countries too. Seaside towns everywhere have a curious, seasonal character, and often slip from wealth to economic decline with a sudden, shocking ease. There's a connection, and one is all I need.

DESCRIPTIONS

Books are made from words. Those twenty-six letters of the alphabet and a few punctuation marks are all we have. That's one reason we have to learn to milk them for all they're worth. If there's one abiding mistake that novice writers make about location it's in the way they create that essential canvas, the living background against which their story will take place. All too often it's approached in a very one-dimensional way, through nothing more than visual description. What the place looks like, precious little more.

There's plenty of opportunity in the case of Charlie's town: the beach, the colour of the sea and sky, the lines of dilapidated buildings, the closed, boarded-up pier and those blackened stanchions, like petrified crane's legs, sticking into the water. All this will be needed but it's only one part of a larger whole. Human beings don't come to know their environment through their eyes alone. We use all our senses: smell and hearing and touch. Fictional worlds need to be a rich brew of sights, sounds, aromas and physical sensations, just like the environment that surrounds us in life. Description, however beautifully executed, is rarely sufficient on its own.

A seaside town offers so much when you move beyond the visual. The salt smell of the sea, the rank stink of seaweed at the foot of the pier legs. Candy floss and hot dogs, bad drains and fetid rubbish waiting to be collected. I want to hear the sound of the waves on the shingle, and I know it will be different depending on whether the tide is coming in or going out. There'll be the jingle of the fruit machines and tinny music from the last working arcade on the promenade, the cries of the seagulls, the shouts of the bingo-callers, the drone of the engines from the fishing boats pulling out of the harbour day and night.

Seasons matter. When I set a story in Rome the time of year is one of the first things I think about. In summer the city is desperately hot and languid, in winter freezing cold and inward-looking. Romans respond to those changes in their moods, the way they live, the clothes they wear.

In Charlie's town it's summer and at times baking hot, the way seaside resorts can be. But I get the impression this town is on the east coast somewhere, perhaps Lincolnshire or Yorkshire. That cruel North Sea wind is going to blow at times and that will leave you shivering if you're wearing too little. There could be morning sea mists, 'frets' we used to call them, which make a hot day gloomy and bone-chilling. Charlie likes to swim. He doesn't mind the cold or the goosebumps on his flesh from time to time. The town is a part of him, and vice versa. Its icy, bleak character infects his. You could state that plainly, and perhaps will.

> Charlie liked this town, admired the way the buildings on the promenade seemed to lean into the blustery wind off the sea as if to say, 'Not with me you won't. I don't bend.' All the other kids couldn't wait to flee, to go to the big cities, to Leeds or Manchester or even London. Not him.

Even better, we can also allow his relationship to the place to be revealed through his own, private experiences.

> The bitter sea fret came out of nowhere. It was as if the waves had somehow risen up and taken physical form, choking the promenade and the streets behind, casting a shroud over the long, wrecked form of the pier, enveloping its shattered frame completely. He was still in his T-shirt and shorts, shivering wildly, teeth chattering, head hurting from the numbing cold. The salty fog entered him, slid through his nostrils, his mouth, wound into his lungs, made him cough and gasp and gag the way he did when he was swimming and something went wrong, a simple mistake, sent him slipping beneath the surface, briefly out of control. This freezing fever racking his body was like drowning on dry land, trapped inside the opaque fog of the sea as it trespassed briefly, hunting for any victim it could find with its cold, damp breath.

This is where those photographs you're collecting in the book journal start to earn their pay. I snap everything when I'm dreaming of locations: street scenes, signs, advertisement hoardings, markets, menus, people going about their lives. I go into cemeteries and photograph headstones. They're always wonderful inspiration for character names. In small communities you can see the different tribes too, surnames that often span centuries. Looking very closely at your preferred location – in real life or through your imagination – helps seal it inside your head. You can refer back to this material later when you need it. After a while it should help make this place so three-dimensional in your own head that you can re-create it in an instant. If it's not alive to you, it never will be to the reader.

When you're writing a story set in a real city, one that is tightly integrated into its geography and buildings, as many of mine are, you will invariably find yourself consulting a map. Partly this is to be 'accurate', if you can use such a word about fiction. Maps help turn a flimsy notion into stone and bricks, streets and landscapes. If your location's imaginary, it will still possess some geographical structure, even if it's one that never progresses from the page.

Why not sketch out a map of it yourself so that you know which way's north, which south, the names of the main streets and topographical features, the look and feel of the place? Fantasy writers do this all the time, and their working map sometimes makes it into the final book. There's no reason why this useful trick can't be used by anyone who needs it. We're not talking publication quality – just a quick sketch like this, one you can add to and amend as the story develops:

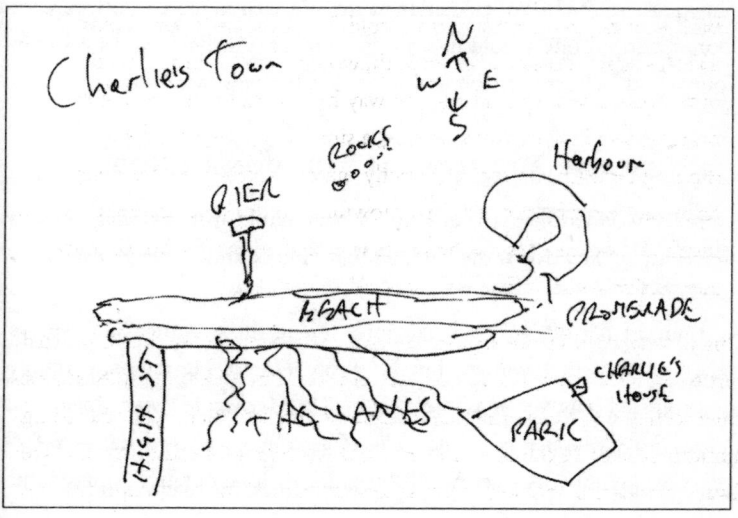

Committing ideas to paper gives you a reference point but, just as importantly, helps flesh out this world in your own imagination. The scribble above may seem meaningless but it's not to me. I've a mental idea of what the harbour looks like, and that tangle of narrow alleys called The Lanes. I can begin to see Charlie's modest terraced house overlooking a rundown park where dodgy drug dealers hang out looking for customers.

Does the town need a name? Not at this stage. If I needed one I'd look at some possibilities later, perhaps by playing with the names of real seaside towns in England. Yarborough or Scarness. It's not important right now. But I'd probably find names for some of those streets, and perhaps an area too. If characters speak confidently and knowledgeably about places – Charlie held out his hand and said, 'I'm going up to the chippie in Belltown. Want to come?' – you add more bricks and mortar to that flimsy invented cosmos in your head.

Whatever kind of location you choose for your story it needs to be an integral part of the book, tied directly to the story. Here we return to a variation of the test you need to use on your dialogue, applying it candidly to your work as it progresses.

Could this story be set somewhere else? Could I move it from, say, Singapore to New York, California to Massachusetts, or Yorkshire to Dorset, and no one would much notice or care? If the answer's yes then your world lacks conviction and substance. It needs more work.

WRITE ABOUT WHAT YOU DON'T KNOW

Here's a wonderful myth, one you'll hear retold from writing class to university up and down the land. It's that old chestnut ... *write about what you know.*

I almost fall off my chair laughing typing those words. Shakespeare never set foot in Denmark but he wrote *Hamlet*. He almost certainly never visited Italy, yet he wrote *Othello, The Merchant of Venice, Romeo and Juliet, Two Gentlemen of Verona, Julius Caesar* and scattered Italian references throughout his work. Was he crippled by his ignorance? You tell me.

Writing about what you know may work for some people. For lots it doesn't. A while back I was teaching at a writing school when someone showed me a wonderful opening she'd written for her book. It was atmospheric, beautifully phrased, had interesting characters and wound up with a dramatic and violent scene that ... died on the page. I couldn't quite believe this. Everything that went before worked fine. What should have been the denouement was written with all the verve of a business report.

I asked this budding author, 'What happened here?'

She looked at me and said, 'Oh, that part's real. I do that job. I see that happen a lot. That's how it is.'

Boring, in other words. To her anyway. Most of us take for granted what we know. We don't see the uniqueness in what lies around us all the time. If we try to turn that world into fiction we may drain it of colour and life because it's so familiar we scarcely notice those essential elements are there.

Except for one book, everything I've written has been set abroad, normally in the Mediterranean. There's a reason for this. The Mediterranean is foreign. To a child from colder climes like me it's exotic, interesting, cryptic, a world waiting to be explored. When I decided to write the Costa books I took the plunge and moved to Rome, enrolled at a language school to study Italian, trying to see the city through the eyes of a native. I was ignorant of the city beneath the surface. I wanted to look more deeply than was possible through some brief visit as a tourist. Most writers who use foreign locations view their stories through the eyes of a fellow countryman, an outsider. I didn't want to do that. I wanted my characters to be, as far as I could make them, Roman through and through.

To write these books I had to turn my ignorance into an interior form of fictional knowledge, building my own private Rome, stone by stone, street by street, vista by vista, so that I could then set it down on the page. I wouldn't have to do that if I located my book in London, a city I've known well for three decades. The foreignness of Rome and my ignorance of its true nature make the eventual story, I hope, more vivid and, yes, more 'real' than it could ever have been if I'd written about somewhere I knew intimately, somewhere I could summon up without a stroke of work.

The operative word there is 'work'. There are books that succeed on ingrained personal knowledge, some real-life situation turned into fiction. But for the most part novels are the product of a fertile and adventurous imagination. Setting your story somewhere new, somewhere different, somewhere you have to invent for yourself, tasks your resourcefulness with the creation of a world that will come to enthral and absorb the reader. I can't imagine doing that with the street round the corner or a place I've known for years.

Shakespeare wrote about what he knew in one respect: he knew people, their foibles, their strengths, their weaknesses and cruelty. That insight into the nature of humanity is irreplaceable, essential in anyone who wants to produce writing that strikes a chord with the reader. When it comes to location and plain fact then familiarity all too easily breeds contempt. Sometimes the best stories are not found at home. You have to go out and hunt them.

Just not too much.

GETTING TOO CLOSE TO YOUR SUBJECT

Yes, I have cop friends. Yes, I will spend some time researching police procedure, usually in Italy. And yes, I have ways of finding out how cops would respond to a situation in real life. But I don't hang around cops seeking inspiration or some mythical kind of accuracy for my books. I don't feel I need to. I don't think it would make them any better. It doubtless works for some people, but for me hanging round cops could prove to be very bad news indeed. Here are some of the reasons why.

You start to like them. A writer I know once spent six months shadowing a real police force and then wrote a book in which every cop character was so nice the editor threw it out of the window. Writers should not become overly fond of their subjects. That affection can warp your perspective. It stops you doing nasty things to them and them doing nasty things to other people. Fiction, of all kinds, is often about cruelty, our bafflement at why it happens, our struggle to stop it, our tendency to reach for the cruel button ourselves when things go wrong. Take a look at children's literature and see how much nastiness is there.

Anything that is an obstacle to your portrayal of one human being's wickedness to another, a portrayal which must be accomplished with the distant, aloof nonchalance of the little deity you are when writing, has to be avoided. Readers need to feel sympathy for your characters. An author requires sufficient detachment to be beastly to them, without the slightest pang of regret, should the occasion demand.

No one really cares how law enforcement agencies work, or wishes to. My stories are usually set in Italy. The law enforcement system there is so complicated that the average Italian has no idea how it functions. Two national police forces, one civilian, one military, local forces, specialist forces, an anti-mafia unit that's not quite police depending on which way you look at it . . . Italy seems to invent a new law enforcement agency every year.

If I reflected 'how things really are' a third of the book would be spent explaining the structure of the Italian policing system. Who wants to read that? Would it make the books any better if Costa's arrest procedures mirrored the official state police rulebook down to the last letter? Would anyone really notice? No.

Real policing happens at a snail's pace, and that sluggishness seems to be getting slower all the time. In the UK some DNA samples can take weeks or months to come back from the lab. Statements have to go through a variety of internal procedures then are placed in front of Crown Prosecution lawyers. In fiction we tend to be obsessed with justice, nailing the culprit, finding some resolution to a tear in the fabric of society. You'd be naive if you thought that's what police officers do every day. If in doubt, find a few and ask. The guilty regularly walk free for a variety of reasons, from insufficient evidence and an unwillingness on the part of prosecutors to bring the case to court to a procedural error or some local political difficulty.

It's possible to write fictional stories that take these factors into account, but if you do they have to become at least part of the story. This is what I attempt in *The Garden of Evil*. We know very early on who the bad guy is. The book is about both the battle to bring him to justice and a broader, hazier struggle to define what, in these circumstances, justice actually is. And I tell some big lies about the speed with which forensic science can take place in that story by the way, alongside some real and accurate chunks of science too.

You can't have the average mystery, crime novel or thriller enter the confusing, jargon-ridden and highly frustrating arena of the real-life justice system as a matter of course, running alongside the rest of the story on equal terms. If you do, the time frame of your narrative is likely to become unsupportable as your characters sit around twiddling their thumbs, waiting for the reports to come in – as real-life cops do all the time.

You're in grave danger of forgetting what this whole business is really about. Remember what the word 'fiction' means? We make it up. It's a fable, a damned lie, a warped mirror held up to the real world in order to make it appear more interesting. Readers understand this implicitly (though you'll always get a few pedants pointing out so-called 'inaccuracies' – that goes with the job). It's a writer's imagination that makes a novel work, not his or her strict adherence to that dull old thing called reality.

There's a wonderful saying in Italian: *meglio una bella bugia che una brutta verità*. Better a beautiful lie than an ugly truth. Storytellers are in the business of beautiful lies. If you want the ugly truth go and buy a newspaper. Speaking of which . . .

NO NEWS IS GOOD NEWS

There's a common line you see in thriller reviews sometimes: 'Straight out of tomorrow's headlines.'

I always wonder when I see that: does it really sell the book?

Fiction and real-world current affairs make awkward bedfellows. I had a really bright idea for my third novel, *Solstice*. I started writing it in 1996.

That meant it was probably going to come out in early 1999. By that time millennial fever was going to be gripping the world, wasn't it? So why not write a story about the end of the world? How cool would that be? Good timing or what?

Well, *Solstice* is certainly an end-of-the-world tale, but it's not tied to any date or event in history. Just as well really. Because being topical in a book is about as dumb as you can get, as an editor cheerfully pointed out to me when I raised this possibility. Time and time again would-be writers make the mistake of thinking real-world news can generate unreal-world fiction. Mostly it can't.

One practical problem has to do with the calendar. That thing moves on. Your book won't. Example: the global economic crash of 2008. I'll bet agents and publishers got a flurry of submissions in the middle of that for popular fiction set directly inside the curiously uncertain world we suddenly found ourselves in. On the surface the idea of a story from that time looks attractive. It's everywhere: in the papers, on the TV, in people's heads. When you start writing nothing may make less sense.

Nine months later you finish it. The crisis is still going on. People are thinking, yawn . . . Even worse, if a publisher accepted your book it would take perhaps twelve to twenty-four months to bring it to the public. The odds are that by then no one in the world will want to read yesterday's news. Something else real will probably have happened that may have drastically changed the premise of your story. What publisher wants to take that risk?

Here's a related truth too: people usually read fiction for the internal veracity of a book, not its relation to the real world. When London suffered that ghastly terrorist attack in 2005 some unfortunate soul had a book out just a week or two before, a thriller that depicted a very similar event, bombs and all. I remember someone at a book festival saying to me at the time, 'What timing – that will sell loads.' No it won't, I thought. And it didn't.

There are some recent events that are just too close for comfort. Writing about terrorism in general is one thing. Imaginary terrorist attacks are fair game too – I use one in *The Blue Demon*. But the real world is different. No one wants to read much about London getting bombed, about 9/11, Afghanistan (directly anyway) or swine flu. Escapism is a strong motive for picking up a book. Yes, miserable books do sell. But normally they're miserable in themselves, not miserable about external matters we're all miserable about already.

It's certainly possible to set fiction around real-world events. But far better to make them something historic – the collapse of the Berlin Wall, the Bay of Pigs crisis, even the first Iraq war – than something that's happening right now. And do remember that, if you're lucky, that book will have a long life. You may only be able to see them a year or two out. If they work they will be around for a lot longer and may get a second wind when they're republished a decade or so later. Tying them to some specific topical thread or event in the news is like dressing them in today's fashions. You guarantee that very soon they'll look jaded and out of date, of interest primarily as a curiosity.

Books exist in a space all of their own. Best to leave them there, not try to drag them kicking and screaming into ours.

VOICE AND STYLE

Whilst one might argue that a dynamic and developing sense of event-led drama forms the central core of the literary narrative, it behoves the embryonic novelist to be cognisant of other, more ephemeral concepts that serve both to create and nurture the fictive bole that must lie at the heart of any convincing narrative exposition. If one accepts that all literature is, in essence, eschatological – that is, concerned with the ultimate end of things, with death and destruction, finality and . . .

Whoa, whoa, whoa. Who grabbed the keyboard there and how many dictionaries has he swallowed? Did you notice? Something changed. This is a non-fiction book. Dictates about point of view don't really count here. You could regard this as a first-person narrative throughout. But it still has something it shares with fiction: a voice. I just altered that voice. A lot. It briefly belonged to someone else, someone who uses words I'd never write without a very good reason: 'whilst' and 'cognisant', 'bole' and 'eschatological'. I sound like some pompous retired lecturer trying to show off his vocabulary, not 'me' at all.

Except that the 'me' you have here isn't 'me' either. From the outset I decided to adopt a particular voice for this book in an attempt to give it some character and establish a relationship with you, the reader. Your novel will attempt the same. This is the voice of the book, not a character, though that comes into play. An overall tone, a feel, a sense of style.

For my chosen voice here I decided to present myself as a frank, argumentative, occasionally tetchy writer of popular fiction, one trying to make practical points in plain language in a classroom full of interested but slightly baffled beginners.

Practicality apart – it should make the book more readable – I did this for two reasons. I want you to understand that writing is a personal matter, and enormous fun once you let your own identity meld with that fictive – whoops, there he goes again – *fictional* voice on the page. I also need you to understand that everything you read here is opinionated and designed to be challenged. This isn't one of those 'The Top Ten Secrets of Writing a Bestseller' tomes that attempts to construct a formula to take you from obscurity to the top of the charts in a flash. As you should know by now, I don't believe in rules and formulae, and neither should you.

I'd also have to wonder why someone who knows the secrets of writing a bestseller isn't writing one of them instead of a non-fiction work that will clearly shift considerably fewer copies.

More than anything though I need you to question everything you read here and ask yourself, 'Is the old curmudgeon right?' To prompt you to do that I try to take on the tone of one of those interesting but eccentric teachers you used to get at school, the sort who'd come up with insights but happily lob chalk at anyone who wasn't paying attention. And usually miss.

Narrative voice shapes the reader's response to a work. If it's pompous, long-winded and overburdened with archaic and obscure words, most will tend to shy away, particularly when it comes to fiction. If there's an aspect that interests them, something they can warm to or even a facet of the book's tone they find horrifying in a fascinating way, they will be more inclined to extend sufficient patience to allow you to reel them in with your story.

The tone of the overall book needs to be fixed as much as possible from the very beginning. Those first few pages will tell the reader what to expect from your tale. You should have a firm grasp of the tenor and style of your narration from your opening paragraph, and of the different approaches that signpost how the audience will react to your story.

WORD CHOICE

Here are the opening two paragraphs of Thomas Hardy's gorgeously melancholic tale, *Far from the Madding Crowd*, first published in 1874:

> When Farmer Oak smiled, the corners of his mouth spread till they were within an unimportant distance of his ears, his eyes were reduced to chinks, and diverging wrinkles appeared round them, extending upon his countenance like the rays in a rudimentary sketch of the rising sun.
>
> His Christian name was Gabriel, and on working days he was a young man of sound judgment, easy motions, proper dress, and general good character. On Sundays he was a man of misty views, rather given to postponing, and hampered by his best clothes and umbrella: upon the whole, one who felt himself to occupy morally that vast middle space of Laodicean neutrality which lay between the Communion people of the parish and the drunken section, – that is, he went to church, but yawned privately by the time the congregation reached the Nicene creed, and thought of what there would be for dinner when he meant to be listening to the sermon. Or, to state his character as it stood in the scale of public opinion, when his friends and critics were in tantrums, he was considered rather a bad man; when they were pleased, he was rather a good man; when they were neither, he was a man whose moral colour was a kind of pepper-and-salt mixture.

There's a wonderful authorial voice at work here, confident, informed, absolutely in touch with what he's trying to do: begin the work through a portrayal of a character who will be central to the whole narrative.

There's a 'but' coming. You can hear it. You know what it is too.

What does 'Laodicean' mean? And the 'Nicene creed'?

Hardy was a good Victorian, one who grew up with the Bible, went to church regularly and, as a young man, wrote a sermon. In Revelation 3:14–16 Laodicea is revealed as a town with a lukewarm attitude to religion, and gets a suitable Old Testament comeuppance for yawning when God is looking.

> I know your deeds, that you are neither cold nor hot. I wish you
> were either one or the other! So, because you are lukewarm –
> neither hot nor cold – I am about to spit you out of my mouth.

From that short entry we have acquired the knowledge that 'Laodicean' is a very obscure adjective meaning 'half-hearted towards religion'.

The Nicene creed is simply the creed of the Anglican church, the declaration of belief that runs something like this, depending on the version: 'We believe in one God, the Father, the Almighty, maker of heaven and earth, of all that is, seen and unseen . . . '

Simple question. If you were writing this scene today would you use those same words? My guess is not – unless you were deliberately creating a literary work replicating the literary style of late nineteenth-century England.

There's nothing social or judgemental in avoiding Hardy's language. Those terms simply lack the ability to communicate they once had. Victorians who read novels were middle to upper class and educated. School education was not made compulsory in England until 1880, and public libraries were confined to urban areas. Even if the rural poor who featured in Hardy's work could read, they would find it difficult to be able to borrow or buy a contemporary novel. The privileged minority who spent the evening with a book in front of them had much the same cultural background as the authors they read. Many doubtless understood what Hardy was talking about without a second thought.

Publishing is quite different in the twenty-first century. Books sell to a mass market around the world. They're a form of entertainment as much as a cultural art form – one more branch of that amorphous beast we know as 'the media'. Consumers are besieged with information and possibilities from all directions. They're perpetually short of time so many never pick up a book at all.

Hardy's readers sat down by candlelight for a long evening with a weighty novel, trapped by their social circumstances, with no easy or quick method of escape. Today's authors must battle with TV, the internet, a busy social life, and the car in the drive for people's attention.

If you want to write a literary novel pitched at a literary audience, one that will understand biblical and arcane references without a second thought, that's fine. But be aware of the course you're taking. Popular fiction is designed to appeal to a general audience. The books that become huge blockbuster sellers only reach that status because they're bought by people who don't usually purchase books at all. The words and the style you use act as the gatekeepers for your story. Popular fiction demands a voice that welcomes all-comers. An archaic, 'literary' approach will limit your appeal, to publishers and readers alike.

Hardy could write as he wanted and be confident that most of the audience would be sufficiently well read to understand his allusions. Modern authors cannot make that assumption. You can look on that with regret or see it as an interesting challenge: how do you create a rich and textured fictional world populated by believable characters using a vocabulary that is, next to Hardy's, necessarily somewhat restricted?

There's more than a touch of snobbery in this area. 'Literary' fiction will on occasion look down on the 'popular' simply because it sells a lot better. I'd just ask a simple question. Imagine you want to write a story that has the depth, texture and resonance of a piece of good classic storytelling. Which do you think is easier? Managing that with a restricted vocabulary and a stylistic approach that is understandable and liked by a mass audience, some of whom rarely read books? Or producing a 'literary' novel for a small, intellectual readership, many of whom will know its arcane language and context already?

It's tougher to be great in five hundred words than a thousand any day, and that is the test facing the popular novelist.

Choose your language carefully. If you want to reach a general audience use words that are commonly understood over obscure, archaic or – let's admit it – flashy ones. Few people will be impressed by an author hell-bent on demonstrating his mastery of an arcane vocabulary. The line between being clever and coming across as a smartass is decidedly slender at times and easily crossed. That doesn't mean you can't challenge your readers from time to time or spark an idea that might set them off looking up something you've introduced into your narrative. But don't push your luck. Their patience isn't what it was.

The best modern writing is invisible. We barely notice the skill and structure behind it, preferring instead to enjoy the story building inside our heads. Unknown words and awkward phrases are narrative speed bumps, needless hiatuses that can, if they begin to happen too often, jolt the reader out of the work altogether.

Try to write good, clear English. Avoid linguistic howlers such as split infinitives – 'to boldly go . . . ' Inverted, prolix sentence structures aren't fashionable any more, or long paragraphs divided by colons and semi-colons, a practice common in Hardy's day. Modern English is less ornate and complex than the language used in the classics of a century or more ago.

I wouldn't get hung up about grammar. So yes, you can start sentences with the word 'and'. And your characters, in dialogue, are free to mangle language as much as is necessary in order to reveal their character because grammar and speech do not necessarily mix. Writing is about communication, and in general fiction it's the story that matters. You don't need an academic tome on syntax by your side in order to write a popular novel, though it's worth remembering that ugly prose is ugly prose in any context (not that clumsy writing has ever stopped a few people entering the bestseller charts).

Hardy's style would need a little tweaking to join them now. If those opening paragraphs were submitted as general fiction today any decent editor would surely get back to him with two simple suggestions: change

'Laodicean' to something along the lines of 'lukewarm and sceptical' and ditch that word 'Nicene' altogether.

Would anything be lost? Let's be honest. No. The change would actually make those two opening paragraphs better from the point of view of the average twenty-first-century reader. It would stop you scratching your head over a couple of obscure words that get in the way of focusing on the important matter: the character of Gabriel Oak, which is surely going to be central to the coming story. And you wouldn't be thinking to yourself, 'You know if this chap's going to use words I'm not sure I can pronounce let alone understand perhaps I'm too stupid for this book and should be reading something else.'

PACE

Few writers have never heard the complaint, 'I'm worried about the pace here.' Yet pinning down what exactly a 'lack of pace' means can be very difficult beyond the obvious: 'I'm in danger of getting bored.'

I doubt anyone nagged Victorian writers much on this subject. The classics of the nineteenth and early twentieth centuries are full of linguistic habits that will generally be frowned upon today. The use of extended and complex sentences, for example, is not a habit that will endear many writers to editors or readers. Take this very long sentence of Thomas Hardy's from the extract we've looked at already:

> On Sundays he was a man of misty views, rather given to post-poning, and hampered by his best clothes and umbrella: upon the whole, one who felt himself to occupy morally that vast middle space of Laodicean neutrality which lay between the Communion people of the parish and the drunken section, – that is, he went to church, but yawned privately by the time the congregation reached the Nicene creed, and thought of what there would be for dinner when he meant to be listening to the sermon.

Perfect and elegant Victorian English. Hardy's use of the colon is absolutely correct if a touch archaic. The punctuation of a comma followed by a dash looks more than a little odd to modern eyes. More than anything, though, it's the prolix construction that gives away the age and the conspicuous artistry of the writer.

Far from the Madding Crowd was Hardy's fourth book. It was first serialised in the popular *Cornhill* magazine and proved to be such a massive success that he was able to give up his job as an architect and begin to write full time. To readers of the day he was a successful and much-respected mass market novelist. Today he's deservedly revered as one of England's great Victorian writers. But emulate his style and you will be marked out as an oddity, beyond the mainstream of fiction. We don't write that way any more.

What's changed?

Modern writing tends to be much closer to spoken English. When we talk we do not speak in long, complex sentences. We construct ones that are short, pithy and much more direct than the flowery and intricate language that was once the *lingua franca* of fiction. We do this for a simple reason: people are much more likely to understand us this way.

A sentence like this – 'Having wheeled his pushbike down to the seafront, Charlie looked around for Sally; nowhere was she to be seen' sounds arch, unnecessary and jarring. Instead, a modern reader would prefer: 'Charlie wheeled his pushbike down to the seafront then looked for Sally. She wasn't there.'

Remember: fiction is now very popular in audio. Most commercial novels will end up being read by professional actors for the growing download business. Storytelling has, to some extent, rediscovered its roots in oral poets like Homer. It's worth bearing that in mind and listening to your words as they appear. Hear them in your own head as you type. Even read them out loud before a final edit. It's another way of experiencing the text. That word 'perspective' again.

The right words and some straightforward sentence construction will help your narrative flow. The precise style will have to be tailored to the nature of your story.

Back to Charlie and his town:

Inkerman Street was deserted as the boy wheeled his pushbike down towards the sea. The flat tyre was a problem he could deal with later. It was a heavy Thursday afternoon in August. The sky was heavy and unsettled. In the south a line of black, angry thunder clouds hung over the ragged green ridge of the Littledown hills. He thought he heard a distant rumble coming from beyond the Dunstaff spur. Then, as he wheeled the bike out into the open space of the Beggars' Arms car park, he saw, a couple of miles out over the rolling, purple sea, a jagged spike of fork lightning arcing down to the angry waves.

Alternatively: 'The bike had a flat tyre so Charlie wheeled it down to the promenade. The weather was turning. It looked as if a storm was on the way.'

Two takes on the same scene. Which is better?

Once again it's an unanswerable question. That depends entirely on the kind of book you're trying to write.

The first approach might suit a work that's going to be full of atmosphere and foreboding, one that hopes to build a highly detailed world, perhaps with a series in mind. If the novel's to be a fast, linear story the second would be better: straight short sentences, little in the way of atmosphere and description, lots of movement.

BOOK DIVISION

Another factor that determines the tone of a book is the structural device you use in order to divide it into different sections. Take a look at the novels on your own shelves and you will see that novels are broken down in different ways depending on their nature.

Stories are made up of component parts. Splitting them into logical and manageable chunks makes the reader's job a lot easier. They can think, 'I'll read one more chapter before I go to bed.' Another reason for logical divisions is pace. Linear, direct thrillers may have a simple, dynamic structure, with something like a cliff-hanger ending marking the close of each section. More complex stories will tend to be rhythmic in nature, moving from fast to slow, teasing the reader a little from time to time. If your work fits the latter category, marking its natural pauses will allow people to break in the right places. They can stop on a reflective moment, and think about what they've read. Or they can halt on a fast action scene and look forward to unravelling what's happened later.

Think of your own reading habits. How often do you flick ahead to see where the next pause is, then aim for that before putting the book to one side? Divisions help the reader enjoy your story. It's a good idea to give your audience a hand whenever you can.

There are three standard building bricks for a story: scenes, chapters and parts.

Scenes

The fundamental element of any story mosaic is the scene: a singular continuous piece of action or description seen from the same point of view. The end of the scene is marked by a change of point of view to a different character or a shift in location or tone. For example: 'Charlie goes to the pier. Afterwards he rides off to see Sally's grandfather and talks to him.' These are two separate scenes. Because the point of view remains the same they could be run together in the book.

Or you could divide them: 'Charlie goes to the pier. Afterwards Sally goes to talk to her grandfather.' These are two separate scenes with two different points of view. They would not normally be run together. Some kind of divider is generally essential.

Chapters

Chapters are collections of scenes tied together by some aspect of the story, such as a plot element, a time frame or a location. They can include scenes with different points of view and different locations.

Parts

These are collections of chapters gathered together to form longer divisions within the book. Parts will normally have some overall thematic connection which links the chapters it contains. You could label the first structural act of a story 'Part One', for example. Or if you were writing a historical novel you could set a specific time period in a part: 'Part Three – Prelude to War (1817–1821)'. Or simply, 'Day One'.

Every book has scenes. Many will have chapters. Parts were once very common but nowadays tend to be restricted to more complex stories.

Let's imagine you're writing a fast-moving linear thriller, one that takes place over a short period of time, perhaps in the first person. The format: scenes and scenes alone.

➢ Scene: Charlie goes to the pier, sees promenade, gives us some background on himself and town. Then sees girl in water.

➢ Scene: Talks to girl in water, persuades her to come out.

➢ Scene: Bad guys come along in black car and make girl get in car.

➢ Scene: Charlie sets off after them.

For something a little more complex we might stick with chapters and scenes alone. In this instance we could enclose all the above scenes in one chapter, perhaps with a label 'Chapter One – Charlie Goes to the Pier'.

If this were a bigger, more prolix project we could adopt the parts methodology.

➢ Part One: A Mermaid in Distress.

➢ Chapter One: Charlie Goes to the Pier.

➢ Scene ...

Do we need titles such as, 'Charlie Goes to the Pier'? That's entirely up to you. Depending on the writing software you're using it may be necessary to label an outline heading for your own convenience when navigating the book. This will be required in Word since you will need those labels for your navigation bar. You can easily remove them later for submission. The same goes for chapters and parts. If you feel the titles add something, use them. If you think you're putting them in just because you're 'supposed to', you're mistaken. Should an editor feel they're needed, it's easy enough to ask for them (I suspect you never will be, by the way).

How about numbers? Do you need them as well? Not always. If I were writing a breakneck thriller designed to be read in one go I'd skip them and offer the reader nothing but short scenes. No one will complain. Dividing scenes without numbers is very simple. If you're delivering a manuscript to an agent or publisher you just type a hash mark # in the text. This is a sign for a scene break. In the finished book – or your own formatted ebook if you're self-publishing – they will be replaced with a line break. Then, in print and sometimes in ebooks, the first line of the opening paragraph of the next scene will be set full out, without an indent (like paragraphs following section breaks in this book).

You should have that separator whether your book is composed of nothing but unnumbered scenes or scenes within chapters. You could if you like set up your word processor to have an opening paragraph style. That would have no first-line indent and an extra line space above it to set it from the final paragraph of the preceding scene. But that's not necessary. That hash mark will be recognised as having the same function.

One slight oddity should be mentioned. There are two conventions for numbering chapters within parts. One is to run the numbering on across the book.

Part One

 Chapter 1

 Chapter 2

Part Two

 Chapter 3

 Chapter 4

Or you can restart with each part (which is what I do because I always find it odd to read something like 'Part Three, Chapter Forty-Four').

Part One

 Chapter 1

 Chapter 2

Part Two

 Chapter 1

 Chapter 2

The division format you use is a personal choice. Just make sure it's consistent and, in the case of most popular fiction, breaks up the book into manageable chunks. Which brings us to ...

SCENE LENGTH

Whatever division method you use it's a good idea to stick to some rough benchmarks for length. In my own work scenes tend to run between fifteen hundred and three thousand words, though occasionally they will be short snatches of seven or eight hundred, usually in action sections. There are no fixed rules about length for scenes, chapters or parts. Let common sense guide you. A fast-moving story will demand short, punchy scenes. A reflective and complex one can be more relaxed.

But be consistent. Readers will be confused if one scene is nine hundred words and the next five thousand. The same goes for chapters and, in some cases, parts. It's usually best to try to aim for some rough conformity over length. You want your reader to break off from the book at a point which leaves them wanting more. Making it easy for them to judge when a moment for pause is about to emerge will help keep them engaged in the story.

SEX, VIOLENCE AND SWEARING

The subject of fiction is life, and life at times is pretty grim and nasty. How you deal with that nastiness in your story will have a strong influence on the voice of your book, and may limit or increase its appeal. 'Dealing with adult situations' – as if these issues only rear their heads when everyone under the age of eighteen has left the room – is something most writers will have to confront at some stage. Do you take the graphic route reluctantly? Do you dive in and wallow joyously in acts that, in real life, would have the police knocking on your door?

I can't tell you. That's an author's individual decision. All I can do is tell you how I approach this subject – and try to knock down a few of the 'adult situation' myths out there.

★★★★ ME! WHAT'S THE DEAL WITH SWEARING?

From time to time I get an email from a reader saying something like, 'I do so admire authors who can write a great thriller without cussing and swearing in it.'

Ah yes, foul language. You hear it everywhere these days, and read it too. Most newspapers still blank out common swearwords. Follow some of their columnists on Twitter and you'll find a good few there who curse like navvies in ways they'd never be allowed in print. Authors have been known to swear too, honestly. Should books exercise self-censorship? Do we really need 'bad language' in fiction?

In my earlier work, and the first three Costa books, you'll find swearing, the f-word usually, not used over-liberally but present, spoken easily by the characters concerned. After that it's pretty much disappeared.

Swearing is very like sex and violence, something writers use because they feel it's expected of them. I also included bad language in the early Costa books for what I felt were linguistic reasons. I moved to Rome for a while to study Italian because I wanted to write books that reflected a little of the modern city. And contemporary spoken Italian is full of slang and profanities.

Anyone wanting to understand the filthy nature of the modern colloquial tongue should track down a copy of Daniela Gobetti's hilarious and compendious *Dictionary of Italian Slang and Colloquial Expressions*. I can guarantee it will open your eyes about the *bella lingua* and how it's used in real life. In truth Italian has always been like this – there are endless smutty sonnets from Caravaggio's time.

I loved this book but it was impossible to translate any of its real-life colloquialisms into something an English reader would understand. One example: any idea what *dare acqua alle fave* (to water the fava beans) actually means? To kill someone. 'He's gone to water Giovanni's beans' is slang for 'The poor guy's going to get murdered.' Take my point?

There was swearing in the early books because they made a conscious attempt to mirror the slangy, colloquial, occasionally foul-mouthed nature of working-class Roman speech. When it came to book four, though, I'd changed my position on this subject. I felt I was straining to make a point most people never noticed. Also Italian slang is bafflingly varied and regional. What works in Rome is incomprehensible in Naples. Why bother with this minefield? So I elected to write speech that simply sounded natural, like ordinary unaccented English. And I thought . . . what if I drop the swearing altogether?

As always with writing, the best way to test an idea is to back up your original and leap in with the scalpel. I cut out the profanities. It didn't make a blind bit of difference to the text. Even when I needed people to swear I could get them to do it without uttering a single word that might offend someone. They simply curse under their breath or mutter some quiet imprecation. For my books that's enough. You get to know they're cross or under stress, which is why I had used swearing in any case. The constant use of the f-word in particular never really suited my style.

That's not to say it's wrong. If you watch the Coen Brothers' movie *Burn After Reading* (which I liked, though many didn't) you'll find an opening in which John Malkovich's Osborne Cox loses it spectacularly when he discovers, in a formal interview, that his employer, the CIA, is about to demote him because of his drinking problem. Malkovich gives a wonderful performance of a man breaking up in the stiffest and most unexpected of circumstances, and swears with great gusto. No problem with that at all. And once it's over it's over.

What grates with me is the constant use of swearing, so much that it becomes repetitive and meaningless. I never did it to that extent, even when I felt swearing was part of being a modern popular writer. The f-word does reappear once in book nine, *The Fallen Angel*, uttered by a character you'd least expect, in pivotal circumstances where I think its revelatory value is essential. Note that word: revelatory. I didn't say 'shock'. Bad language has absolutely no shock value these days. If anything it may have the opposite effect, generating a yawn, not a frisson.

You will occasionally hear the argument, 'But they need to swear because people do in real life.'

So what? As I hope we've now established, fiction and real life are different. The argument 'because that's how things are' is a cop-out.

Fiction is invented. The only reality that matters is the one an author builds in the reader's head.

My advice to would-be writers about swearing is simple. Don't feel it has to be in or that using it will make you look cool and clever. Do try taking it out to see if its removal makes a difference. If the cursing really has to be there, use it. If not, hit the delete key.

VIOLENCE

A note to photographers everywhere: I don't pose with guns. Ever. Not even silly toy plastic ones of the kind some snapper brought along to a photo-shoot in Singapore once, hoping to spice up the usual boring author picture with something a little 'exciting'.

There's a reason for this. Yes, I depict violence in my work, graphic violence at times. But I do it to shock, not titillate. I hate violence, and I hate guns in particular, as do my protagonists. As one of them puts it in one book, they may have to use force but when it results in someone getting hurt or killed they feel a sense of failure. They were supposed to do the job differently, to get a result without people getting injured.

Not every author feels this way. In some books violence itself is meant to be thrilling. When the hero beats up the bad guy the reader becomes that hero, exacting justice on behalf of a bloodied innocent world. Order is restored. Good defeats evil till the next bout. That kind of reader-as-hero model has worked well for centuries, and will continue to do so for many to come.

Then there's the Quentin Tarantino theory of violence, which is that it's all a big and wonderful buzz, the reason some people go to the movies in the first place. Well I don't go to the movies for that. Nor is extreme brutality something I want to be central to my own writing. My attitude to violence is simple: it's reprehensible, usually avoidable, an extension of the dark side of human nature that we would all, in ideal circumstances, like to suppress.

Critics sometimes moan about the amount of violence in modern fiction and film, arguing that it provokes similar acts in real life. I've never been much impressed by that argument, though there are certainly movies and books out there that turn me off through excessive brutality. Art reflects society. It doesn't do much to shape it. The idea that 'the pen is mightier than the sword' is pretty ridiculous. I don't think Hitler spent many sleepless nights fretting about writers.

The fictional bloodshed that worries me most is the old-fashioned kind – bloodless deaths, gentle poisonings among the aspidistras in the hothouse, Hopalong Cassidy shooting some bad guy who doesn't even bleed, just clutches his shirt and says, 'Ah, you got me.' That kind of fake, sanitised violence was understandable in its day. When Agatha Christie was writing in the 1930s crime was something that happened to other people and those who committed it were exterior creatures, beyond the norms of 'civilised' society. What is often called classic crime tends to treat criminals the way gardeners treat greenfly. All you have to do is identify them, locate them, spray on the right kind of insecticide/justice and everything turns right again.

It's difficult to justify that kind of portrayal today. Crime is everywhere. Most of us will know someone who's been the victim of violence, perhaps even murder. In the classic crime template all that is required for justice to be enacted is the simple matter of identification. The villain is unveiled, he puts up his hands, the police come along, a trial ensues and the world is put to rights. Does law enforcement in the twenty-first century feel that way to you? Probably not. Today justice is truly blind. Even if a perpetrator is found he or she may well walk free through failures in process or the intervention of very clever lawyers.

Ordinary decent citizens no longer feel safe. At the same time more and more start to think, 'If they can get away with it, why shouldn't I?' The world's a greyer, less certain place. When I depict violence I try to reflect that. So my violence may well not be the work of 'criminals'. It's unpredictable, hard to understand, random, even unplanned. And it has consequences – lasting ones that affect all those involved. I can't pretend that murder is simply a plot device, not when violence and crime, fear and a lust for retribution are everywhere around us.

Here are a few ground rules I try to apply when depicting brutal acts:

➤ I keep violent scenes short. The impact they have on the reader bears no proportion to the number of pages they take up. I well remember one book event where the moderator wondered out loud, 'Why is there so much violence in your book?' I asked him, 'How many violent scenes do you think there are?' He said, 'Lots.' I went through it with him. There were just three. It's not the quantity that matters, it's the impact. You can achieve more with a few well-written paragraphs than with ten pages of graphic, gruesome scalpel-wielding.

➤ I avoid extensive physical detail. It adds nothing to my kind of book to be told what tendons are severed, what part of the brain is lying on the pavement. I'm squeamish in real life. I don't want to know, and I don't see why the reader should. This may be different for those writing from, say, a medical point of view or reaching for revulsion as an effect.

➤ I always ensure that I describe the emotional effect of the violence on those involved, the person who inflicts it, the victims, those who've witnessed the act and those charged with bringing the perpetrators to justice. Particularly the culprit sometimes, because I know from experience as a journalist that extreme violence does affect many of those who use it. They can be as shocked by what it achieves as anyone else. And if they're not – as happens with a character in *Death in Seville* – that needs to be depicted and explained too, since it says something about them.

There are a lot of myths out there – fairy stories about 'closure' and the like. One such fable is the idea that people, police officers especially, become 'inured' to violence in the sense that it no longer affects them. I think it's true that they may not let its effects show after a while. But they're usually there, even if they're invisible to the person concerned. And again if they're not that tells you something about that person.

In many standard forms of popular literature violence is seen as a regrettable means towards a justifiable end. In my work there's a touch of that, but I want more. I want my characters to feel touched by brutality, damaged and tainted by its cruelty and injustice. Force may resolve the problem, but what interests me as much as the event itself is the aftermath, its cost and its consequences.

And that is why you'll never find a picture of me with a gun.

SEX — DO YOU NEED IT?

There's an odd literary prize in England called the Bad Sex in Fiction awards. I've never been nominated myself though I'm sure I'm qualified. Sex in fiction is an odd thing. Many, perhaps most, wannabe authors of mainstream fiction have sex in the book they are trying to sell. Why? I could be disingenuous here. I could say because sex is an integral part of human life and it would be hypocritical to ignore it. I could argue it was essential for the story I want to tell. Or even the most important part of all.

All these things may be true. But let's be honest. There's a grubbier, more common reason. It's plain desperation. People believe that without sex no one will publish the damned book. They reach for those buttons in the belief they need to be pushed in order to succeed. Is this true?

This is a big subject and I'm well aware that some people will be thinking, 'But I never want sex in my books at all'. Bear with me. Exploring the topic does tell us something about the nature of writing too. Let's try and break this down to four basic questions. First . . .

Does your story need sex or not?

Human beings have sex. We all know that. Most of us have got a pretty good idea what goes on in the bedroom. I'm sure there are authors desperate to introduce new and more physically improbable forms of sex for their readers. But for the most part sex in books is, well, sex. It's not a revelation. It's a physical thing. So is going to the toilet. There are writers out there who describe that too, though for the life of me I can't imagine a good reason (not that I feel they should stop trying if they're so minded).

Sex is rarely novel or, in terms of physical detail, particularly illuminating. Why write it then? One reason – and it's quite a common one – is to titillate. I'm always slightly bemused by this use of sex since we live in an extraordinarily graphic age. When you can see people having actual sex in mainstream cinema you have to push the boat out pretty far to match what's out there nationwide on twenty-feet-high cinema screens.

I'm not going to get prissy here. If you want to titillate, go for it. But go for it with gusto and be aware that it will change the tone of your overall book. Readers aren't stupid. They know and may appreciate smut when they see it. What they will spot a mile off is if you switch into poetic allegorical mode straight after and try to do the 'yes, but it's all in context – I wouldn't do it otherwise' thing.

The real reason for sex, though, is in order to explore character. To show love between people, whether it's established love, developing love or love that's falling apart. Desperate sex between two people whose genuine love is disintegrating can be heartbreaking. The moment a couple fall into bed the first time can be touching too and make the reader think, 'Finally . . . '

Sex between steady couples . . . I'm not so sure. If the relationship is firm, unthreatened, friendly, I don't know if you tell the reader anything by showing they have sex too. They would, wouldn't they? One reader put it to me this way: she wanted to know the good people had sex so that they were happy. But she didn't need to know the details, only that it was going on. As always the basic question is the same: can I take this out without materially damaging the book? If the answer's yes then it has to go.

If you're going to write sex how graphic should it be?

You have to work that out for yourself. There are delicate and sensitive lines here that can so easily be crossed. I squirm with embarrassment when I read a passage in which a male authorial voice is clearly salivating over the physical characteristics of a woman. No one (well, not many people) likes to listen to one human being pervy over another, and that's what this can sound like all too easily.

Graphic physical detail is dangerous. I've done that but not for a long time. You leave yourself open to getting a guffaw from the reader just when you'd like something else. It's also a very difficult call to make. With most work you can gauge whether it's good or not. Once you're in the bedroom it may not be just your characters who are faking it.

I don't use sex very much these days. There was one short scene in *Dante's Numbers* where the reader was in the room when it started. I felt in that case it was necessary because it established something about the relationship between the two people concerned. But most of my recent books, if they feature sex at all, have depicted the moment before or the moment after (and frankly that can tell you just as much as some blow by blow bedroom account). I tend to treat sex as I do violence – keep these things short, to the point and, hopefully, powerful. I'm not enamoured of lingering sex any more than I am of lingering violence. But that's my choice. Others will feel differently. Maybe I'm just getting old.

Do readers want to read about sex?

Some do. I have had people complain about the way sex has tapered off in my books over the years. But not many. If some hot scene is part of your unique selling point you'd be crazy to abandon it. But if it is *that* important your editor will know and be the first to demand it. It won't be something you need to think about much.

Do publishers expect sex in order to sell your book?

Many years ago a former editor of mine in New York picked out a passage in an early book and said, 'I like hot writing as much as anyone. But what does this add to the book?'

Nothing, if I was honest. I just felt I was keeping up the sex quotient demanded of new writers. So it came out.

The straight answer is: publishers expect a good book. I'm sure there are occasions when some have said, 'This would be better with some more sex in it.' But I'd guess it's not often. Experienced editors will have seen it all over the years, every different description of every variation on the act, every euphemism there is for the various appendages of the human body. For them it's going to be the story that counts. In most popular fiction sex is not going to be a make-or-break issue however much wannabe writers feel they have to write it in at some point.

If I was starting out now I'd probably be very wary indeed about putting prominent sex scenes in any prospective manuscript. At least if you leave them out you know you're going to be offering something different to most of the other stuff on the slush pile.

HE, SHE OR IT

Let's deal with one more subtlety to do with sex, or more accurately gender, in terms of your book voice. Should you treat female characters differently to male ones when it comes to describing them in the third person? Do you automatically refer to male characters by their surnames and female ones by their first names?

Example: 'Giordano crossed the room and opened Charlie's filing cabinet. Sally followed him.'

There are people who think that writing a sentence like that is sexist. The reasoning I can see. Why should men and women be treated differently? Isn't it condescending? Akin to referring to grown women as 'girls'? Or, as pop songs invariably do, 'babe', a word I've never actually heard anyone use in that context in real life?

The honest answer is . . . it depends. Yes, it would be possible to write a book using these conventions and be highly condescending to the story's female characters. But I also think you can slip between first and second names over gender and age with good reason.

Charlie is fourteen years old. His schoolteacher may think of him as 'Harrison'. I can't. So Charlie he is.

Sally's a touch older. I think I'm going to be writing this book from a third-person subjective point of view, usually Charlie's. He likes Sally. He's probably attracted to her. He wouldn't think of her by her surname for a moment. When Sally is in a scene she's going to be called Sally.

What about an older character? Say Sally's grandfather? Charlie doesn't know him well. They're not on first-name terms. To Charlie he would be 'Mr Whitby'. So in a third-person subjective scene he would be that too.

If Charlie's dad had a girlfriend, Rosemary Wilkins, a woman Charlie knew well, she'd be Rosemary, not Mrs Wilkins.

And our bad guy? Surname throughout. Charlie doesn't like him.

Does this make sense? To me it does, and I'm the one who's going to write this thing. If you try to create a rule to cover this logic I think you'd fail. But the real test is: does it work in terms of the book? Does the reader feel, in each scene, that he or she is sitting on the shoulder of the POV character and viewing what's happening through their eyes, not as some distanced, anonymous observer? Most important of all, does this allow the book to be read without prompting those 'hang on?' moments that disturb the rhythm and force your audience to ponder unnaturally over some stylistic device?

I think that would happen if, on the grounds of some strange notion of political correctness, I referred to all adult characters, male and female, by their second names, regardless of their relationship to the point-of-view character. Charlie's a young English schoolkid. He'd never think of any woman by her surname. If your protagonist was an adult, working in a big company or a government department where everyone referred to everyone else as a surname it might be different.

The key for me, though, is not corporate behaviour but what's happening inside a character's head. People who establish relationships with one another, romantic or otherwise, tend to move to first-name terms somewhere along the way. Forget so-called correctness. Write what feels natural.

A SHORT TYPING LESSON

Nothing shouts 'Amateur!' so loudly as flying fingers hitting the wrong parts of the keyboard. Let's put to bed one of the most common errors seen in rookie manuscripts: the use of typographical elements to emphasise or dramatise parts of the text. There are those who will tell you this matter is subject to a simple rule: never do it. As usual, things aren't quite as simple as that.

Example: 'EEKKKK!!! Desmond! DESMOND!!!! Colonel Farquhar' just been found DEAD face down in the hothouse aspidistra!!!'

'How *very* inconvenient, darling. I'd only just pruned it.'

There are some stinkers there. But there's also something that is rather handy and worthy of use – as always with the caveat 'in moderation'.

Let's deal with the shockers first.

Exclamation marks and other typographical fluff

Some people say these should never be used. I disagree. Exclamation marks are long-standing elements of punctuation that serve a purpose. They add that extra sense of power at the end of a sentence: 'I don't care. I'm going to do it anyway!' I don't have any problem with that so long as exclamation marks are used very lightly indeed, not sprinkled around like confetti.

What you mustn't do is think you can enhance the process by adding in more than one. Multiple exclamation marks – or question marks for that matter – are bad punctuation, ugly on the page and look childish. Even worse, never, ever throw in other typographical marks – • ★ # – thinking they add even more emphasis. They don't. They just make you look banal.

Writers should stick to the letters of the alphabet, common punctuation marks, and foreign accents when needed. There is no reason why you need worry about formatting at all – someone else will take care of that. This applies to dashes by the way – type them as two short hyphens like this if you like -- and the publisher will set them correctly in the end.

Avoid CONTINUOUS CAPITAL LETTERS. Shouty, inelegant and ineffective.

Exaggerated spelling. For example: ' Eeekkkkk! Wooooo-o-o-o-tttt! Begorrrrrhaaaah!' You don't really need me to say it, do you?

The use of **bold**. Bold is a typographic style principally used in functional non-fiction such as computer manuals, and in journalism as a design feature. It's not there to emphasise individual words in a narrative work. Fiction, particularly popular fiction, emulates the oral storytelling tradition. Punctuation, used properly, signals the pauses and effects used by someone reading a story. Bold has no place in that process.

The use of italics

Finally something I can and will use. But isn't it just like bold, you say? A typographic convention? Well, yes, but the italic style is long-established and fulfils several readily understood purposes in books.

Here are some ways you will see italics used.

For emphasis – compare ' Are you the only one who's going to turn up today?' with 'Are you the *only* one who's going to turn up today?' Same words, slightly different tone, through nothing other than the italics in the second. I can't think of any other way to achieve that, though perhaps an italics jihadist out there can suggest one.

For foreign words: ' The *abbacchio scottadito* was perfect. 'You'll often see this in my books since they take place in Italy. But I don't italicise everything otherwise there'd be a lot of italics around. Very common words such as Questura I leave in Roman (i.e. plain) text since they appear so often they don't seem so foreign. You wouldn't want to italicise pizza, would you?

For interior thought. '*Does he really love me*, Rebecca wondered.' Or simply on a line of its own: '*Does he love me?*' The first is popular and house style for many publishers, but far from mandatory. The second sounds OK because it represents an entire interior spoken thought, which the first doesn't. But, like anything, it would quickly become annoying if overused. You decide.

Book titles, newspaper names, ships . . . *The Times*, *Moby-Dick*, the *Queen Mary*. All OK.

To represent historic passages. You'll find in some of my American editions, notably *Lucifer's Shadow* and *The Seventh Sacrament*, whole sections printed in italics. Nothing to do with me. This was the publisher's editorial style. I don't like it. Italics should be used for a single sentence or two at most. In big chunks italic text becomes unreadable. Under no circumstances submit a manuscript that contains more than a paragraph or two of italic text at the most.

If you genuinely feel a historic or separate element needs to be differentiated visually, just set it in a contrasting font. If your body font is a sans style, say Helvetica, Arial or Calibri, then you could choose a serif font – a more ornate newspaper style one – such as Times, Garamond or Cambria for the separate sections.

But I wouldn't spend a lot of time agonising over decisions like this. If your target agent or editor chooses to read the manuscript on an ereader – and they probably will – your font decisions will be overridden and they probably won't see them. Better to put a covering note in with the manuscript suggesting these contrasting sections could be marked by some typographic design in the final book. You'll be judged on your writing talent, not your ability to format Microsoft Word prettily. Keep things simple and avoid exotic typefaces too (your intended customer may not even see them).

One oddity about italics that people sometimes forget: if you want to italicise something within an italic sentence you revert to the plain Roman style. For example: '*Perhaps we should put a notice in* The Times.'

I use italics sparingly, principally for unusual foreign words and for emphasising single words in direct speech. They can give text a rhythm and texture that's difficult, if not impossible, to achieve through any other means. If your work ends up appearing as an audio book, italics will also help the narrator understand better the rhythm of the prose.

Remember: punctuation and typography are effective in fiction when they suggest the flow and balance of the spoken word. The rest of the tricks here are best avoided unless you're writing one of the rare books that genuinely need them.

SOPHISTICATION AHEAD: PROCEED WITH CARE

An American writer friend of mine, late one night in a bar in New York, leaned over to me once and whispered, 'You know the trouble with readers? They're dumb. You spend a chunk of your life making your books all rich and sophisticated and full of hidden meanings for them to stumble on. And they never get there. They just read the story and then they're done.'

Here's another perspective on that viewpoint. Authors can sometimes be very stupid. They assume a level of knowledge, sophistication and commitment on the part of their readers that is simply unrealistic. They become obsessed with small details no one notices. They lose themselves in the trees and forget that people are there to see the forest.

I know. I've been there.

Florian is a famous Venetian café in the Piazza San Marco. I used the place – sparingly – in *The Cemetery of Secrets* (or *Lucifer's Shadow* depending where you are in the world and when you bought the book).

That story got a lot of acclaim. Here's part of the review by one of America's veteran critics Dick Adler writing about it in the *Chicago Tribune*:

> Tasty little insider jokes abound: The 1733 hero wonders in a
> letter why the pompous owner of a popular coffeehouse called
> Triofante 'doesn't just name the place after himself and have done
> with it.' The fact that the 1733 owner's name was Floriano
> Francesconi, and the present-day coffeehouse (now the home of
> the $20 cup of espresso) is named Florian's, is part of the book's
> pleasure. Vivaldi is a sadly grotesque but still powerful musical
> force, and even the French writer Rousseau comes in for his share
> of needling.
>
> Add horribly believable scenes of violence, enough sex to
> ensure the city's reputation for romance, as well as great gobbets
> of food and scenery both splendid and squalid, and you begin to
> see why *Lucifer's Shadow* is unputdownable.

Great review. Dick Adler, though, knows Venice well. He used to live there. I reread that book shortly before it was republished in the UK as *The Cemetery of Secrets*. I was amazed at the number of in-jokes I'd stuffed in. Why? For the old mountaineer's reason I guess – because I could. That work was written under extraordinary circumstances. It was to be the final book in my then publishing contract. I seriously believed it might be the last novel I ever managed to publish. So I bunged in everything I could to see what it looked like.

I don't do that now. The problem is that those in-jokes only made sense to someone who knows Venice, and knows it very well. No casual visitor was likely to get them. You had to visit the place, read some serious history books, become absorbed entirely in the city. Here's the catch: that's what I'm supposed to be doing on behalf of the reader, then re-creating it for their imaginations. They shouldn't have to bring much more to the party except some spare time, a willingness to read and an open, receptive mind.

It is terribly tempting to be over-sophisticated when writing fiction – to assume a level of knowledge on the part of the reader that is simply impractical. As we've established, readers in Victorian times could devote themselves to long and complex books because they had nothing else to do. Today they're fighting not to be distracted by something else before they turn the page.

So in-jokes and arcane sophistication are, for me, out. I write fairly long and complex books in the first place. They also demand that the reader be willing to imagine themselves into another country, and become acquainted with unfamiliar aspects of history. I doubtless tread a fine line and cross over it on occasion. But you can't push those poor souls too far. They simply won't go there.

WRITING A SERIES

Series books are very popular, with publishers and authors. Many – my own included – started out as standalone novels, then turned into a series because a publisher asked for more. It's flattering to find that something you thought was a one-off book provokes sufficient interest for readers to want to return to your characters time and time again.

What makes a book the start of a series instead of a standalone?

➤ An interesting protagonist or team of protagonists who solve the problem in the first story but remain somehow unresolved as characters by the close.

> A world that's vividly painted and so 'real' that readers will want to return to it time and time again.

> A commitment from the writer to devote himself to the same kind of book, and the same characters, over several years without getting bored, without worrying that he runs a serious risk of being typecast, successful or not.

If you think the book you're embarking upon could be the start of a series here are a few issues to consider first. For those of us already in the game they probably fall into the category of 'things I wished someone had told me before it all began'.

THIS GUY DOES WHAT EXACTLY?

Readers will sometimes whine about the number of series based around cops or secret agents or people connected to law-enforcement agencies in some other way. Perhaps you're even of this mind yourself. You have a bright idea. Something completely original.

Here's a tip: when you can hear the sentence 'No one's ever done this before' forming in your head, flee the computer and do something else for a while. There's usually a reason why others have walked away from that same bright notion.

Series books hinge upon characters who, time after time, find themselves in situations that spark a story. For that to work they have to do something professionally or in their private life that makes it natural for trouble to find them.

Let's imagine you've set out to create a 'different' kind of crime series. Your detective is a floral arranger. She goes to deliver a very expensive bouquet to a rich family mansion and walks into the scene of a horrendous murder. Whoever did it ordered the flowers in the first place. He was setting her up for the blame. All of a sudden her biggest worry is no longer 'Will the chrysanthemums look fresh?' It's 'How do I find the bad guy, reveal him for what he truly is and get back to the boring little life I had before – if that's possible?'

That could work for a story. And next time round? Well it's hard to get away from the idea that she's going to deliver a bouquet and find she's surrounded by dead bodies again. Perhaps the readers will forgive you once. Come book three they'll surely be screaming, 'Why the hell do people use this woman? Every time you buy flowers from her someone winds up dead.'

You could try and broaden things a little. Let's say our florist discovers there's a hot detective in the cops, someone who believes her and gets into trouble for it. She could still be fancying him in later books, perhaps even pursuing an on-off relationship. Since he's a cop he could get into trouble. Oh, but hang on. We're back with cops, aren't we? Not florists at all. That 'original' idea just fell by the wayside.

Inventiveness is a very good thing, provided it's sustainable and believable. There's a point at which the struggle to be ingenious in differentiating your protagonist becomes untenable. Trying to define a character through labels – 'I know . . . he could be a black/gay/psychic/war veteran/disabled wedding planner with vampire tendencies' – rarely works. Most crime series are set around people working in law enforcement for a reason: it's natural that they should meet the problems that will provide new stories.

The same goes for fantasy. If you're a trainee wizard or a vampire hunter your day is never going to be boring. Ordinary citizens are fine for a standalone book in which they come face to face with the dark side of human nature. If it happens on a regular basis readers will very soon begin to think . . . these people aren't normal at all.

The best way to differentiate series protagonists is through character and the world that encloses them. With Nic Costa I wanted to buck the trend for middle-aged, melancholic, divorced, alcoholic, shabbily dressed detectives who are somehow perennially attractive to women and trapped in a grim urban environment. So Costa is young, full of integrity, bright and determined, terrible with women and working in Rome. His character manages to work on those around him who are cynical. It's a twist on the old way of doing things. Evolution not revolution.

AVOIDING SHERLOCK

Arthur Conan Doyle famously killed off Sherlock Holmes at the Reichenbach Falls in *The Final Problem* in 1893. Two years before he'd written to his mother, 'I think of slaying Holmes . . . and winding him up for good and all. He takes my mind from better things.'

His mother responded, 'You may do what you deem fit, but the crowds will not take this light-heartedly.'

Within a decade Conan Doyle disinterred Holmes due to popular demand. He had a clever old mum.

Authors who write series books frequently fall out with their protagonists after a while. For the first couple of books you love them. By book three they're old, familiar friends. Come book six they're the much-loathed house guests who never want to leave and sour everything with their presence, including the books in which they appear.

How do you avoid Conan Doyle syndrome?

Like most authors I came into a series by accident. I wrote the first Nic Costa book as a standalone. It was turned into a series because my publishers saw an opportunity. I was, however, very aware of series drift and ennui. I never set out thinking, 'I'll write six of these books then try something else.' Some people can manage that. I'm not sufficiently organised. The only way I could approach a series was in the belief it would somehow run for ever, with other standalones threaded in between. I wanted the books to have sufficient variety and texture built into their fabric to allow me to improvise and switch perspectives from title to title. The principal way I sought to achieve this was through the introduction of a team, a family of characters surrounding Nic Costa, who was very much the protagonist in the first story. So in the second book, *The Villa of Mysteries*, I amplify two minor characters from the first book and introduce a new key player.

From that point on we have Costa, his boss Falcone, the pathologist Teresa Lupo and his sidekick Gianni Peroni. Four people who love and respect one another and give me a lot more opportunity to stretch with each story. Series books that run out of steam are often based around a single dominant character and follow the same kind of format from title to title. A case floats into the in-tray, gets investigated, then placed in the out-tray at the end. The protagonist occupies the same desk, the same office throughout. Tedium lurks around the corner.

What I try to do with a team book is shift the camera constantly. We see Costa progressing in his career as his older colleagues start to flounder in theirs. We observe changing relationships happening beneath the single story that's the focus of each book. The ensemble approach to a series – even if it encompasses nothing more than a simple partnership such as Holmes and Watson – allows the author freedom over the stories to come.

In a way the Costa stories aren't a series at all. I write standalone stories that just happen to involve the same set of characters. You don't need to worry about any of this too much with book one. Just remember to build in some interesting minor players from the start. Later on they could save you a trip to the Reichenbach Falls.

DEALING WITH TIME

When it comes to fiction, and series fiction in particular, time stinks. It's a blight on us all, a nasty chunk of so-called reality that tries to poke its ugly head in where it's not wanted. Let's leave aside those books that use time the way statisticians use chart paper, as pegs on which to hang an argument. You know the kind. The ones with the *X-Files*-style chapter headings – 'Peter's pantry, 11.09 a.m., Thursday 13 August, Stoke Newington, London, England, The World.' Nothing wrong with that. I wrote one myself once.

There are often practical reasons for marking down a timeline as your story progresses. That doesn't mean you have to use those time slugs in the finished version. Readers don't obsess about the passage of time. Try to remember the last book you really liked. Then ask yourself: over what time period did it take place?

My guess is you don't really know. A few days. A week. Years. Mostly time doesn't matter. Yes, readers want to know what comes next. But that's because they're keen to know where the characters are going. They're not stopping you in the street and asking you to check your watch.

Yet writers still agonise over time. They nag people who make writing software to include some kind of timeline feature so they can map out the chronology of their story to the last second. They – you may wish to look away here – plan their tales in sad columns in Excel spreadsheets as if they were lines on a P&L statement (and may the Lord have mercy on their souls). They worry that, in the real world, it may take a DNA sample two to three months to come back from the lab, when in the pages of their story it happens in a couple of days, not that the reader is any the wiser either way. Use time in a book in any real sense and it will, more than likely, complicate matters unnecessarily and run the risk of making the whole thing as dull and full of languid pauses as 'real life' itself.

If you're thinking of going down this path, let me plead with you now: don't. It's ridiculous. Books stay around for years. If your series works you'll find that, after a while, absolutely no one reads them in order anyway, so your artificial timing habits will either go unnoticed or baffle them. At the same time you're inevitably building in continuity gotchas that will come back to bite you. Imagine you're at book ten and want to do something but can't because of some concrete timing event you placed in book three. Why burden yourself with this? Isn't writing hard enough already?

Time is important only in so far as it makes, or keeps, your story credible. All fiction is a whopping great lie. The secret is to lie so well that your fabrication takes on the mantle of truth. Objective reality is dangerous bunkum that belongs to newspapers and TV stations (not that you'd know it some of the time). Subjective reality is, to the novelist, everything. If it seems genuine enough to touch inside the page, then it's real inside the reader's head, and that's the only place that counts.

In practice this means that all you need ask of time is that it sounds feasible. You can't fly from New York to Beijing in a couple of hours. You mustn't put someone in hospital with multiple fractures one day and have them walking round biffing people on the nose the next. The moments in your story must add up in the sense that they shouldn't contradict one another, or make some other event impossible or improbable. But that really is it.

Let me give you one concrete example in which time trips up writers. I write a Costa book a year. Like many series authors, I started off thinking this meant the year between books meant a year between the lives of the characters in them.

This is insane.

After three books Nic, who was twenty-four or so in the first book, was twenty-seven. His colleagues, who were much older, were suddenly entering their fifties. I love writing these books. I could write them for ever, alongside other things, of course. But I can't age my people one year every year. Otherwise very soon Peroni and Falcone would be up for retirement and Costa would be looking to settle down, breed children and wonder about which brand of safety seat to buy for the back of the car.

Treating time literally will kill any series. I deeply regret all indications I've given in the earlier books that will allow readers of a sufficiently anal bent to add up the warped and highly inaccurate chronology of the series. You won't get those clues again. They're needless and confusing.

Here's the real rub. I do need time in one very specific way. These stories are very much about Nic Costa and his entry into adulthood. The growing up of a decent yet naive young man as he finds the world's a rough place where you have to cut corners from time to time. I need him to age just a little. That shows him experiencing changes in his life and adapting to them. But at the same time I need my older characters to stay where they are before they get pensioned off.

You see the dilemma? You see the solution?

No? Well, here it is. Lie and lie big. Throw the whole space–time continuum out of the window. Nic gets older. Falcone and Peroni don't. The later books mention Nic's age but blur theirs. If you were picky you could go through the books and work out how this process is going on numerically. No, I'm not going to do this for you. All I will say is that at his present rate of ageing Nic, if I spelled things out, would overtake mid-thirties Teresa Lupo in age about six years or so from now, and do the same to early-fifties Falcone and Peroni somewhere around 2019. Ridiculous? Maybe. But it's fiction, and fiction fundamentally is ridiculous. The only thing more ridiculous is the literal. I am not going there.

And if you want proof here it is. This two-stage process of ageing has been going on for six or seven books, one a year. Until I point it out to people no one notices.

That's how important time is in the great swing of things. Not at all.

EVERY BOOK'S A NEW BOOK TO SOMEONE

Once in a while a reader emails me to say something like this.

'I love your books. I've read every one of them. I just enjoyed the latest. But why oh why do you keep telling me what Costa/Peroni/Teresa look like? I know by now. You don't have to keep repeating that information.'

Oh but I do. Once a series starts to become established you will pick up new readers who will never experience your stories in the sequence they were written. When you have two or three books out it's easy for them to keep up if they want. Those titles should be on the shelves. People can sift through them, spot the first and start with that. That won't last when you're up to book four or five. Very few stores will keep an entire series in stock. So when people discover your work they will tend to buy what's in front of them which, after a few years, will usually be well into the series. That's why you have to describe your characters in each and every book. Many readers will be meeting them for the first time. You can't just pitch your titles at people who know them already.

This leads on to a more difficult question: how do you get your backstory – the things that happened before – into later books? There's no easy answer. My approach is to leak small amounts of information into the present book that give a hint of what's happened before. But I don't do any more than is necessary. I really want to avoid the kind of preface you see on some TV programmes that spend a few minutes at the start telling you what you missed earlier.

It's very important to me that no one should have to read one title in order to understand another. There's a continuing story beneath the surface, primarily that of the relationships between the principal characters involved. But each story is an individual tale. That's very different from something like Harry Potter, say, which is a series of books set in direct chronological order, joined by linked events and themes, travelling towards a fixed conclusion.

Whatever kind of series you're writing, make sure you keep character and location notes in your book journal as you go along. They're going to be priceless as your world and its people develop and you refer back to them to inform a new generation of readers as they appear. Long-term fans are fabulous. We all love and appreciate them. But to be honest they'd get as fed up as everyone else if we wrote for them and them alone.

PRE-FLIGHT CHECKLIST

I have an idea of the mosaic of characters, events, places and possible narrative threads that ought to get this book off the ground. Every piece of that mosaic is essential. But that doesn't mean they're all equally important. When you're locked into the tunnel-vision process of putting words down on the page it's dangerously easy to get obsessed about one small, simple issue. Allow that to happen and that single detail could hold up an entire project when, in a sane world, you'd just pass it by and mark it as something to fix later.

What we need as we begin is a set of priorities. Here are mine, and note – this is very important – they come in what some would regard as reverse order. First of all I want to know what I don't want to do, so that I can focus on what truly matters.

OBJECTS OF MINOR SIGNIFICANCE

These are things that can be fixed quickly and easily once the main work of a book – the manuscript itself – is complete. If I get some good insight into these issues while I'm writing, fine. If they have to wait till the final revise, or get dealt with during the post-editing process, it's no big deal.

Titles

These can and sometimes will change, even after a book is accepted. I make a note of potential titles all the time in a little entry in my book journal. Usually the right one will become apparent during the writing process. But if it doesn't I'm not going to lose any sleep, and I certainly won't halt the writing process to puzzle over a few words for the cover.

Character names

Search and replace is a wonderful thing. I often try out three or four different names to see which one works best.

Transitional moments

By this I mean those bits of a book that lead from one passage to another. If I don't know how but I'm sure what comes after this missing piece, I write that instead. Usually the transition itself becomes apparent during that process so I then go back and fill it in. Sometimes it becomes clear I don't need much of a transition at all. It may be a single paragraph at the end of the preceding scene. Or nothing at all.

Dialogue that doesn't work

Speech is easy to fix at a later date. It can be cut or rewritten very easily. If I were really stuck I'd just put in a note describing what the speech in particular needs to relate and then move on.

Awkward text

Does something sound rough and clumsy? So what? These are just words. When you delete them no fairies die. Graham Greene used to say that the first thing he did when he finished a book was to go back and take out all the adjectives and adverbs. He'd then read it again and insert the ones he thought necessary, then reread once more to try to get a final version. Revision is a vital part of the book-writing process, as we shall see. If something doesn't quite gel, mark it for another look later and move on.

OBJECTS OF MAJOR SIGNIFICANCE

Here are some things I must have established in my head, even if they're rough and hazy.

Story flow

I don't write conventional 4/4 common time stories. The pace and the tempo vary very deliberately, from fast to reflective. But at the same time each piece needs to fit – or contrast – with what goes before and what comes next. Minor transitional moments I can set to one side. But the feel and fit are different. I find it hard to progress unless the relationship between the different elements of the mosaic is well established and there's no accidental, awkward jar between one passage and the next.

Characters

Yes, I come to understand them better as I'm writing the book. And yes, they reveal mysteries to me that I hadn't guessed in the beginning, when I created them. But I still have to know them to some extent from the start. They need to feel familiar, capable of being 'seen' in my mind's eye, heard with real voices in my head. Without that they don't have the promise of inner, hidden substance, something waiting to be discovered during the progress of the book, like an iceberg slowly revealing itself, not added artificially with daubs of deliberate paint masquerading as 'characterisation'.

Locations

Again, if I can't see them, feel them, smell them, I can't describe them. I need to establish the canvas firmly in my head before starting to create the narrative it will one day enclose.

Key event detail

By this I mean things you can't skip, fudge, make excuses for. At some stage all stories come to pivot on certain central facts: this happened and these were the consequences. You may not know them fully before you begin. But at some stage those events become so central they have to move front of stage. You need an inkling about what they are. These elements are the levers that will trigger and move the mechanisms of the finished story.

I've an idea of the kind of tale I want to write. It's not going to be conventional crime or a thriller. It's destined to be something that is somewhat looser in definition, mixing a few elements of the two: a mystery. This is a coming-of-age story about a decent young man taking his first few steps into the adult world and discovering it's more complicated, and more threatening, than he could ever have imagined.

Minor items aren't project stoppers. I can leave them and fix them even after a first or second revise. This second set are, for me, matters that have to take prominence, top priority when I'm writing. Without them I'm lost in the desert, and that's a place no one wants to be.

I have the first act now. *Charlie and the Mermaid* has attained the status of 'work in progress'. Here's the story so far.

FIRST–ACT SYNOPSIS

Charlie Harrison is a fourteen-year-old kid living alone in a rundown English seaside resort with his father, a surly and uncommunicative police officer whose wife left him years ago. Charlie's a good kid, studious, honest, fond of swimming in the sea and athletics. One summer evening he walks down to the beach for a swim. In the shadows of the pier, a scary structure half-destroyed by fire, he sees a figure. A young girl, about his own age, standing in the water, her back to him, staring out to sea. She's fully dressed, soaking wet and looks as if she's about to walk into the waves. He races in and stops her. An exchange takes place. He doesn't know if she was trying to kill herself or not. She's pretty, she's fascinating. He has an odd thought: she looks like a mermaid.

He talks her out on to the beach, still concerned. Then a long black American limo draws up by the road and a man in a suit gets out and barks at her to join him. The girl refuses. The man comes closer. He's big and scary, threatening ... and very odd too, staring at both of them in a controlling way. His right hand is covered in a black leather glove, so thick and heavy it seems artificial. Charlie knows something's wrong here and stands up for her. There's a confrontation. The car drives off. The girl, Sally, walks off without a word of thanks. All she does is turn round and say to him from some distance away, 'Stay away from me. You don't want trouble.'

It's the summer holidays and Charlie's bored. The next day he goes to the dilapidated town swimming pool, a place he never normally visits because he much prefers to swim in the sea, whatever the weather. The girl's there, working as a lifeguard. He realises she's a couple of years older than him. She doesn't smile. She's even prettier than he remembers. She doesn't look pleased to see him. She's running a life-saving class, showing people techniques such as mouth-to-mouth resuscitation on a dummy. Charlie takes part. There's a bully from his class at school, and a couple of his mates. They obviously have an interest in the girl. When Charlie has his turn on the dummy the bully asks, 'First kiss, Harrison?' Sally looks at him sympathetically. When the others start to rib him some more she bawls them out very forcefully.

'There,' she says, when they're gone. 'We're even.'

But they're not. The bullies wait outside and sock him one. His nose is bleeding so Sally takes Charlie home for tea. She lives with her grand-father, Eric Whitby, an old seaside children's entertainer, comedian, magician, ventriloquist – you name it. He's a likeable, talkative old man with a glint in his eye. Sally is transformed around him. He's funny, clever, observant, full of life. Eric shows him what he says is the best magic trick in the world. He clicks his fingers and flames appear at his fingertips. It's so easy, so real it does feel like magic. Sally smiles when she sees this. Her mum's dead. She doesn't mention her father. Charlie thinks of the long black car and the man in the suit but doesn't say anything.

When he leaves she sees him to the door and says again, 'I'm trouble. Stay away from me.'

Charlie is shocked to find he's wondering what it would be like to kiss her. And why she keeps asking him to stay away in one breath but asking him into her life with the next.

When he gets home his dad bawls him out. He's furious. Livid and scared too, Charlie thinks. It's all to do with the man in the black car, who's complained to him about Charlie somehow. Who is he? Charlie asks. Only Matt Giordano, the man who owns the town. The man everyone answers to. Even the police, it seems to Charlie.

He listens to his dad for a while, telling him to steer clear of Giordano or get a good hiding. Then Charlie goes for a walk. Back down to the beach, wondering if he'll see Sally again since it's the evening. Charlie's puzzled. He's a dogged, inquisitive kid. When something sticks in his head it's not easily dislodged. His dad is always calling him out for that.

He walks up to the pier and squeezes through the gates. No one's supposed to go in this place and normally Charlie, the *old* Charlie, wouldn't dream of doing anything he wasn't supposed to. But he goes in this time because the old Charlie was a kid, and the new Charlie isn't. The place burned down years ago, and whoever's trying to reopen it seems to be running out of money. Most of it is fire-blasted, ruined. At the end is a small theatre, half-rebuilt but covered in chains and security fencing. Charlie walks there. On the outside wall, charred, only just visible, he sees a poster from years ago, before the fire. It's a variety bill. Top of the list is a double act of children's entertainers: Whitby and Giordano, the funniest duo this side of Blackpool. Eric Whitby, the comedian. Giordano, the straight man and – it makes a big play of this – a hypnotist too: 'The Man Who Can Make You Do Anything'. There are pictures of the two men in suits, with top hats and props, Eric grinning, Giordano scary and with the same staring eyes Charlie's already seen. Behind them is a beautiful woman in a showgirl's costume with a feathered headdress. She looks very like Sally.

Something's wrong here, he thinks. He goes back and squeezes out of the security gates. As he does so he realises he's been seen. The American limo is there, parked in the road by the pier. The window winds down. A long arm comes out, a black leather glove on the hand. It makes the gesture of a gun being cocked then fired directly at him. The car drives off.

Charlie stands there and wonders how he feels. Frightened? A bit maybe. More than that he's angry. Something bad is going on and it affects Sally, makes her miserable, which she doesn't deserve. He's got the school holidays ahead of him and nothing to fill them supposedly. He has now.

THE SECOND ACT: FORKS IN THE ROAD

At this point we enter dangerous territory. The storytellers' ancestral graveyard, a bleak, grey landscape littered with the corpses of half-abandoned projects. Cinema folk wail about this stage of the process endlessly. Wander into any bar in a fashionable district of LA and you don't have to wait long to hear some wannabe writer bemoaning his second-act angst to a bartender who can't wait to respond with a whine about his failed audition. Novelists suffer the same agonies, though usually in silence. We know this pain is coming and the wise will anticipate it.

To recap: the second act begins at the point where our protagonist has seized hold of his or her problem and determined to solve it come what may. In Charlie's case it's his realisation that there's something seriously bad going on in Sally's life, something that scares her to the point where she may even be considering suicide. Charlie's going to do something about that. He doesn't have a clue yet what it might be.

Think of *Hamlet*'s second act, our melancholy Dane wandering around trying to work out how to respond to the news that Claudius murdered his stepfather. What to do? Go mad? Commit suicide? Wander round being a perennial pain in the butt for anyone willing to listen?

Hamlet, unusually for a protagonist, is aware of his own second-act dilemma. He speaks about it openly in soliloquy – here in Act 2, Scene 2:

> O, vengeance!
> Why, what an ass am I! This is most brave,
> That I, the son of a dear father murdered,
> Prompted to my revenge by heaven and hell,
> Must like a whore unpack my heart with words
> And fall a-cursing like a very drab,
> A stallion! Fie upon't, foh! About, my brains.

You see the problem? The second act is discursive, fickle, uncertain, as you too must 'unpack your heart with words'. This phase of the book is about characters wandering around in search of answers, and mostly failing to find them. It may require dead ends and red herrings, but not too many to confuse the plot. Characters will begin to reveal themselves, locations will grow richer and more convincing. And events . . . The possible steps and staging posts on the way to the next and final part of the journey will multiply constantly, trying to tempt you into countless different directions. There is, in short, enormous potential to turn the whole thing into a flabby middle of unresolved doubts, cul-de-sacs and circuitous meanderings.

Expect no short cuts, no easy solutions. You've probably sprinted to this point. Now you need to keep up a steady, measured pace to conquer the long, marathon laps that take you to the final dash to the close.

Let me repeat: writing a book requires focus and control. Those essentials are needed more during the second act than at any time during the creation of this tale. Perhaps without noticing it you've found some of that focus already. It's certainly there in the synopsis for *Charlie and the Mermaid*. I don't need to cry, like Hamlet, 'About, my brains.' Not yet anyway.

WHY CHARLIE DIDN'T GO TO LONDON

When I was throwing around some early ideas for this story I had a closing point for the first act in mind. Charlie and Sally would flee their unnamed seaside town and head for London, there to discover the world of magic and theatre, the threats and excitement of the metropolis.

Hmm . . . nah.

Charlie's seaside town grew on me the more I thought about his scenes there. That burnt-out pier, the blasted promenade, the sense of decay and poverty in a place that once was grand and perhaps hoped to return to those glory days again before long – these were all ideas and images I felt I could play with and extend, hope to turn into something real. The place didn't even have a name, but I was starting to see it, to hear the amusement arcades on the promenade, smell the salt tang of the sea overlaid with the greasy stink of the fish and chip shops.

Writers don't just create that story on the page. We're its first audience too, and you have to listen to your people and your world as they start to emerge from the shadows of your own imagination. Charlie's town soon struck a chord as I thought about how it might look. I checked a few photos of other, real seaside resorts that could serve as models and pretty soon my mind was made up. London's a great and wonderful city but there are a million different stories set there, and a million more to come. No one's ever written about Charlie's town. It's *mine*.

If a location is vivid early on for the writer there's a greater chance you can pass on some of that sense of place to your audience. Just as importantly, I've now narrowed my field of possibilities. We progress through this second phase of the book not just by developing ideas but also through killing those we don't want. I've ruled out London from the story entirely. It's gone for good. I know that Charlie's town is all I have. The story begins, develops and ends here. I've *focused*.

As a matter of course I always check myself if I begin to wonder whether the story should move elsewhere. Sometimes – by no means always – that shift in location is a sign of desperation or bewilderment about the direction of the narrative. You find yourself thinking, 'I don't know what might happen if they stay here, but if I take them somewhere else something's bound to come up, isn't it?'

Possibly. But not, I suspect, for me. It's not my style.

Some authors are telescope writers, constantly searching the distant horizon for fresh locations to inspire them, the linear narrative bumps you get when your protagonists are snatched from one world and placed in another. Telescope writers like rapid scene shifts, people getting on planes and trains, fetching up somewhere new and different where they're strangers in a strange land. They're excellent at chases that race across different landscapes, never standing still.

I've learned over the years I'm a microscope writer. I like looking at one small part of the world in very fine detail, then saying to my characters, 'This is your stage. Make the most of it because it's all you're going to have.' So when I set a book in Rome I deliberately fix on an area and lock the story pretty much to that place throughout. Most of the books happen in a neighbourhood you could walk around in an hour or so. They're Roman stories, but the canvas is much smaller than the sprawling, polyglot city that encloses them.

I like the fact that, in ten books or so, my people have only got on a plane once. Working this way forces me to draw on their characters and the developing story, nothing else. All gardeners know that some plants require feeding, and some do best if they're made to grow in stony, infertile soil. There's something of that in the storytelling process too. Try to work out which side of the fence is your natural territory.

Now to get a grip on some control.

BRING ON THOSE UNPLACED SCENES

Depending on where we do our outlining we now have an Unplaced Scenes folder or heading. In a book journal or a word processor your plan for the book would look something like this . . .

Part One

(now complete)

Part Two

Part Three

Unplaced Scenes

I would probably have populated that last heading with a few ideas already. By the time I'm a third of the way through this second act, it should be bursting with potential ideas. This folder or heading applies to the remainder of the book. Most of the possibilities I will place in there will affect the second act. Some will never be used at all. A few could find their way into the third act. I'm not worried about positioning at the moment. This is note-keeping and brainstorming pure and simple. Since it's in outline format it's easy to rearrange anything there and move it into the book itself just by dragging the entry to a new location.

All I'm concerned about is setting down some potential events that will drive this story forward to the moment where Charlie, at the close of the second act, sees a solution to the problems that have beset both him and Sally and, through his own interference, started to become progressively worse. Charlie, you see, isn't just the protagonist here. He's the catalyst too, and during the second act he will become increasingly aware of that fact. At first he will be driven by his desire to do the right thing. But after a while, as he matures, he'll come to understand that part of the wrong thing he wants to fix stems from his own meddling, his interest in Sally, his desire to be an adult, not a kid.

Some of the challenges ahead are so general I don't need to write them down. I know I have to expand on the characters of all the significant players – Charlie, Sally, Eric Whitby, Matt Giordano and Charlie's rather weak and probably untrustworthy father. Two characters will, I suspect, need particular attention. I need to develop Matt Giordano a lot more, since it's obvious he's the antagonist in this tale, the bad guy, the one who wishes Sally ill for some reason. He's the dragon that Charlie must slay in order to free her. I need to get inside his head and understand why he has turned out that way.

The other difficult player is Sally herself. At the moment she's somewhat slight, even unlikeable. She needs to find an individual voice, a sense of humour, a spark of indignant rage. Cold and unfriendly won't work. Spiky will. It's not enough that Charlie finds her very pretty. There has to be something else that makes him interested, some sharp, interesting aspect to her character that hasn't yet come across in what I have for the first act. When I understand how to achieve that change I will need to go back to the first act and start the process there. She needs some warmth early on, through characterisation – the way she speaks and behaves – not through direct events. I can't leave it till the second act. So a note will go into the 'to do' list in the book diary: make Sally more likeable early on.

It's clear too that the world they inhabit will have to become more vivid, a touch claustrophobic perhaps. It's a rundown, miserly place, one where they're all trapped. But it's Charlie's home and he's not the kind of fourteen-year-old who will easily take against somewhere he's known from birth, the only town with which he's familiar. He likes that cold sea and the way it enfolds him, pushes his limits, when he goes swimming.

He enjoys his pushbike and the biting breeze against his face. I need to bring out the architecture of the place too. It wasn't always dilapidated and grim. Some of the buildings are reminders of greater, glorious days, when England took to its own seaside and enriched those who owned the hotels and theatres they patronised during the summer. There's a lost world here and I need to find it. The key to understanding Matt Giordano – and through him the true nature of the problem – lies somewhere among the ghosts left behind by the death of that rich and elegant seaside resort from another era.

Plenty to work with there. What else do I need? Waypoints. All stories are a kind of journey. Sometimes it's a cerebral one, from ignorance to knowledge, adolescence to adulthood. Sometimes it's a literal voyage, starting at one geographical point and visiting several others on the way to the end of our quest. Whatever its nature, this journey will consist of sections and pauses, a continuous line of discrete events that come to form the shape of the narrative. In the first and third acts the journey is usually short and straight. In both we know where we're going and can't wait to get there. In the troublesome second act the storyline will meander constantly as our protagonist struggles to see clear day through the fog of possibilities surrounding him.

Let's try a different analogy. Imagine a book as an attempt to climb Everest. The first act is the march out of the foothills to the low mountain station where we'll pitch camp. When we get there we stare ahead and see a panorama of higher peaks calling for our attention as they lead further and further towards the final destination. The battle we now face is choosing the right course through that endless landscape and, if we make a wrong turn, spotting the error soon enough to correct it without endangering the entire expedition.

That 'Unplaced Scenes' folder is where we list our potential waypoints, in no particular order at this stage. The first will be obvious. A few will be speculative in the extreme. All will lead us on to that great peak in the sky. But it's best we don't spend too much time staring at that right now. We may have an idea what it looks like and what we can expect to find there but there are more immediate matters at hand.

Here are some possibilities for unplaced scenes in the story ahead:

➢ Charlie goes to the library to unravel the story of Eric Whitby and Matt Giordano.

➢ Charlie's father gets really scared about what's going on.

➢ The story of the pier is revealed – and the fact that Sally's mother disappeared in the blaze, just a few months after Sally was born.

➢ Eric Whitby shows Charlie more magic. He's entranced, and surprised that Sally can perform magic tricks she's learned too.

➢ Matt Giordano tries to force Sally to come with him again. He's her father, he says. He wants her to live with him in the one remaining big, posh mansion in the town.

➢ Charlie tries to kiss Sally. He's so bad she laughs at him, nicely, but not in a way that gives him much hope. This is unfortunate because he's becoming progressively more obsessed with her.

➢ After another confrontation Sally tells Charlie she thinks Giordano killed her mother that night when the pier burned down. Now he owns everything – but not her, much as he wants to compel her to live with him. Giordano doesn't like the idea there's something he can't possess.

➢ Charlie thinks there's more to Giordano's interest in Sally than this. He hears rumours about Giordano, and his obsession with children.

➢ Charlie tries to talk to his dad about Matt Giordano's past and what goes on in the big house where Giordano lives. His dad clams up.

➢ Charlie will discover that his trust in his father may be misplaced.

➢ Giordano *does* make Sally go with him into the big house. Charlie follows. There's another confrontation, a shocking one, that will trigger Charlie's determination to bring Giordano down.

➢ At the close of the act Charlie hits upon a plan to entrap Giordano and make him confess to killing Sally's mother.

The first three sound fine as openers for this section. Since this is a piece of fiction let me wave a magic wand and say: those scenes are done. The closing scene, vague as it is, looks right too.

Now what?

Now it's the second act. We go away and write, trying to sort those unplaced scenes into an order that makes sense and invent more so that we can uncover our narrative.

We are, before long, stuck. Becalmed in an empty grey ocean, racked with doubt, unable to decide whether what we've produced is good or bad. Don't fret. Every writer's been there. It's entirely natural to feel this way about your manuscript, especially at this stage.

I'll pick up Charlie's story at the end of this section. In the meantime let's think of a few tricks to put some wind back in those sails when you find yourself becalmed.

WHEN YOU'RE STUCK

Many things shoot down a book in the second act: a lack of self-confidence, too little time, poor advice from someone you've turned to for an opinion. Oh, and laziness too, or perhaps more accurately a dispiriting sense of fear over the size of the task ahead.

I told you not to look up at Everest, didn't I? This is a time to focus strictly on the waypoints, making sure you choose the right ones. The big peak will let you know when it needs your attention – probably sometime around the sixty- or seventy-thousand-word mark when you look up out of the blue and think: 'Oh, there it is.'

Don't forget one other lurking time bomb: perhaps this really is a bad idea, something best junked to make way for a project with more potential. I wrote one much-rejected book and started several others before I finally found a publisher for *Semana Santa*. There's no shame in deciding a project isn't worth pursuing, even though it seemed a good idea when you started it. The real pity is in pursuing a lost cause, whether it's a book that's turned up its toes halfway through or a finished manuscript that simply can't find a buyer. I've lost track of the number of would-be writers I've met who've produced one book that won't sell and then spent years rewriting, retitling and resubmitting the manuscript to a dwindling band of agents and publishers, all of whom know a dud when they see one.

Don't get sucked into this cycle. A turkey's still a turkey however much you try to pin peacock feathers to it. If the world says your work stinks the world is probably right. Kill the thing and start something else. Don't throw it away. You can always return for a second look later. Ditching ideas we at first thought exceptional is part of the experience of becoming a writer. Career authors obsess about many things but longevity is close to the top of the list. The heartless, ruthless abandonment of stories we once cherished is one way many of us stay published over the years.

Not that this is the biggest reason people give for giving up on a book project. Usually it's something else altogether . . .

THE PERVASIVE MYTH OF WRITER'S BLOCK

You never walk into a supermarket and have the person on the till say, 'Sorry, I can't serve you today. I've got checkout person's block.' Yet every day, every minute it seems, someone somewhere in the world dashes their hands to head and shrieks that the muse has mysteriously departed them.

At events I get asked all the time, 'What do you do when you get writer's block'? As if it's a given, we all suffer from this strange and perhaps mythical ailment. Do I? No. There are times when I struggle for something to write. That's not the same as being unable to work on a story at all. But the block thing is so commonly written about it must, in some sense anyway, be 'real', in the way Father Christmas and Bigfoot are deemed to exist too. I've even seen published writers bewailing their block in public, which is odd indeed. A word of advice: public bewailing by writers on any subject is best avoided, not least because we've got a very cushy job compared to many.

What should you do if you can't think of something to write? Anything but stare at the computer pleading for help. In case you haven't noticed, *it can't hear you.*

Take a break. Mow the lawn. Walk the dog. Learn to speak Croatian. Give your aching brain a rest from being banged against the narrative wall. Do that and my guess is the solution will one day leap into your head at the most unexpected of moments and you'll be kicking yourself over how obvious the solution sounds.

The 'I don't know what happens next' ailment is the easiest to deal with. It's like unblocking a drain. You just have to work to find where the obstruction is, then clear it. A more insidious kind of block is marked by a sudden collapse of confidence, a feeling that everything you've written so far may be inadequate or downright rubbish, coupled with a conviction that you have no way forward even though you may actually have a storyline written down somewhere that suggests otherwise.

Both are common signs of classic second-act angst. It can manifest itself over a simple mechanical turn in the story, but really that's a symptom, not the disease. When you reach this state everything is starting to become more metaphysical: what the hell is going on here and does anyone care? Seen objectively – which is usually pretty much impossible for those infected by this condition – the whole idea is clearly ridiculous. Books don't die halfway through; they get killed. By laziness, by ennui, by a lack of self-confidence, planning or care.

When people talk about block what they are often saying, it seems to me, is that they fail to have a direction for the story in question. They may have an end in mind. What they lack is a confident string of staging points. This is one reason why we're putting down some possibilities in that 'Unplaced Scenes' folder. Simply thinking about how you get from A to B is one way of loosening the jam. You could even write that future scene, or the climax of the book if you like, just to keep you going.

Yes, you did read that correctly. There is no law that says a narrative, even a fast-moving and linear one, needs to be written in the order in which it is to be read. If the next five scenes are hazy but the sixth is clear then go and write that. You'll probably have to change it by the time you fill in the missing steps to get there but so what? You'll be back in the game. There are even people who try and write the final scene of the story part way through, or even at the beginning. Not me, though I could imagine doing that for a short story. We're all different. If it works for you, use it.

Then there's the book diary. Always remember: this is one way you can work on your novel without having to write it. If you're keeping this, faithfully and lovingly, there may well be a note somewhere that fires an idea in your head. Even if there isn't, you can go over your thoughts about the work as it progressed and try to understand where things went awry. Was a story thread lost somewhere along the way? Did you deviate from your intended path? If so, how can you recover the original route?

Blocked writers need to be dragged away from staring at that blank last page in the manuscript. Reading and learning from your book diary is one place you can still stay connected to the project without being constantly reminded of your inability to hit the daily word-count target.

Another tactic. Make a backup copy of your book so far then take an axe to a second version and slash out everything you don't like. That's right. It's called editing. Cutting stuff is good for the authorial soul. It forces you to think about what's important and what's not. I once went to Italy with a 30,000-word manuscript and came back with it whittled down to 12,000, happy as could be. I told one of my author friends of my delight and she thought I'd gone mad. But that was progress. By pruning away the unnecessary I found what it was that I wanted to say.

Counting words is one thing. Counting words that matter is another. Cutting like crazy will also teach you one of the most important writing lessons there is. If you are blocked on some seemingly insurmountable problem on page 182 you can bet your last penny the problem, and its solution, actually lie way back in the history, probably around page 131. Tackle it there and you've a hope of finishing. Keep banging away at page 182 and you may well go mad.

Print out the pages so far and try and see them through the eyes of a reader. You'll be amazed, too, how things look when they're ink on paper, not dots on a screen. Moving from computer to a physical page will give you a fresh insight into the story and keep you engaged with it.

Ask yourself how it would look if it were written differently. What would it be like if you switched, say, from first person to third? If some of your characters were male instead of female, young instead of old, black instead of white? Dream a little, go off-piste.

Finally, use that outline function to the full. Drag some scenes around the timeline. What if this happened here instead of there? When authors wrote with pens and typewriters they would produce scenes and chapters in separate parts. They could play with the running order very easily – they just renumbered the page. It's even simpler on a computer – so experiment and try to work out how your story might change if the narrative were rearranged.

This kind of problem can affect writers at any stage in their career. There's a different kind of 'block' that's reserved for the start. I wrote my first two books, *Semana Santa* and *Epiphany*, in a whirl. The first took a whole summer, the second just six weeks to produce a 160,000-word draft. I was on a roll. After years dreaming of being an author I finally discovered I could produce a book. It was hard work – I was holding down a full-time job in journalism at the time too. But it was achievable.

Then came book three, the final one in my then contract. I sat down and I had absolutely no idea where to go. There wasn't a storyline. There wasn't even a frame of reference. I didn't know what kind of writer I was trying to be, what kind of book I was hoping to produce. The clash between journalism, which was paying the bills, and fiction, which I hoped would one day do so, was getting unbearable. I was working too hard at both. So I banged out something that was rough, misshapen, unpublishable, and got it thrown back at me. What was going on?

Something pretty much every author will encounter somewhere along his or her career once you begin to get published. Most writers spend years dreaming of finishing a book before they ever get to complete one. When you reach that milestone you think you're there. Truth: you're not. You've scarcely begun. The hardest part is still ahead because your first one, two or three books are works that have been sitting festering inside you for years, waiting to be vomited up into the world. The core material is there already. Once you find the gagging trick it will come out relatively easily. Then, after a while, there's nothing left inside. Suddenly you're dry-heaving and that's never going to be pleasant.

What happens at this point? Let's be honest: a lot of people give up. They find it too hard to get past that rock. They look at the meagre amounts of money they've made for all the work put in and wonder if it's really worthwhile having to start from a truly blank page.

Stubborn old sods like me persist (stubbornness is a key virtue for writers in case you hadn't guessed). I dragged myself out of that pit the hard way. I read the manuscript I'd produced, worked out that somewhere in it there was a kind of sci-fi thriller, then rewrote the whole thing several times until it resembled something like a conventional story. It came out as *Solstice*, did pretty well and got me published in the US for the first time.

If you hit that rock and want to get past it the only way is to grind your way through. Learn the basics of the craft, which probably escaped you in the mad rush to produce your first couple of books. Try to work out what kind of writer you are and how much that matches what kind of writer you want to be. Get your head down for the long term, because chances are it *will* be long – have you noticed how few of those authors who have big hits with books one or two are still getting published at all ten years later?

Make sure you keep the ideas tab in that book diary open. One day – and it may be years away – you could be very grateful for it.

KEEPING A PROJECT ALIVE

Lots of people struggle to find the time to write. I know because I've seen them in their thousands going on Facebook and Twitter to tell the world how very difficult it is.

My advice here is going to be brutally short. If you can't make the time to write a book then there's no point in trying. Writing is about commitment and hunger. It doesn't matter whether you're doing another job, engaged with a family, or have some other responsibility that takes up a chunk of the day. If you can't find the space to write, the book won't be finished.

When time is short – as it often is for all of us – what matters is that the work remains alive in your head, even, or perhaps especially, if you're not writing a word. We need ways to keep it bubbling away somewhere, getting richer, firing your imagination, gathering more possibilities that will draw you back to the page.

How do you maintain some life and enthusiasm in these circumstances? You keep it with you, always, like fluff in the pocket, something that never goes away. Serious writing must mean the dividing line between work and leisure is pretty much gone for ever. If you're not willing to accept that, give up now.

I take a little laptop wherever I go. I also have a note-taking application on my phone, a camera and, when things get desperate, pen and paper (though since I lose physical notepads all the time those definitely come last). When I see or think of something that's relevant to my current work I make a note about it there and then. No procrastination. No 'I'll do that later after I have lunch or mess around on the internet.'

I'm deeply lazy at heart. If I postpone things either they don't happen at all or turn into an afterthought that's nowhere near as complete as it was when the bright spark first lit up.

We have so many ways of setting down thoughts these days. Through a computer, a phone or just a simple voice note. By keeping that idea you do two useful things: preserve it for the future, and subtly remind yourself there's still a work in progress.

Budding authors come up with a million excuses why their books stay unfinished. No time, someone sick in the family, a crisis of confidence, problems at work, someone else's manuscript to read in the book group. But the biggest reason book projects die is a very simple one: people simply stop working on them.

Yet you can still keep that idea alive very easily, without writing a word, away from your desk, sitting on a bus or a plane. If the book means so little to you that it doesn't merit that amount of attention, do you really think it's going to work in the long run?

Here, though, is some good news.

YOU DON'T NEED TO WRITE EVERY DAY

I once heard a fellow author say out loud that a daily bout of writing is essential for anyone who wants to be an writer as if it were jogging or some other muscular exercise. If it works for you, fine. It doesn't work for me, or lots of other professional writers I know. Not only do I not have to write every day; I deliberately avoid doing so. This is a job, one I do five days a week, Monday to Friday, from around eight in the morning to six at night. Weekends are for other things. I need a break from the book. I want to go back to it on Monday morning feeling fresh and enthusiastic.

That's not to say I don't think about the manuscript at weekends, or do some other work then. Research, thinking, reading. But not writing. The Monday to Friday, morning to evening thing, is a habit I've got into over the years, and I happen to think that habits, when it comes to work, are very good ideas.

Are there exceptions? Rarely. When a book is approaching its conclusion I will sometimes work weekends because I can't drag myself away from the narrative. Equally when I'm on the road normal patterns go out of the window so every day becomes a potential work day. But even then I will always try to make sure there are days when I do not write. I like the idea of separation, of some temporary distance from those tens of thousands of words.

When I was running two careers – as a journalist and an author – I would sometimes set books to one side for two to three weeks because of newspaper assignments. At the beginning I worried about ever being able to pick them up again. In truth if the idea's strong enough, leaving it for a while poses no problem. Sometimes it improved the manuscript because I came back with better, fresher ideas.

Writers are all too often portrayed as dreamers staring into the distance, like our old chum Dante Alighieri, musing away on a hillside. But consider this: Dante was a trained pharmacist, a diplomat, a politician, a soldier. He read obsessively, in Italian and Latin, as you can tell from the obscure and scattergun references in his masterwork, *The Divine Comedy*. Would he recognise the standard portrait of him, as an aesthete whiling away a sunny afternoon with his head in the clouds? No. We all need thinking time. But without doing time it means nothing. Dante was too busy to spend much of his life staring into the distance.

Busy. A great word to describe what turns wannabe writers into actual ones. Here's another: *routine.* You don't have to write every day, but you do need to set aside some part of your life as time for writing.

Here is what routine means for me.

For almost the first ten years of my writing career I did two jobs – as a journalist for the *Sunday Times* and as a writer trying to produce one book a year. This isn't a situation I'd ever want to go back to. It was hard work, involving long hours, seven-day weeks and few holidays. But I had no choice. Writing novels didn't pay the bills. It was either two jobs, give up the dream of being an author, or starve.

Most people will try to start off this way. You'd have to be pretty brave or foolish to abandon the day job and declare to the world you're going to be a writer. Even if it works, you're probably looking at a couple of years before you see much income, so best make sure there's plenty of money in the bank. Let's assume you're like most writers and start your novel alongside another career. How do you make both work?

You need a routine and you need to stick to it. Mine worked like this. I angled my way into freelance journalism after a staff career on national newspapers. Freelancing meant I controlled my time, not someone else. After a while it resulted in a contract with the *Sunday Times* which meant I could rely on guaranteed income each month in return for a guaranteed amount of work.

Once I got into that position the division between books and journalism almost defined itself. When it comes to fiction I discovered I work best in the mornings. That's when the creative side of me is most alive. So I gave over mornings to the novels. In the afternoons I worked on journalism. Five days a week. Seven when necessary. It was difficult at first. After a while it became second nature.

It's important to integrate the job – or chore if you like – of writing fully into your life. To allow that part of the day or night or both will be given over to working on a novel and nothing is going to get in the way.

We're surrounded by so many distractions these days it's easy to lose sight of priorities. For the writer there's only one: keeping the work in progress alive and kicking, and growing organically a little each week. Anything that drags you away from that necessity is the enemy, a monster that can leave you a wannabe author for ever.

My distractions are different these days – emails from readers, events, promotions, interviews and the necessary task of communicating through the web. But they're still distractions that need to be contained, pushed always into parts of the day when I would never be writing on the book.

Here's my home routine, Monday to Friday, around eight a.m. to around six in the evening when I knock off.

➢ First hour of the day. Deal with overnight email, read newspapers, check the web.

➢ Around eight-thirty till twelve-thirty. First, read anything I wrote the day before, revise it, try to cut what's not needed and add in anything that should have been there but wasn't. This will usually take me to ten. Break for a coffee briefly. Come back and write, maybe a few hundred words, maybe more, until I feel the day's output has taken hold to the extent I know where it's headed. Take dog for a twenty-minute walk around eleven, then back to work. Around twelve-thirty break for lunch till two.

➢ Afternoon: two till six. Email again, though nothing substantial is written during this period except the book. Will be hoping to hit two thousand words if this is a writing phrase. Pleased if it gets to three thousand, which it does maybe one time in five. Always pack in at three thousand. Always end on a scene conclusion, not mid-scene if possible. I hate picking up unfinished threads the following day. At six, knock off and do nothing more on the book though I will come and check emails in the evening since they come in from all places and time zones.

➢ Weekends: be a normal human being mostly, but do the maintenance stuff – filing, websites, any boring work.

And that's it. The timing doesn't change much any more because, well, it works. This is my routine. Yours will be different. Find it, then stick to it.

Why are routines successful? Because once you find the one that works you no longer have to ask yourself, 'Shall I write?' You do it because that's the time of day you devote to your novel. Routines take away the conscious decision to write or not, and if you're as fundamentally lazy as I am that's a wonderful thing.

Did Dante have a routine? You bet. Just wish I knew what it was.

BEWARE OF BIG SECOND-ACT IDEAS

If you're keeping that book alive, it's inevitable that you will, before long, find a very bright light bulb going on in your head. You have an idea. Not a small, developmental one. A *big* idea. One so huge that it changes the nature of the project entirely, transforms it into something else.

It may not be much to write. Perhaps a morning's work at the most and your struggling narrative is set on a new track.

Here's the dilemma. Do you ... (a) step in straight away and commit that change to paper. Or (b) sit on it, think about the change for a while, then try it out tentatively another day?

Those of you who answered (b) go buy yourself a lollipop. The (a) people can stand in the corner and ask yourself: '*What have I done?*'

Trust me. I'm an airhead whose mind is constantly spinning with ideas, possibilities, changes, alternative versions. I have been through this quandary a million times. And if I've learned one thing over the years it's this: never, ever act on impulse.

First reason: you may just be plain wrong. Today's bright idea is tomorrow's 'How could I possibly be so stupid?' revelation. Impulsive notions always seem attractive when you have them. We're built that way. It's our brains rewarding themselves for being so clever in coming up with the idea in the first place. It doesn't mean they're right. And the worst thing of all is this: bright ideas invariably mean some substantial shift in the direction of a story which we'd hoped, only the day before, had been firmly set on track. A new facet to a character. A different way forward for a narrative thread or even the whole book. Commit that idea to words and you'll find you can rarely undo it just by taking out the bits you wrote after the idea hit. You'll usually have to unpick all the difficult threading that went before and was rewritten to make the genius notion feasible. This is rarely a good use of your precious time.

Second reason: bright ideas mid-story inevitably involve adding things. Making something longer and, yes, more complicated. As a general rule books are improved more by subtraction than addition.

When I have bright ideas I treat them like this. They go in my book diary immediately as a possibility. I sit on them for a day or two. Then I look at them in the cold, hard light of day with the slightly jaundiced eye a little time brings to that bright spark moment. If I'm really convinced they're worth trying, they go in. If I'm not sure, they either stay out or I save a copy of the draft as a backup and try a fresh version with the spark in to see if it works.

Bright ideas are great before writing and after you've finished. But when they crop up mid-book they need to be treated with caution because sooner or later you will hit that 'I know – the guy could be an alien zombie!' moment.

Best avoided, honestly.

UNDERWRITE, NOT OVERWRITE

I hope you spotted the good news in the preceding section. I was, believe it or not, encouraging you to do less work on your book, not more.

When I was starting out as a writer I felt that every word was precious. There seemed something magical and fragile about every paragraph. I was grateful they even appeared at all. That made me very reluctant to mess with them beyond rewriting, and incredibly loath to cut them out altogether. They did get excised in the end, of course. Those manuscripts went on to sell and when they met a publisher an editor turned round to me and said, 'This needs to come out.'

That doesn't happen so much these days because I write from an entirely different perspective. Instead of trying to put in everything I want in a first draft, I try very deliberately to leave things lean and spare. Physical descriptions, dialogue, action . . . the lot. I try to keep it shorn of detail as much as possible, instead of throwing in everything I have as I used to in the early days.

The main reason for this is practical. Putting things in is easy and more productive than taking things out. If you read your first draft and think, 'Hmm . . . I need to paint this character a bit more clearly,' you're engaging the creative right side of the brain and introducing, hopefully, some new texture into the project. If you spend your time hitting the delete key then . . . you're just cutting stuff. Slashing verbiage is a good idea but better still if the verbiage isn't there in the first place.

And here's the truth. Work this way and you will end up with a tighter book than if you overwrote and tried to slim it down afterwards. Honest. As a general rule every book out there is capable of being cut without suffering any harm. Underwriting is one way you can get closer to the goal of not a single wasted word.

There's also the issue of simple artistry. I'd rather spend the hours available to me on work that is creative and enriches the story, not ploughing through every paragraph thinking, 'We can do without that, do without that . . . '

Think about art. Painters don't produce a finished canvas and then start improving it by removing what they've just produced. They can't. So they work slowly, building up their vision first with pencil, then with a little ink, then, when they finally know what they're doing, coming up with a finished version.

In writing this is an imprecise process. There's always, always something that can be cut. But if you set out to underwrite you will spend less time slashing and more working on the parts that matter, putting some finesse on the bare bones that are already there.

Here's another argument for being spare with your prose. When your work reaches an editor, he or she will have important input for you, advice that should help you produce a better book in the end. Editors, like writers, have limited time. I want to hear from mine how I can improve the book I've given them. I'll get much better value from them if they're telling me I need a little extra here and there rather than listening to them list the bits that ought to be removed.

Underwriting should get you much better advice from an editor. Overwriting simply burdens them with needless hours spent wielding a red pen.

AVOIDING PEER PRESSURE

When I wrote my first real book, *Semana Santa*, I did so in secret. Told no one – no friends, no colleagues, not even my wife. This was primarily because I didn't want to admit to anyone it had failed, as fail it must because every other attempt I'd made at writing a novel wound up that way.

Today not much has changed. When I'm working on a book it's just me in there. I rarely show part-finished work to anyone. I don't see the point. I'd never try to sell a book on the basis of an opening few chapters. Seems a bit odd to me. How does anyone know you're going to finish it?

More than anything I do not seek opinions until there's an actual manuscript, beginning to end, to be read. Lots of professional writers I know work this way. Probably most. Lots of people who want to be writers don't. They constantly share scraps of work with each other in writing groups or informally. Is this a good idea? Or is it a way never to finish a book?

It depends, of course. I've never been part of a writing group. I've never attended a writing school except to teach. To my mind everything you need to know about the craft of writing is out there already, freely available in a very obvious format. It's called 'books'.

I learned to write by reading them. Yes, I've picked up ideas along the way listening to other writers talk about their working methods at public events. But I've never set out to 'learn' writing, or to seek assurance from others, part way through a work, that I'm not barking up the wrong tree.

Yet writing groups abound. Sometimes they produce authors who go on to greater things. Sometimes they simply seem to involve an endless round of work for enthusiastic novices, many of whom never quite get round to finishing their novel. You write a chapter, hand it to twelve people to read – then, while waiting for their opinions on your work, read their draft in return. I find the whole idea baffling. It's difficult enough for me to hold one book project of my own in my head at one time. Writing group members seem to attempt to stay on top of multiple nascent manuscripts by different authors, often in a range of styles, and get on with their own stories too.

It's not all bad news. One of the great benefits of writing groups is the companionship they provide and the discussion that takes place about style, working methods, tactics and the rest. They obviously provide support and confidence, and I'm sure that if you have someone on board who is a professional author, able to give you the benefit of their experience, that can be useful for insights and tips.

My principal misgiving is a practical one: what most budding authors lack more than anything is time. Writing groups can, if you're not careful, devour that in spades. If they overload you with so much reading that it interferes with your own writing, they're counter-productive. And – sorry, I have to say this – you have to weigh up what those mutual opinions are worth. This is a bunch of people who usually haven't made it as writers yet and probably don't even work in publishing.

Why is their view on where you've succeeded or failed relevant? How do you know if they're right or wrong? Even professionals in this business – seasoned writers, agents and editors – disagree over what constitutes a worthwhile book. If they can't manage a consensus, what real value can you place on the views of people who are still looking to be published themselves?

If you're in a writing group do ask yourself occasionally: is this helping me finish my book? Or would the time I'm spending going to meetings and reading other people's work perhaps be better spent working on my own instead?

Like it or not, the business of writing is essentially solitary: it's between you and those words on the page. Best get them down first then invite the world in to see what it thinks.

TREAT THOSE WORD COUNTS CAUTIOUSLY

There's a little fairy tale that runs through the head of every budding author when they start writing. It runs something like this . . .

A book is one hundred thousand words. I can write two thousand words a day and work five days a week. That means ten thousand words a week. In ten weeks I have a finished novel. Yippee!

Yes, we've all been there. You don't honestly think it's as simple as that, do you?

We all want to know how well we're doing, whether we're writing a book, working on a painting or just doing the day job. The question, always, is how do you measure that? Particularly with something as oddly intangible as a novel.

The blunt way is that daily word count. Hit your target and you're bound to get there in the end, aren't you?

No, not really. Word counts are useful because books are finite objects. They will run to a certain length – in my case usually between 105,000 and 125,000 words – and must do their job within that span otherwise something has gone wrong. Any way you look at it you need to monitor the extent of a book and its individual components – scenes, sections, parts.

Let me repeat myself because this is an important point. Books aren't simply written. They're *created*. Writing means putting words on paper. Creating entails building a story and polishing it to something hopefully approaching perfection. Cutting five thousand unnecessary words from a draft manuscript is a creative act. Writing five thousand wrong ones isn't.

A blunt word count will whine that the former is a backward move and the latter a successful one. This is the first step towards self-deceit, a trait the author above all people must avoid since you are your first reader and editor, two jobs that demand frankness above all else. Daily word counts in particular can be highly deceptive. That number is useful but not vital, and certainly not an infallible indicator of how a project is proceeding.

Instead of obsessing about word counts you might want to try basing your writing habits around scenes. I find it difficult to leave a scene in mid-air at the end of the day, whether I'm writing or editing. Generally speaking, my scenes run anywhere between 800 and 2,500 words. So I'll tend to crack on until that scene is finished, or left with sufficient notes to complete the following day.

Yes, I keep an eye on the scene word count. But that's mainly to check it's the right length for the book, not to convince myself I'm getting some work done. I generally set a 1,500-word median length for the average scene (or chunk of scene). I want to know I'm not going too much above that or below it (usually the former) too often.

Possessing some idea of a project's direction and eventual conclusion is much more important than counting the number of words you're typing. Change your measure of productivity from words to an assessment of scenes and you will get a more accurate measure of how well the book is progressing.

SMALL CHANGES, BIG DIFFERENCE

Here's a familiar situation. You've got a few sequenced scenes leading to some pivotal event, say the close of this second act. The content works fine. The people are right. So are their actions. But there's something not quite there. An indefinable element is missing. The manuscript needs more work before you can go on. What do you do?

The temptation is always: something big – introduce a new character, rewrite an existing one to be someone else, scheme in a new key event that will reshape the narrative.

All of these actions can work, and may be necessary. But before you embark on what is, inevitably, going to be an enormous amount of work, possibly derailing the original concept for the book, ask yourself this: isn't there an easier, *smaller* way?

Stories are delicate, complex constructions. Chaos theory applies to them just as much as it does to ecosystems. A tiny shift in something in one place can occasionally have a direct and welcome effect elsewhere.

Here's an example. During the writing of my last book I hit just such a problem. The scene in question took place during the morning, directly after a pivotal event in the previous chapter.

When I thought about it I realised there was nothing wrong with either scene in principle. What drained them of their effect was something very simple: the time of day. So I fiddled with the timeline to make them occur at night. This made the drama more atmospheric and better suited to the kind of section denouement I had in mind.

Moving those events by just eight hours also left space for a brief scene at the front of the next section that served a few useful purposes. It allowed me to feed in some essential information for the narrative. It also acted as a buffer to the rhythm. The previous scene ended at quite a pace. Some writers try for a constant beat. I like variation. This was the ideal way to get a reflective pause in before the next rush of adrenaline.

The whole change entailed little more than one morning of rewriting. Small changes, big effect. Remember the mantra: there's no way to make writing easier, but you can make it less difficult. Look for simple, easy solutions to narrative problems before you embark on long, complex and possibly dangerous ones instead.

OVERCOMING THE SECOND-ACT DEMONS

A series of compelling events, revelation of character, place and the gradual unfolding of the mystery that will lie at the heart of the story – that's what I would be looking for from this second phase of the book. Success will demand that you overcome some classic second-act demons such as story drift, lack of confidence and a growing awareness of the size of the task you've undertaken. That's why I've tried to focus on stratagems and ploys to get you out of the hell of this stage of the story. Most of us need a little help at this point in the game.

After a few stabs I've worked out what I think is going to happen to our cast of characters as they progress through this section of the narrative. The second act began with Charlie taking on the job of finding and fixing the dark mystery surrounding Sally, his 'mermaid'. It progresses as our protagonist searches his world for a solution. It ends when he thinks he's found it.

SECOND-ACT SYNOPSIS

Charlie sets out to unravel the story of the pier, of Sally, Eric Whitby and Matt Giordano. He tries to talk to his father who gets even more scared at the mention of Giordano. So Charlie goes down the library and pulls out old newspapers. It's all there. Sixteen years earlier the pier burned down in mysterious circumstances. One body, that of a man, a pier musician, was found. Nothing more. Whitby and Giordano were the two big acts that year, popular performers with their own TV show for children. They never worked together again. Sally's mother, who had a baby the paper says, disappeared in the blaze, which started in the theatre just after a performance. She was a bathing beauty, winner of a number of diving medals and – Charlie shivers when he reads this – nicknamed 'The Mermaid'.

Charlie reads on. Eric Whitby's career enters free fall afterwards. Matt Giordano leaves show business and begins to buy up hotels, restaurants and pubs, houses and shopping arcades as they come on the market at rock-bottom prices when the seaside resort economy collapses. Eventually he even buys the pier. Charlie begins to understand why his dad is scared. This is Matt Giordano's town now. He lives in the biggest house, a sprawling mansion in a park at the edge, once a kind of stately home. Charlie starts to see things differently, not as a schoolkid any more. He's aware he's growing up and he's not sure what he thinks of the process.

He goes back to the swimming pool repeatedly, trying to get to know Sally better, trying to get out of her what she was doing in the dark water beneath the pier that night. She doesn't say, but she doesn't put him off. One time, very awkwardly, he tries to kiss her. She laughs and pushes him away. The idea's too ridiculous. After this light moment the black car emerges and Matt Giordano orders her to get inside. Charlie stands in the way, though it's difficult. 'The Man Who Can Make You Do Anything'. Giordano, a big brute, full of power, leans down, extends his black leather fist and asks: does Charlie want more trouble with his dad?

No, Charlie says. I want more trouble with *you*.

Giordano laughs him off, as Sally did when he tried to kiss her. Then he turns on Sally and says: 'I am your father and you'll do as you're told.'

She's in tears, Charlie tries to stop her. But she runs away, with Giordano trying to follow. Charlie loses them both but thinks Sally escaped.

He goes to Giordano's mansion, breaks a window and gets inside. It's a creepy place, full of old show-business memorabilia. And photos everywhere of the three of them – Eric Whitby, Matt Giordano and Sally's mother. Smiling in that artificial way show-business people smile. In strange clothes. Sally's mother almost naked in some of them. Charlie walks around the place, horrified as he comes upon photos of Sally, some clearly taken surreptitiously, some at the pool, in her bathing suit. Prurient, nasty photos. He hears Giordano coming back, then starting to rage like a madman around the vast empty mansion. Sally did escape him.

Charlie manages to get out through a window. He goes to see Eric Whitby and demands the truth. About how Eric and Giordano were partners, but Giordano cheated on him in so many ways: with money, and by pestering Eric's daughter, Sally's mother, constantly. Then, that night on the pier.

What happened? Charlie asks. Eric says he doesn't know. There'd been a row between him and Giordano. Sally's mum was staying with Eric. She wouldn't live with Giordano. She'd come to hate him but money meant they had to work together. She stayed behind to clear up in the theatre. The place burned down. She was a good, strong swimmer. Everyone assumed she could have escaped by jumping into the sea after the boardwalk collapsed. But she was never seen again. Sally took after her in many ways: pretty, headstrong, loving the water. Eric is aware that Giordano's been telling her he's her father. She still wouldn't go to live with him, even though he has so much money. She was the last part of the town Giordano couldn't buy, and the part he valued most.

Charlie tells him what's just happened. About Giordano following Sally around. About how she walked into the sea looking suicidal, and how she's run away. And about what he found in the house: the photos, the obsessive ranting of Giordano, crying out for Sally.

Eric takes a deep breath: he knows he's got to do something and regrets he didn't face up to this years ago. He treats Charlie like a child, says thanks and tells him to go home, a grown-up will deal with it. Charlie bridles at that and insists he *is* a grown-up. This is a big moment for them both. Charlie's fed up with being treated like a kid – by his own father, by Sally, by Giordano. He's also aware he's responsible for making a bad situation worse, and feels guilty about that.

Eric looks at him and sees something the others don't. Then he tells Charlie that what he's about to hear now is a secret between them. Sally doesn't know and mustn't. Matt Giordano isn't her father after all, and Giordano knows it. Sally's mother was two-timing Giordano, having an affair with another man at the time, a musician in the band. A bad man, like Giordano. Sally's mother had a liking for bad men, which is something Eric would rather keep from his troubled granddaughter. Giordano knew about the affair, knew she was someone else's child, and that made his possessiveness all the worse.

Eric thinks that her mother and Giordano had a row at the end of the pier, with the musician too. 'Did he kill them both?' Charlie asks. Eric just says it was the musician whose body was found. He was a rough, unreliable type. A few thought *he* was to blame for the fire.

'We have to do something,' Charlie insists. 'I will,' Eric Whitby promises. He thinks he knows where Sally is. He says he'll find her, then confront Giordano and tell them this has to stop or the police will become involved. 'My dad's a good man,' Charlie tells him. 'Scared of Giordano like everyone else in town, but not the kind who'd stand by and allow something wicked to happen.' Whitby smiles and says, 'Best leave the police out of this, Charlie.' It's as if he knows something.

The next morning Charlie wakes up to the news that Eric's house has burned down. Charlie races round there on his bike. His father is there with the fire officers. Eric's dead. Sally is distraught outside the house. Matt Giordano is with her. In the brief time they're allowed to talk she tells him, not looking in his eyes, that she spent the previous night in Giordano's mansion. He caught her in the end. Now he looks as if he owns her – and she's nowhere else to go.

Charlie is convinced the fire was started deliberately, just like the one on the pier. Giordano has murdered Sally's grandfather, as he murdered her mother and her lover.

Later, at home, Charlie takes his dad to one side and tells him everything he knows. He appeals to him: you're a policeman. This is *wrong*. Even if Giordano does own everything he doesn't own the law, does he?

His father's torn. Scared. But appalled too. We can trap him, Charlie says, making this all up. We can make him confess, he says.

How? his father asks. He's Matt Giordano. This is his town. I know how, Charlie insists. His father listens and agrees. A trap will be set.

In the dead of night Charlie rides out on his bike, posts a note through Giordano's door, rings the bell then rides away.

THE THIRD ACT – THAT'S ALL FOLKS

Congratulations. You're now in the final strait. If the preceding acts have gone to plan you have the end of the tale in sight and can't wait to race to the finish. It's pleasurable watching a story take shape. It's a relief to negotiate the stormy waters of the second act. Finding that finished book in your hand is a moment of deserved pride. But you know what? Nothing, absolutely nothing, beats finishing the damned thing.

The third act is the section that begins when your protagonist believes he sees a resolution to the problem that lies at the heart of the book. It ends, naturally, at the close of the book. This is often a fairly short section, as was the first act. The act structure is sometimes summarised this way:

➢ First act: cat runs up tree.

➢ Second act: protagonist throws stones at cat in effort to get it down.

➢ Third act: cat falls.

This part of a conventional story should feel confident and fluent. By this stage we know – or think we do – where we're headed. The race is on to get there. Do books fail in the third act? Of course – they can fail anywhere. But most books expire in the first and second acts. Many die at the beginning because they carry insufficient weight and conviction. Even more fall apart in the second act when they drift off course and lose momentum.

Provided the preceding story elements are in place, the principal problems with the third act are likely to be quite basic. Instead of worrying about structural issues you should be able to focus on delivering what the reader expects: a satisfactory conclusion. And that, in itself, is a contradictory exercise because if you give them the ending they want, they'll turn around and say, 'I saw that coming.'

The third act is an exercise in balance – between speed and exposition, between delivering some unforeseen bombshell and confirming the reader's expectations. It can make or break the book with just a few well-timed or misplaced paragraphs. You are on that last knife-edge walk to the summit of Everest. It's not a long way and you can see the peak very clearly. But there's an abyss on either side.

Here's a suggestion.

TAKE A BREAK

Usually if you're bursting to write something it's worth sitting down and getting it out of your system. There's a cathartic element to writing. Sometimes ideas are best expelled. The third act works that way occasionally. If you have the time and the patience, though, I'd sit back from the project at this point. You've been through a lot to get here. You deserve some respite from hammering the keyboard.

As always, the story won't disappear in your absence. If you're lucky it will get richer and deeper, for which your readers would thank you if only they knew. At this stage of the game we're dealing with small yet crucial elements. The last 5 per cent you add to a book's character and texture can turn a middling project into an exceptional one. Given the labour you've put in to get this far, there really is no point in dashing to the end, however tempting that may sound.

I will often set a project to one side for a week or two and do something else. The story is always working away in my imagination and from time to time I may return to the computer to make some notes or check something. At some stage I'll usually print out the draft so far and read it on paper. As we'll discuss further when we come to revision, everything will look different when we see it this way. I'll also make several very careful passes through my book journal, noting what points I took up along the way, what I rejected and asking myself how wise some of those decisions were.

When I sit down to start work on writing this closing section of the story I want to know that everything leading up to it is in as good an order as I can make it. Minor tweaks will always be possible later, but I don't want major, structural blips at this stage. They will dislodge the direction and momentum of the third act, and by doing so damage the entire book. I do not want to be midway through the denouement only to find myself dogged by some nagging worry that an element a few hundred pages back will derail the whole exercise.

There's no rush here. You've waited years to write this book. If it works it will still be years before it appears. A week or two of reflection costs nothing, and can add greatly to the final manuscript.

WRITING LIKE THE WIND

When you do reach for the keyboard, things are likely to happen very quickly. In my last book my normal daily target was 1,500 words. In the final week of writing I produced 15,000 words in three days. I knew every step that would be taken towards the end. I could scarcely wait to get there.

Should you be worried when writing becomes this easy?

No. You should be thankful. Work that comes this easily is often better than work you have to slave over. But you do have to keep an eye on writing produced at speed. Here are some of the problems to look out for.

Literals and typos

When writing quickly you're setting down the words as they form in your head. They may be right in your head, but wrong when they pass through your fumbling fingers. All work needs reading carefully. Passages that have been written quickly deserve proofing with special attention. Spellcheckers are useful up to a point, but they won't pick up issues of sense. Take extra care to read the previous session's work before starting a new one.

Deviations from the script

Speed can mean stray ideas keep popping into your head. Treat them with even more caution than they received in the second act. If your third act is still loose and open in some respects, they may work. But if you set out with a plan and decide to divert from it halfway through because the idea just seems too good to ignore you may be setting yourself up for a logistical fall.

Missed opportunities

I'm a great believer in squeezing scenes for all they're worth (in moderation, if that makes sense). When you're writing quickly that doesn't always happen. Simple example: in the last book I had a key climactic scene which happens in an unusual Venetian location. In the first, rapid-fire draft this was on ground level in a deserted little square near the Rialto in the dead of night. Fine, but looking at it, and reading the first effort through, it was immediately obvious how much more resonant this scene would be if it took place in an underground room – a basement, a cellar, somewhere out of the way and hidden from view. Had I been writing at a more considered pace I would have seen this immediately. Hammering away to get to the end, that possibility escaped me.

Writing quickly is good. But never forget books consist of nothing more than text. Architects have to tear down walls to correct their mistakes. Film directors have to reshoot or recut scenes. All we need do is find new words at no cost to anyone but ourselves.

So keep your eye on them, especially when they're flowing.

ADJUSTING THE RHYTHM

Another issue with that race to the finish is pace. We want it, of course. But do we want nothing *but* pace? The third act is our readers' reward for sticking with the book. If it's just one quick, straight dash to the finish might it not appear a touch mechanical and cheat them of a little depth along the way?

Shakespeare had some interesting ideas on this subject. In *Macbeth* he has our eponymous villain murder the rightful king, Duncan, offstage in a bid to usurp his throne. Pretty soon both Macbeth and his evil wife are wandering, deed done, trying to wash the monarch's blood from their hands. The audience knows we're heading for a key moment in the play: the announcement of Duncan's death.

Does Shakespeare go straight to this climactic moment? Not a bit of it. Duncan's murder is 'discovered' and unconvincingly blamed on some servants Macbeth then happened to kill, supposedly out of fury at their deed. But the scene in which the unwinding of Macbeth's bloody plot commences actually starts with a ribald, knockabout comedy act. The castle porter opens the door to Macduff and Lennox, two thanes who will eventually bring vengeance down on Macbeth, and embarks upon a cheeky riff about the effects of strong drink:

> . . . nose-painting, sleep, and urine. Lechery, sir, it provokes, and unprovokes; it provokes the desire, but it takes away the performance: therefore, much drink may be said to be an equivocator with lechery: it makes him, and it mars him; it sets him on, and it takes him off; it persuades him, and disheartens him; makes him stand to, and not stand to; in conclusion, equivocates him in a sleep, and, giving him the lie, leaves him.

What's going on here? We're aware Duncan's dead even if Macduff and Lennox aren't. We know all hell is about to break loose. The two perpetrators have just been waving their bloodied hands around like lunatics, which doesn't bode well for a convincing performance of grief. And Shakespeare's got a minor character performing a dubious nightclub routine with a couple of important players, one of whom is due to behead Macbeth at the conclusion of the play.

In a word: tension. Instead of taking us straight to the place we expected – the bloody murder scene – Shakespeare teases us with the last thing we'd expect, a brief moment of rude comedy. He's playing with the rhythm of the piece, slackening the pace for a moment in the sure knowledge that we'll sit up on our seats even more as a result, wondering what black deed is round the corner.

Not all stories can play this trick. If you're writing a very direct, fast-moving linear tale, some diversion is probably the last thing you need. Nor is ribald comedy a device most modern writers would use. There are plenty of alternatives. A row among the cops before they go in to make an arrest. Some unforeseen interruption in the narrative – traffic, weather, the intrusion of a world that is utterly unaware of the drama taking place within it. Sudden, swift changes in point of view can jolt the pace in a way that will leave the reader nervy and on edge. So can flashbacks revealing key plot elements that might otherwise have been handled in a more conventional form of explication.

It's important to realise, however, that ploys like this must be used sparingly. Shakespeare lingers with his hungover porter for little more than a minute before Macduff drags us back into the drama with the line, 'Is thy master stirring?'

A minor diversion can have the unexpected effect of drawing the reader into the story more closely. The danger is that, if you dwell too long on your cleverness, you may make them think, 'What on earth's going on here?' Brevity, please.

IN SEARCH OF A CONCLUSION

It's axiomatic in this business that some people will find your ending unsatisfactory. If you're beastly to your protagonist and leave him in a hole a few will accuse you of cruelty. If you let him win the day unreservedly others will say you lack the godlike impersonal distance all writers should feel towards their creations.

You can't win with everyone, though you can try to comfort yourself with the idea, 'They're just mad at me for bringing their much-loved story to an end.' Perhaps. The plain truth is there's no perfect, universal way to close a book. Two complaints are particularly common. Someone will say, 'I saw it coming .' Or 'Nice book but the ending is unbelievable.' Let's deal with the first one.

Is it really a complaint? Not always. Some readers see books as puzzles to unravel. They're familiar with their genre and understand its conventions. They may *want* to be able to see the ending, and be made to work their way through the maze of possibilities you've presented in order to find the right solution. They won't like it if the puzzle is too easy or the riddle too cryptic. But they won't mind so much if they get the right answer. It may even make the book better for them. This applies particularly to the procedural form of classic 'whodunit' crime story which sets up five or six possible culprits and, after many twists and turns, unveils one as the bad guy. If your reader can spot the right one that reaffirms how smart they are. If they don't you're in danger of meeting that second objection, 'It's unbelievable.'

Both these comments relate to the way an author manages the expectations of his readers. We focus constantly on how to bring some element of surprise into our work – and rightly so. It's less often appreciated that a smidgen of predictability is essential in popular fiction too.

Think of the basic three-act structure – setup, pursuit, denouement – as a silent conspiracy between storytellers and their audience, entered into a couple of millennia or more ago when Homer was touting his tales around the eastern Mediterranean. Readers begin a story with a clear idea of the kind of journey they've embarked upon. They want to be entertained and have some twists, thrills and shocks along the way. But much of what they encounter will be expected. A horror story will entail terror, a ghost story a ghost. Crime books invariably entail a hunt for the perpetrator of a misdeed.

Popular fiction is, in many ways, an improvisation on a set, classic theme. Originality matters, but it's not open-ended. The context of the tale is important to readers because it defines the landscape through which the story is supposed to take place. When they say 'This ending is unbelievable' what they usually mean is they feel an author has broken that context or extended it beyond limits they find acceptable. You can't lead your audience down a path they think they understand and then, at the very end, remove the veneer of your fictional world and reveal that – aha! – it was actually something else all along.

Take *Charlie and the Mermaid*. Can I close out the book with Matt Giordano whipping off his human head and revealing that he's actually an alien/vampire/Arcturus Sprout, Beelzebub's chosen lieutenant in the Seventh Circle of Hell?

Of course not. I exaggerate a touch. Among the seven billion or so people currently alive on the planet as I write this sentence there may be one out there who could pull off a trick like that. Best work on the assumption it's not you. Most of us should work within accepted limits and try to make something unique and original inside those boundaries. No one wants the old clichés but they will love you to bits if you can provide them with a few new ones.

If aliens or vampires or demons had a place in this tale they should have made their presence known earlier. It's all very well to end a story with an unexpected twist – but not one that turns everything that's gone before completely on its head. Authors sometimes try too hard to find an ending they regard as inventive. Most crime stories end with the bad guy getting his comeuppance in some fashion, and the mending of that tear in the fabric of the universe. It's fine to close a story in this field with failure too – the criminal escaping, the wrong one going to jail. In truth, though, all the reader expects at the end of a story is some sense of finality. A feeling that the wound in the world has healed a little, perhaps not perfectly or for long, but at least for a while.

It's also worth pointing out something that's rarely conceded, by authors or readers: endings are important but they're not a make-or-break factor. Books are judged in their entirety, not on their finales. Sometimes those last few pages will disappoint, but not enough to spoil your overall enjoyment of the story. Try for the best ending you can, one that surprises, if that's what you want, but doesn't generate a groan. And be aware that someone, somewhere will always find it wanting, whatever you write.

MORE SERIES CONSIDERATIONS

If you hope your book is going to be the start of a long-running series you need to give a little extra thought to its conclusion. The story must come to an end, but you have to leave some element of its characters sufficiently unresolved that readers (and publishers) will want to know more.

You can try that old stalwart the cliff-hanger, but if you do you must accept it will be at least a year, and possibly more, before the reader gets the next episode – which you still have to write. Will they remember enough detail of what went before to allow for any direct, linear connection between one book and the next? Possibly. But even so, if your series works, before long much of your audience will be reading it out of sequence.

Unless you are writing a very specific, sequenced series, tying the end of one book to the beginning of the next will make no sense whatsoever for someone picking up something mid-series. Readers hate to feel they're being denied knowledge they need in order to understand the present book. They think they should have everything they need in the title they just bought – and they're right.

It's much easier to look to a more general and subtle sense of unresolved issues. It might be an awkward 'will they, won't they?' relationship between two characters. In a cop drama it could be the growing realisation on the part of those involved that, though they may have fixed one tear in the universe, there are a lot more out there waiting for them than they realised. What you ought to avoid is specifying what exactly that next tear will be. A weekly TV series can try to do that; an annual book will struggle to maintain the continuity.

If you're writing a series and produce on time publishers will have the opportunity to insert these come-ons more effectively for you by printing the first chapter of your forthcoming hardback in the paperback of your previous book. That's their job, not yours. Write the book you want – not one you think the 'market' needs.

Some stories simply don't lend themselves to a series. *Charlie and the Mermaid*, the way it's developing for me, is one of them. This is a coming-of-age tale, about Charlie's brave and painful entry into adulthood. Once he's crossed that threshold he'll be rather less interesting, I suspect. You could return to the scene for another look at these characters a year or two on. But I'd rather deal with them here and then go on to something else. There's a lot to be said for that old show-business saw, 'Always leave them wanting more.'

Had the story taken on a different character there could have been a series here. Imagine the young adult thriller scenario. Charlie finds himself in the midst of a bunch of spies and turns out to be so good at the job they recruit him at the end of the book. The fantasy idea could spark a quest which, once Charlie and Sally complete it, only reveals a larger, deeper mission. The possibility of a series, then, lies in the nature of the book as much as in the characters that populate it.

Some writers hate the idea of writing a series, of course. If you're one of them there's a simple way to try to avoid being pushed into that episodic corner: kill your protagonist in the final scene. The trouble is publishers are smart and persuasive people. If you do that and they still think there's a series you're likely to get a contract tempting you to dig him out of the ground and rewrite that ending so that he lives, poised to enter the second book firing on all cylinders.

You will, of course, bite off their hands with gratitude.

ANSWERS THAT CONVINCE

We've established that popular storytelling revolves around a pressing problem of some kind. The answer to a problem is usually a solution, something that closes the door on what went before. An answer, as firm and unequivocal as a mathematical sum – one plus one equals two.

But this is fiction, not algebra. Are we really looking for something quite as certain as that? In some kinds of books – stories for small children, for example – we might expect a closing line indicating that everyone lived happily ever after. Most fiction inhabits a world that's a touch more realistic and grey. We may dream that our problems will one day be solved. The adult realist in our heads tells us it's more likely they will be *re*solved, in other words brought to a conclusion but not necessarily the one we'd prefer.

Murderers get caught if we're lucky, but that doesn't help their victims. Damaged relationships can be healed, but there are usually a few scars left behind. Happily-ever-after sounds attractive as a concept. It carries an inherent idea of justice, of symmetry, of good triumphing over evil, right over wrong. In execution this can be difficult to carry off with any great conviction. Resolutions tend to be more like the world we know: asymmetrical, awkward, incomplete and occasionally unjust.

Fifty or a hundred years ago it was acceptable to produce a popular tale that defied conventional resolution altogether and dared the audience to interpret it. Think of Hitchcock's movie *Vertigo*, made in 1957 and often acclaimed as one of the finest pieces of cinema ever made. It reaches a tragic and heartbreaking close as Scottie, the detective, sees the woman he seems to love fall to her death.

But nothing's quite as simple as that. Hitchcock leaves the storyline open to interpretation in several different places. How morally culpable is Scottie in his obsession? How guilty is the woman who pretended to be Madeleine Elster? He never tells us. We, the audience, are left to decide. Logically, seen as a procedural crime story, *Vertigo* scarcely makes sense at all. Yet it's a wonderful movie precisely because it leaves several key questions unresolved and challenges us to fill in the gaps.

Twenty-first-century popular fiction can, on occasion, be less than tolerant of this open-ended approach to the conclusion of a narrative. There's a feeling that every question raised in a story must, at some point, be answered. You need to strike a balance here. If your narrative entails key 'who did what and when?' questions as it progresses then the answers will need to be injected into the narrative at some stage. That doesn't mean there isn't room for doubt in modern storytelling. You may not be allowed to be as free with the exposition of your tale as Hitchcock was with *Vertigo*. But you don't need to explain every last motive, every decision or statement a character has made throughout the book.

We're back to algebra here. It's not the same as storytelling. There's one very good reason you should be wary of an ending that boasts, 'And now all is revealed.' Exposition of this nature can come across as very artificial indeed. The most primitive form of all is to lay out the plot flatly at the conclusion, in a series of exchanges between the characters who retell the 'truth' of the tale, ostensibly for one another, in fact for the reader. It's a bit like an extended, concluding version of the 'exposition in dialogue' problem we discussed earlier. This kind of thing:

> Charlie listened to his father, amazed. 'You mean you've been following Matt Giordano all along, Dad? And I never knew?'
>
> 'That's right. Ever since Giordano started going back into that pier I knew he was a bad 'un. I've been tailing him for a week, day and night.'
>
> 'So the mystery man I saw down by the beach? The one I told you about? It was you?'
>
> 'Correct. Why do you think I came on that scooter? I couldn't let you see the car. You'd know.'
>
> 'And that poster I saw?' Charlie asked. 'The one with Mr Whitby?'
>
> 'I made sure you wouldn't miss that one. I knew you wouldn't be able to keep quiet about it. Once you'd told Giordano we had him.'

Artificial, forced and wrong. I repeat: you can't put big chunks of exposition into the mouths of your characters in some quick wrap-up section like this and expect readers to believe it. Stories need to be revealed through action, behaviour and character, all the more so at the end.

That doesn't mean you can't have conversations between characters in which answers appear. In the instance above we could cut the revelation down to a single fact and make it appear in Charlie's head as a sudden epiphany.

> Charlie remembered that pitch-black evening on the beach, the faceless man sneaking off beneath the pier as if he had something to hide. Things were starting to fall into place.
>
> 'That was you the other night, wasn't it?' he said. 'Not Giordano at all. You breaking into the pier?'

'Maybe,' his father muttered.

'You ought to tell me why, Dad. I've got a right to know.'

Written like this, the exchange has conflict, which is a good and gripping element in any narrative. More important, Charlie becomes an inquisitor, someone who's genuinely curious about the truth through his own character, not as some proxy device for the reader, there simply to generate the necessary explanations required for the plot.

Avoid disgorging your mysteries all in one go, ticking off the answers like some pub quizmaster. Spin out the resolution process, feeding the revelations into the action. Try threading them into the narrative directly so that they spur what comes next. That way your characters can discover them, untangle the problem and move to the following scene naturally. If your revelations come across as little more than one long recap scene, tidily tacked on to the end of the book, they're likely to be unconvincing and leave your climax feeling distinctly anticlimactic.

FALSE ENDINGS AND EPILOGUES

Sometimes stories don't end at the obvious moment. If you read books – and I trust you do – you're familiar with this trick already. We see the bad guy taken down, we're led to believe the world is back the way it should be. Then there's a sudden about-turn in the plot and the last person we suspected – or so the author hopes – turns out to be the villain after all, triggering a final confrontation. False endings are an established narrative device and may even present us with several red herrings before we see the actual resolution. They can be very effective. As always, don't push your luck by stretching them too far. False-ending sequences that extend much beyond one or two fake conclusions can become tiresome.

An epilogue is very different. This is a chapter that happens after the denouement of the story and offers some reflection and perhaps explanation of what has gone before. Sometimes an epilogue will run on directly from the preceding action. Sometimes it could take place years later, or be in the form of a letter or some kind of false document.

Epilogues can serve a variety of purposes. They can elaborate on the preceding plot or tell you what happens to characters in the book after the main story. If you're planning a sequel the epilogue can point the way forward to the coming book. Note I said 'sequel' – in other words two books designed to be read as a pair, such as Robert Graves's *I, Claudius* and *Claudius the God* – not a series. If there really are only two books involved you are entitled to raise hopes for the second at the end of the first. If this is just an open-ended series you should avoid this link, for the reasons I've outlined already.

I like epilogues, but then I write stories that are often suited to them. They can change the pace of the story and offer you the chance to insert insights that aren't easily added any other way. In my part-historical Venetian standalone, *The Cemetery of Secrets*, the epilogue consists of a false document, a diary entry supposedly written by Jean-Jacques Rousseau describing his accidental encounter with the book's protagonists years after the main story. It gives me the opportunity to describe what happened to them and, at the very end, insert a surprise link to the modern half of the story which connects both sides of the tale. I can't think of any other way this could have been achieved. But if your story has no need of an epilogue then don't write one.

HOW LONG SHOULD YOUR FINISHED BOOK BE?

That depends. In the UK we usually measure books in terms of words. In America some people still doggedly use the term 'pages', going back to typewriter days when everything was written on typewriters, with a monospaced font and double line spacing. Some software can try to make an estimate of page length. But I'd still ditch the pages idea – it's increasingly meaningless and both agents and editors on both sides of the Atlantic are now familiar with the concept of words instead.

Most of my books tend to come in at up to 125,000 words these days. That is somewhat shorter than some of my earlier work, which often ran to 160,000 words or more. But books were bigger in the nineties, and those early ones could have used some judicious editing. I'm probably coming in a touch longer than most of my peers. In the UK the average book length for popular fiction is between 90,000 and 100,000 words.

Budding writers often ask about word counts in a rather meek and tentative fashion. They've written something that's come out at 60,000 words or so and they're wondering whether anyone will publish it. Probably not in the UK, where thin novels are a rarity. In the US, though, publishers will consider some kinds of book, such as romance and light mystery, at this length.

The market for novellas, say of 40,000 words, is pretty much nonexistent for unknown writers, and pretty thin for established ones too, though the rise of ebooks, where length seems less of a consideration, may change this. Unless you are brimming over with confidence, I'd think twice about delivering some gigantic doorstopper of a quarter of a million words or more unless you're in a field, such as some areas of fantasy, where massive tomes are occasionally acceptable.

The honest answer to this question is: as long as the book needs. Market conditions will demand a minimum length, say from 90,000 words up in the UK, and deter you from writing something massive. But let the narrative flow naturally to its own rhythm and work out when it is starting to call for the resolution. You can't pad out a thin book with verbiage as a makeweight – everyone will notice. Stories have a natural balance and cycle from beginning to end. Publishers will be looking to see that you've spotted this rhythm and stayed with it throughout the story. Bucking the feel of the piece by inserting needless chapters and diversions will be very obvious, hopefully in the first instance to the writer. You should know when you're faking it, so stop.

The wild card in all this, of course, is the ebook. Novellas and long short stories, sometimes selling for peanuts, do seem to be reaching readers through digital sales, though how sustainable that market is remains to be seen. If you want a conventional publishing contract, deliver a book that comes in at a conventional length.

Charlie and the Mermaid seems to me a relatively straightforward story, linear, with a single location and a small cast of closely linked characters. My guess is it would fit comfortably into that 90–100,000 benchmark with a first act of around 25,000, a second of 45,000 and a third of 20–25,000. No epilogue either. When this story ends, it's over.

THIRD–ACT SYNOPSIS

Here we go ...

Sally is still with Giordano. Charlie sends him a message saying he knows what's happened and they need to meet. There's a final confrontation on the pier. Charlie's dad hides while Charlie puts it all to Giordano. Matt Giordano is a big man. He's brought Sally with him 'to finish this once and for all'. They're in the wrecked theatre where the fire began, charred posters on the walls, gutted seats, a chill wind whipping through the roof. Sally listens and starts to chime in. Giordano responds in a strange and unexpected fashion, talking wildly about murder, calls her mother a whore, a *bad* mother. Not loving and caring like him. She was selfish, like her father too, who'd come round the night before asking for her back, *demanding*. No one demands anything of Matt Giordano. Not even Eric Whitby, and he admits to killing Sally's grandfather. Says he had to. He was going to ruin it for them all.

Charlie hears this and calls for his dad who's been hiding with a voice recorder. He reveals himself and hands the recorder to Giordano. He's been intending to do this all along. There's money involved and Giordano says, 'I'll look after the boy from now on. I'll keep him straight. Good man.'

Sally looks into Charlie's eyes and he realises. Matt Giordano really does possess everything. This is his world. Charlie's dad leaves. Charlie, for the first time in life, stands up to his father and refuses to leave with him. Now it's just the three of them. Giordano is mad but scarily serious all at the same time.

Giordano says he's got something to show them. Something to prove who he really is. He leads them to a magician's cabinet at the back of the fire-blasted dressing rooms, opens it and inside is a body, charred, but not so much you can't see the showgirl's costume and the remains of a feathered headdress: Sally's mum. There's a look on Giordano's face – a look of insane, obsessive love.

We break to a flashback. It's fifteen years before and we're in Giordano's head, seeing the real events, realising that his confused words about murder weren't quite what they seem. It was Sally's mum and her musician boyfriend who were trying to murder him, Giordano who was fighting for his life against them. He hits the boyfriend, knocks him unconscious. Then turns to face Sally's mother, telling her he loves her, wants her, will do anything for her and their child.

'It's not your child,' she says, then performs the magic trick we know from Eric Whitby, clicking her fingers, bringing flames to the tips, and approaches him. But the flames brush against one of the velvet drapes by the stage and in an instant we're amid a sea of flames.

Back to the present. Sally is looking at Giordano intently. She clicks her fingers the way her grandfather did with that magic trick. Flames appear. Matt Giordano is frozen to the spot. She looks at Charlie, glances at something in her bag. He sees a bottle of some kind of liquid there, gets the messages, reaches in and sprays the stuff on Giordano. Sally reaches forward and touches the man.

Second flashback. We see that Giordano is trying to save Sally's mother but she's crazy and won't accept his help. He burns his right hand badly as he reaches into the fire as she's consumed by the blaze, explaining the black glove Charlie has seen.

Back to now. Giordano bursts into flame, and so does the pier around them once more, the fire reaching the raw wood of the boarding and building work Giordano had been ordering as he tried to bring it back to life. There's another inferno. Giordano retreats screaming into its maw, to his death. The cabinet with the corpse of Sally's mum shakes and the corpse inside shatters on the floor.

Final brief flashback. Giordano searching through the wreckage the day after the first fire. Finding her corpse. Hiding it, dressing it in a costume, going over the edge with his obsessive love.

Back to now. Sally disappears. Charlie is lucky to escape with his life. Breathless, anxious, he makes it back to the beach.

There's only one place she can be. Charlie just sees her disappearing beneath the waves. He dives in to rescue her, but it takes an agonising time to find her still, cold body in the waves beneath the stanchions. Charlie rescues her half-dead from the sea and places her on the sand.

He's fighting for what to do, then remembers the first time he saw her in the swimming pool. Mouth-to-mouth resuscitation. Sally recovers, coughs up the salt water from her lungs, turns away from him sobbing. He stays there all the same, close by. After a while she turns back and they hold one another on the beach beneath the pier as the structure is once again consumed by flames overhead.

Charlie, who'd been aching so much to kiss her, thinks: finally I did, in a way. It wasn't the kind of kiss he'd expected, craved. It was more important somehow. And she tasted like a mermaid.

End of story . . .

This is a bit of a guess, if I'm honest. I'm not the kind of writer who can outline in great detail in advance, so the synopses here are best efforts. They would not, I'm sure, reflect the finished article if I were to write in full the story of Charlie and his mermaid. And I'm not sure the part about Sally's mother's body, a charred skeleton still dressed for the stage, is something I could pull off.

What else might I change on the page if I set about writing? A few things, mainly to do with Sally and Giordano. Is she actually very like her mother, wicked and vengeful? Did she engineer this conclusion in some way? And is there a side to Giordano I haven't explored? A gentler, loving man who was destroyed by Sally's mother in a fashion that – the story might suggest – Sally might one day try to destroy Charlie?

Don't know, and the only way a writer like this one could find out would be to write the whole book and see.

Part 3
DELIVER

FEELING pleased with yourself? You should be. Most people don't get this far. And I know what you're thinking. 'I've written a book! Best send it off to agents, publishers and anyone else I can think of right now!'

Hang on. You haven't written a book. You've completed a first draft. That's not the same thing. You still have to go through the revision process, which is just as important and, at times, just as frustrating as putting that story together in the first place.

There's a saying in this business: there are no good writers, only good rewriters. For once it's an old saw that's got a point. Revision is a crucial part of the process, a final polish of a rough-cut stone, a delicate tweaking act that can turn an everyday piece of fiction into something special. You need to approach this phase of the writing process with care, determination and understanding.

And be patient. The first thing I do when I have a first draft is walk away from the whole thing. For a week. A month. More time if I had it (but I never do). You've waited years to reach this point. Why squander the opportunity to make it as good as possible?

How often will you need to revise your manuscript? My guess is at least three times, each from a different perspective. If it's less than that, I suspect you're dodging work. If it turns out to be much more, you may be getting over-obsessive – editing has to come to an end sometime.

Let's go through each of these steps and assign them some specific objectives.

FIRST REVISE

We all become a little insane at the end of the book. Can't get it out of our heads. Can't see the wood for the trees. There is an argument for believing that the entire process of writing a piece of fiction is simply a thinly controlled and highly internalised nervous breakdown designed, with a bit of luck, to produce something worthwhile at the end. Revision is the part of the game where you wake up and find yourselves strapped into the white jacket, staring around thinking: what next?

For the sake of your own well-being it's best to aim for what audio and video people call 'non-destructive editing'. In other words you should be able to hack away to your heart's content knowing that if you go too far you can always get back to the original. Some word processors, Word notably, will let you track changes in a document so you can see what you've excised and restore it. This is a good idea in principle though I find it confusing frankly – you get a screen full of coloured type with lots of marks through it.

The simplest way to make sure you lose nothing is to copy your finished manuscript and work on it with a new name, say Book Version 1. (I still leave track changes turned on in case it's useful.) Scrivener also has its handy snapshot feature which lets you keep a copy of a scene while you work on a new version. But mostly if something goes wrong, I return to the original and retrieve anything I've cut out.

When I approach a first revise I'm wearing an editor's hat. In other words I'm trying to view the manuscript from the perspective of the professional who will one day see it in front of them and look for tell-tale signs of sloppiness such as mistakes, continuity issues and non sequiturs. I always do this revise on screen because it involves a fair bit of basic typing. Just set up your document in draft mode – you really don't need to see headers and footers – and go through it line by line cutting out the verbiage, trying to spot mistakes and cleaning up ugly language. I'm not trying to do a serious polish at this stage. I'm not even terribly worried about logistical flaws. All I want to do is get a script that is as 'clean as possible'. In other words I'm not rewriting in any serious fashion, I'm *correcting*, dealing with basic errors to get them out of the way so I can concentrate on the bigger picture at a later stage.

This is not a terribly difficult part of the revision process. You're sub-editing your own copy and trying to rid it of glitches. But you're probably feeling a little shell-shocked from having finished the thing at all, so a little light work is definitely welcome. I approach this first revise in a single, concentrated burst. I'm not trying to think my way deeply into the book at all. I'm just hoping to make the thing read properly, nothing more.

Working full time I will usually get through this phase in a week or ten days. After that it's another pause for breath and then I put on another hat.

SECOND REVISE

Can an author step back from his or her work and see it the way an eventual reader will? Not easily, but we can at least try, and that's what I hope to achieve with the second revise.

At this stage I'm trying to evaluate the work as a whole, and to do that I need to look at its chief component, scenes. Three questions need to be asked of every one:

➤ Does it work in itself?

➤ Does it work as part of this section of the book?

➤ Does it work in the whole scheme of things, from beginning to end?

Sometimes you get scenes that are lovely but expendable. A dumb blonde starlet that's talked her way on to the set through nothing more than looks. They have to go. Sometimes a scene reads perfectly well but jars with what came before or what comes after. This needs attention.

And sometimes the thing raises a problem – some narrative link, some unanswered question – that needed to be addressed elsewhere, perhaps miles away in the story, and wasn't. So either that has to be written in elsewhere or the source has to be removed.

One simple, unshakeable fact joins all these issues: you can only see them if you read the whole thing from beginning to end without serious interruption. It's fatal to try to read and rewrite at the same time. The final polish is for the third phase of the revise, or later, not now.

Here's a tip to help you turn from author into reader: abandon the computer and go back to paper. Print out your manuscript, go into a room away from the PC and the internet, and read it from first page to last. Then, if you have the time and energy, print it out again but this time landscape, with two book pages on each page of paper, so that it looks like spreads in a paperback book.

You will be amazed how much you see that is fresh if you simply change the format of your book's appearance. Different typefaces, different sizes and layouts reveal issues and, especially, repeated words that will pass you by on screen. When readers have a book they see two pages at a time, not one. As authors and editors we tend to focus on the paragraph in front of us and check how that works against the three or four around it. That simple change in print format should let you view everything in the broader context your eventual audience will experience.

Can you do this on one of the new ereaders or tablets such as an iPad, Kindle or Android tablet? Yes, up to a point. Getting a Word file on to your reader can be a bit tricky, but newer apps, such as Scrivener and Apple Pages, will save directly into ereader formats. Such devices as Kindle or iPad do a very good job of making your draft manuscript look like a properly formatted ebook, and headings will usually appear as chapter links. The drawback comes when you want to annotate your draft. You're restricted to basic margin notes which can be a bit awkward to type using these small devices. Agents and editors can read and evaluate manuscripts very well this way. Authors who need to make substantial revisions may find the note-taking facilities a bit rudimentary.

Nothing beats paper – being able to sit down with a red pen and scribble away to your heart's content, making changes, notes, highlights and referring back easily to other sections in the book. My preferred revision method is to print out the whole book as double-page spreads, paperback-style, read them, put the ones requiring attention in one pile, and setting the rest to one side. I then return to the computer with the marked pages and type in the corrections. If you own a tablet you should try reading your draft to see if it helps. But I wouldn't buy one solely for this purpose, and frankly it's hard to see a digital device that can possibly compete with pen and paper for author revisions.

During this stage of revision I usually find that around half of the draft pages will need more work back at the computer. If you find you're picking up only a few for corrections you're either a fantastic, first-time talent or perilously uncritical.

FINAL REVISE

However many passes you take at a manuscript you will, one day, find yourself facing a last run-through of the story, trying to apply some final changes before you look to sell it. There's a big difference between how a newbie writer and a seasoned one will approach this revise.

When glitches become apparent the newbie will spend endless hours trying to fix them, rewriting, juggling scenes, often turning a simple knot into a horrible mess of tangles. Let me repeat. Changing anything of substance at this stage of a book is not something to undertake lightly. You always have to check the knock-on effect elsewhere in the narrative.

Think of this in terms of a movie, which is always shot out of sequence, based on location not the movement of the story. Imagine that an actor ad libs a line at some point. It's a great line. Everyone loves it. Everyone wants to see it in the finished film. But the problem is that the line invalidates the content of a scene elsewhere, one that's already been shot. Do you go back and reshoot the earlier scene? Maybe. The trouble is, if you do that another scene is ruined. And then another . . .

It's easier to rewrite a book than reshoot a movie. But it can still be a horrible and complex experience. So let me tell you how an experienced writer will usually respond to bumps in the road, most of which – let's be frank – concern matters that are decidedly minor.

You cut them. Make them gone. Vanished. Disappeared.

It's that word 'edit' again. Here's a definition from the dictionary on my Mac: 'remove unnecessary or inappropriate words, sounds, or scenes from a text, movie, or radio or television program'.

Make those awkward moments go away and see if the story is diminished by their removal. My guess is that 90 per cent of logistical queries – your own or those of a copy editor – can be dealt with more easily by excision than by some tortuous rewrite. So save yourself the grief, and wield that red pen without mercy. Editors – and readers – scream 'less' far more often than they yell 'more'.

So you've read your book wearing an editor's hat, as a reader and now, finally, as the author, trying to fix every problem you can see. How do you know when a work in progress is actually ready to go? What are the signs?

First things first. Books are never truly complete. We simply say, 'That's as far as I can go with this one. Take it please. I want your opinions on it and in the meantime I'll think about writing something else.'

That doesn't mean the book should feel incomplete to the reader. The very opposite. It should read like a rounded piece of work, one that poses a question, takes the reader through the hunt and chase, then offers some kind of resolution. But in terms of writing, 'finished' isn't a word that makes much sense.

When it comes to sending off material to agents and publishers you need some benchmarks. Here are three of mine.

➢ I will never dispatch half-complete stories for consideration, asking, 'Does this work?' That sounds unprofessional and unfair on the recipients. Agents and editors are great sounding boards. They're not there as proxy psychologists. Nor are they clairvoyant. The only honest answer to that question with regard to a half-finished book is either 'no' or 'maybe', because the unfinished part could fail too. Unless your agent or publisher asks – and sometimes they will – 'what's the point?'

➢ I never work the versions trick. You know the one? Send off something one week. Then send an 'improved' version the next. This wastes people's time and makes you look like an amateur.

➢ One final condition: the book goes off when I know I can do no more to it without some outside feedback.

When you look at your draft and think, 'It seems finished to me and I've no idea how I can possibly make this any better than it is' . . . then it's time to think of sending it out into the world.

There are, though, just a few final details to be settled.

TITLES, TITLES, TITLES

We have, by this stage, a complete book telling the story of Charlie Harrison, Sally and dark events in that strange seaside town. We had a working title from the outside too, *Charlie and the Mermaid*.

It's not going to work. If I were writing a young adult story, or some fantasy piece, then perhaps it would be fine. But we have here something very different, much darker and more intense. It needs a title that reflects the tone of the story.

As I write this book I will have noted down possibilities along the way. Usually I will have as many as twenty in there when it comes to completion. The first thing I will do is whittle them down to five or six favourites, then head off to Amazon to see if anyone else has used them recently. There are a lot of books in this world, and a good many share the same title. Ideally yours will be unique, but it doesn't have to be. If an unknown book used the same title a few years ago you're fine to take it on again. Just don't pick *The Godfather* or any other obvious and well-known title.

Very long titles occasionally work – *Midnight in the Garden of Good and Evil*, for example. Single-word ones – *Epiphany*, *Solstice* – can be striking, but will usually have been used elsewhere so you'll need to check for any recent competitors. Titles that play off other books – *The Vermeer Code* – are best avoided unless you are trying to make a very direct point or taking the mickey. Titles that contain foreign names are probably worth skipping too (people still mispronounce and misunderstand *Semana Santa* even though it's simply the Spanish for 'holy week').

You'll have noticed I've just told you what makes a bad title, not what constitutes a good one. Let me be honest: I don't know, and nor do many of us really. My working title for this story would probably be *The Mermaid's Kiss*. It's relevant to the narrative, it's evocative and it gives a flavour of the book.

But here's the good news: while a great title for your unpublished book is wonderful if you can find it, you really don't *have* to have one. Agents and editors will be looking at the quality of the manuscript, not the words that will one day appear on the front cover. A bad book with a great title will go in the bin. A promising book with a hopeless title will simply make an agent or editor think, 'I like this one – and we'll sort out the title later.'

So don't worry about it. In fact you might win yourself a bit of respect if, in your covering letter, you say you're not sure whether the title works or not, and will happily accept better suggestions.

MAKING IT EASIER FOR READERS

I write fairly complex books set in a country that, for most of my readers, is foreign. I have rules about trying not to overburden them with details they might find puzzling. I use Italian words sparingly, for example, and try to avoid mystifying phrases as much as possible.

Even so there are always going to be things you can't do in the text of the narrative itself. Should we make fiction easier to read by adding extra informational material? Possibly. Here are some extras that can work. But if you don't need these additions, don't waste time on them.

First, a map. My UK editions usually have maps now. Overseas ones vary according to the policy of the publisher. I wish they all had maps but that's out of my hands. If publishers asked readers 'map or no map?' I know what the answer for my books would be: 'Yes, please!' If you think your book needs a map, say so when you deliver. You don't have to provide it, but if you're an artist yourself a hand-drawn one inserted into the manuscript could be impressive, especially if your world is a fictional one, say a fantasy land complete with oceans and mountain ranges. If the world of your story is an ordinary urban landscape I'd skip a map entirely.

A cast list at the front, detailing all the main characters? I've only ever done this once, at a publisher's request, for a book with a fairly large cast of players that took place in two different eras. If you're writing a dynastic saga set in Imperial Rome they're doubtless essential. In a modern story, I'm not so sure. Best skipped for now, and you can always add it in later if required.

A table of contents – in other words a chapter-by-chapter breakdown of the book laid out at the front? Old-fashioned novels did this all the same. If you're writing a book in the style of Dickens or Defoe, fine. If not, avoid.

A glossary? Why would you need one in a work of fiction? There may be occasions when the writer wants to use the right words to give you a local flavour or inside knowledge, but knows that, while you may have heard of them, you probably are a little hazy on detail.

I used a glossary in *Carnival for the Dead*. It's set in Venice. I want it to be absolutely soaked in Venetian atmosphere. I can't avoid using words that are local – carnival terms such as *frittelle*, gondola expressions such as *forcola*, architectural descriptions such as *salizada*. If I use 'doughnut', 'rowlock' and 'paved street' instead, it just wouldn't work. In order to drag you to Venice I have to adopt the local vernacular.

So there will be a short glossary at the front of that book, and it will, I hope, contain every word that may raise doubts in the reader's mind. But I won't make a habit of this. Most of the time it's simply unnecessary.

An author's note? I started writing these part way through the Costa series and people seem to appreciate them. They're principally there to separate fact from fiction and to give some historical and cultural background to the stories. I always place them at the end so they won't spoil the story. And unless they add something – like all other extras – they will be avoided altogether.

Finally, reading guides. It's become fashionable of late for some books to appear with sections at the back designed to offer insights into what the author was trying to achieve with his story. These are supposedly aimed at people in reading groups who want to discuss the work in question.

The last time I read Hemingway he came without a reading guide at the back. Why modern writers would need them is beyond me. Are readers supposed to think, 'This book has a reading guide – it *must* be important?' If so, the prevalence of reading guides, often attached to books that are general popular fiction titles unlikely to reach the curricula of schools and universities, is likely to diminish what little currency they have. If your publisher feels your book genuinely requires such a thing they will, I imagine, inform you of that fact. If they do, you might want to ask them why they want to give away what is often little more than a brief synopsis of the book to a paying customer who has either just read or is about to start it.

Call me old-fashioned, but if a book needs a separate section at the end to help you better understand what went before then something has surely gone wrong. Say what you have to say in the book, then shut up.

As a novice author you should not for one second think of including a reading guide along with your manuscript. Most publishing people will sniff a pompous, self-important windbag in the offing and recoil from everything – you, your reading guide and, worst of all, your book.

WHAT HAPPENS NEXT

This is a guide to writing a novel up to the point of delivery. We are pretty much at that point now. There's a lot more to the book business than delivering a manuscript but most of it is outside the remit of this work. The annual *Writers' and Artists' Yearbook* (Bloomsbury) is an invaluable source of information, including names and addresses of publishers and agents you may wish to approach. For a thoroughly informative insight into how to get published I recommend *The Writers' and Artists' Yearbook Guide to Getting Published* by Harry Bingham (Bloomsbury, 2010, ISBN 978 1 408 12895 4).

I should, however, add a brief word of advice about how to deal with the people who may come to hold your writing career in their hands. You doubtless feel unique once you have that finished manuscript in your hand. The truth is . . . you're not. The book business is besieged by would-be authors who think that agents and publishers have nothing better to do with their time but peruse long manuscripts, offer endless free advice, and act as good Samaritans for the many complete strangers who cross their paths each day.

This isn't the case. Act professional and follow the rules. All reputable literary agencies – and a few less impressive ones – will have websites these days. Before you send off a letter of inquiry do make sure to visit this and check their submission guidelines. Some will accept emailed Word documents. Others will ask for printed-out manuscripts (which will not be returned). It's vital you follow these guidelines to the letter. Nothing infuriates a potential agent more than having their own working practices ignored.

All will be swamped with constant inquiries. It's very easy for them to reject first off those that come from people who can't be bothered to check how best to reach them or simply ignore advice on how to deliver. Don't expect instant answers – agents will have a huge reading list to deal with already, and their existing clients will always come before potential new ones. Don't nag by email or expect special treatment if you happen to be a Facebook friend or Twitter follower. If you're going to be considered for representation it's important you come across as someone serious about the business of writing.

Budding writers are understandably fixated on the idea of being published. But ideally you are embarking on the first step of a career here, not simply placing a single book. It's worth taking your time to find the right agent, one who understands what you're seeking from writing and is in tune with your ambitions. Mistakes – in choice of agent or publisher – may take years to correct and can damage or even kill the most promising of careers.

There are sharks in these waters. Among the many genuine and honest agents and editorial consultants out there lurk people with little experience and an avid desire to part you from your money while giving little or nothing in return. No worthwhile agent will demand a fee from you for reading a manuscript. Do not even consider hiring an editorial consultant to improve your manuscript without gaining a good idea of what he or she has in the way of professional experience relevant to your needs. Anyone can call themselves an agent or editor. It's up to you to avoid the dodgy ones – follow the excellent advice in sources such as the *Writers' and Artists' Yearbook* when you set out to seek representation.

Unless you have decided to enter the rather tricky world of self-publishing – a subject outside the remit of this book – you should not have to pay either to see your work appear or evaluated. Finally, if you decide to sign a publishing contract without using an agent – which I would not advise – do consider paying to join the Society of Authors so that their contract experts can vet the deal you're being offered to make sure it's fair. I've heard of some small publishers gulling writers into signing contracts that would give half of any theatrical rights – from TV or film – from a book to the publisher. No agent would countenance such a deal, and nor should you. But any publishing contract is likely to be couched in language the average human being will find hard to understand, so make sure someone knowledgeable checks the details.

Throughout the submission process remember you are one would-be author among thousands. Show civility and a little humility, especially when you meet rejection. Learn from what people tell you when they turn you down. Don't waste your time on so-called 'promotion'. The only thing you have to push is an unsold manuscript. There's no point in putting up a website boasting of your authorial prowess if no one has yet bought your book.

I'd also be wary of putting up too much free material as ebooks. Yes, some writers have had some spectacular successes as self-published authors through Kindle and a handful have found publishing contracts that way. But those success stories are rare. Professional publishers do not spend their time scouring the thousands of new ebooks going up on the web each day, and nor do many readers.

It's highly unlikely your manuscript will be accepted by the first agent you approach. Rejection is inevitable for most of us. My first book, *Semana Santa*, went unread by every literary agency I contacted when I wrote it – none of them was interested in seeing the manuscript, largely because it was set in Spain. Through good fortune and coincidence an agent did finally look at a few pages. She then asked to see the rest – and within a few months I had a three-book contract and a movie deal not long after.

Yet my first agent came from an agency that had already rejected even reading the book when I first wrote to them (not that I told her this when she called). This is, you see, a very haphazard business at times. Learn to live with it and keep your frustrations to yourself.

How many rejections should you take before giving up on your book? Practicalities will probably dictate that. If you've been read and turned down by all the people you think might be interested, it's time to think of something else. And don't, please, simply change a few things, tack on a new title then start hawking the same manuscript around hoping against hope that this time round those same people will suddenly say yes. It's unlikely to happen and you won't do yourself any favours in the meantime.

Once you've finished a book do what professional writers do. Start another. As I said at the outset, career writing demands perseverance as much as talent. Oh, and a touch of good luck. I wish you all three.

Appendix

WORD PROCESSING

Microsoft Word (www.microsoft.com) is the standard text-handling package in the book business. Publishers and agents will expect you to submit your manuscript as a Word file and may handle the editing process through returned Word files with comments and change-tracking. So most writers will find it easiest to own a copy of Word, even if it's not their primary writing tool. Word 2010 for Windows is an excellent novel-writing package, however, with new facilities for shuffling scenes and chapters and seeing instant word counts for the individual parts of a book, something that has traditionally been missing in most word-processing packages. Its Mac equivalent, Word 2011, does not have these functions and remains as awkward and occasionally flaky as earlier versions of the package.

This may be best avoided by using Apple's own word processor, Pages (www.apple.com). This Mac-only program, part of the relatively inexpensive iWork bundle, is fast and slick and can read and write Word files, including comments and tracked changes, so can be used as an alternative to the largely unsatisfactory Word 2011 on the Mac. But Apple's Pages word processor app for the iPad is a pale version of the Mac original, incapable of comments, change-tracking and some other key features needed for book-length manuscript revision. Best avoided.

Writer (www.openoffice.org) is the word processor bundled with the cross-platform free Open Office package. It can read and write Word files but has little in the way of book-length management features, and often resembles a rather old version of Word itself. If you've written your book in something else and simply want to check how it looks in Word this could do the job. There are no easy and elegant ways to manage a long document divided into many scenes and chapters which, in my book, makes Writer a poor alternative to Word for lengthy fiction.

SPECIALIST WRITING APPLICATIONS

These are software programs specially designed for creative writing. Prices usually run between $45 and $75 and may change with promotions. All of them offer free trial downloads which allow you to evaluate the app before parting with your money. They are designed to be primary writing tools which eventually export a final manuscript to Word for sending to an agent or publisher. Several will also export epub files that allow you to proof a manuscript electronically on an iPad or Android tablet.

Scrivener (www.literatureandlatte.com), for Mac and Windows, was the work of a budding writer who turned software developer because he was unhappy with using conventional word processing for writing fiction. It is now one of the most popular apps of its kind, used by both professional and amateur writers alike. It was first developed for the Mac but now has a companion Windows version, though the latter lacks a few features of its older, more advanced sibling. Scrivener has taken the division of a manuscript into parts, chapters and scenes to a fine art, allowing very detailed control of word counts and annotations. Its outlining facilities include a corkboard/index card interface. The program can also be used to write movie scripts. It can appear a little unintuitive at first glance, like most scene-based writing apps, and few writers will need all the tools on offer. Best evaluate the free trial, follow the excellent training videos, then decide if it's for you before buying. If you do go the Scrivener route you may want to consider my short and very specific ebook guide (details at www.davidhewson.com/writing-a-novel-with-scrivener) on using the software for novel writing.

Storymill (www.marinersoftware.com) is another well-established scene-based writing app, this time for the Mac only. It takes a much simpler approach to the job than Scrivener, and includes easy-to-use facilities for characters and event tracking and a timeline feature that can be used to track the development of the narrative.

Pagefour (http://www.softwareforwriting.com/pagefour.html) is a very simple, highly functional scene-based app for Windows only.

Liquid Story Binder (www.blackobelisksoftware.com) combines some very advanced outlining features with image management, mindmaps, journal keeping and the familiar scene-based editing facilities seen in its rivals. A touch on the complex side but worth a look – Windows only.

Ulysses (www.the-soulmen.com/ulysses) is a slightly eccentric Mac-only writing program that pioneered some of the chapter techniques seen in later apps. It is very rigid about the way it – and you – should work when it comes to formatting.

Storyist (www.storyist.com) is a Mac-only Scrivener competitor with similar features at a slightly higher price.

INFORMATION MANAGEMENT

OneNote (www.microsoft.com) comes with even the most inexpensive versions of Microsoft Office for Windows, so if you own Word you will usually have this too. It is one of the most under-appreciated of all Microsoft's products, a very powerful yet simple-to-use information manager that is perfect for everything from maintaining a research library to keeping a book diary or outlining a book project. It also fits in very well alongside Word, allowing you to make notes on a Word project in OneNote and have the exact location in the text automatically saved with the comment. There is no easy way to share OneNote notebooks outside Windows, however, except with a Windows 7 mobile phone.

Evernote (www.evernote.com) is a web service that allows you to store information on its servers then access it through a variety of free client applications for Macs or Windows PCs, iPads, iPhones and Android phones, or through any web browser. Your data is stored behind a username and password so best make sure they are secure. The basic service is free, including client apps, but for more storage and the ability to store Office documents you will need to open a premium account which currently costs $5 a month or $45 a year.

Evernote's client software is developing at a hectic pace and has improved greatly in a very short space of time. It lacks some of the finer features of OneNote, but the ability to type in quick notes on your phone and have them sync back to your PC or Mac automatically is very tempting. Definitely worth a try.

MacJournal and WinJournal (www.marinersoftware.com) are companion inexpensive journal packages for the Mac and Windows respectively. Both are very capable for keeping individual diaries and research files on an individual computer. Sharing them is, at the time of writing, more difficult. If you need that, best look to Evernote.

Specialist writing packages such as Scrivener can store research material alongside your manuscript if you want. Personally, as I've outlined here, I like to keep factual and manuscript material separate, partly because my books involve copious amounts of research. Writers with more sensible baggage may feel differently.

Index

Scrivener is an award-winning word processor and project-management tool created specifically for writers of long texts such as novels and research papers. It won't try to tell you how to write – it just provides powerful tools for getting your words onto the page and finding the structure that best suits your project. Refer to research as you write; restructure your work using the virtual corkboard or outliner; dynamically combine multiple scenes into a single text just to see how they fit; enter full-screen mode for distraction-free composition. And once your text is complete, you can print, export to popular word-processing formats, or self-publish as a PDF or e-book. Scrivener has been enthusiastically adopted by best-selling novelists and novices alike – whatever you write, grow your ideas in style. Available for both Windows and Mac OS X.

www.literatureandlatte.com/scrivener.php

30-day free trial available.

DISCOUNT
for readers of *Writing: A User Manual*

Enter the code 'HEWSONWRITING' in the coupon code text field of our web store to get a 20% discount (regular licence only)

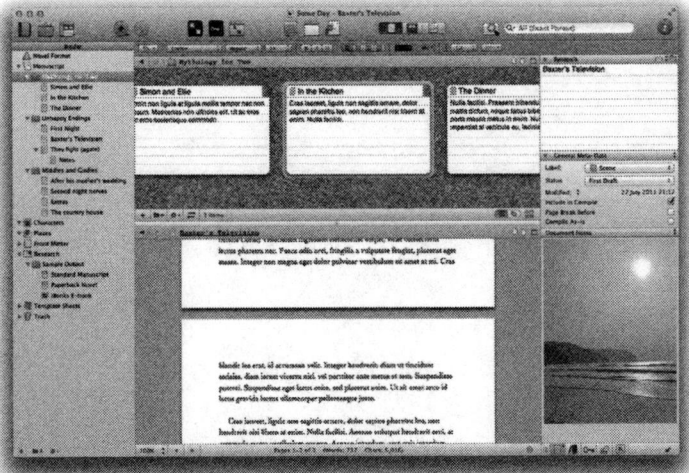

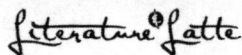

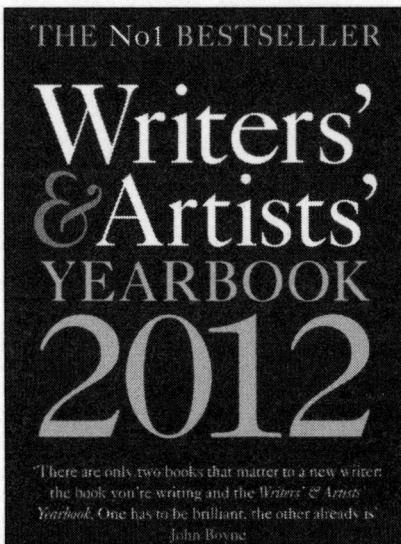